C000227482

RESEARCHING WITH FEELING

Should researchers be interested in their feelings and emotions as they carry out research? Emotion is what it is to exist, to be human, and is present in every sphere of our lives. All activities are infused with emotion, even those that are constructed as 'rational', because rationality and emotionality are interpenetrated and entwined, because all thinking is tinged with feeling, and all feeling is tinged with thinking.

This book illuminates the emotional processes of doing social and organizational research, and the implications of this for the outcomes of research. With contributions from leading academics and research practitioners, it addresses the significant issue of the sometimes intense emotional experiences involved in doing research and the implications it has for the theory and practice of social research. By examining the nature of feelings and emotions, it explores how we might understand researchers' emotions and experiences, and considers the often powerful feelings encountered in a variety of research contexts. Topics discussed include power relations; psycho-social explanations of researcher emotions; paradoxical relations with research participants and the sometimes disturbing data that is gained; research supervision; the politics of research; gender; and publishing, undergoing vivas and presenting at conferences.

This book will therefore be a valuable companion to researchers and research students from the start of their career onwards.

Caroline Clarke is Senior Lecturer in Management with the Open University Business School, UK.

Mike Broussine is a freelance organizational researcher and consultant and a Visiting Research Fellow at UWE, UK.

Linda Watts has worked in corporate management and community development roles in local government and is actively involved in the voluntary sector in Bath.

This vibrant and truly fascinating collection of chapters opens up the normally hidden backstage of doing organizational research. Going well beyond the familiar ritualistic nods towards reflexivity, the authors delve into the complex emotional and social terrain of the research process, emphasizing the dynamics of power and identity that are in play. It will be invaluable reading both for graduate students and more experienced researchers in organization studies and social science.

Christopher Grey, Professor, Royal Holloway, University of London, UK

At last! A research methods book that acknowledges and even celebrates the fact that researchers are human beings with feelings and emotional attachments. Outing the insecurities in research relationships and in the interpretation of data will reassure new researchers that they are 'normal'. I wish this book had been available when I was struggling with my PhD research.

Michael Humphreys, Professor, University of Durham, UK

The book is an excellent and timely contribution to understanding researcher emotion, which will resonate with any reader who has, even only occasionally, ventured into this field of operation. It exposes the academics' very worst fears, but it provides a coping mechanism too that this is not a lonely endeavour and will provide solace and sustenance to researchers at any stage of their careers.

Christine Coupland, Professor, Loughborough University, UK

This book is a 'must read' for anyone with an interest in emotions in organizational research, honest explorations of the research journey, and social science inquiry sensitive to feeling.

Andrew D. Brown, Professor, University of Bath, UK

The significance of researchers' assumptions and preconceptions in the production of social science is now widely acknowledged. This book extends such reflexivity to the emotions – that is, to the emotionality of the researcher, not just the emotions of research 'subjects'. Its contributors offer a series of illuminating insights into all phases of research as an emotionally charged roller coaster ride fuelled by beatific (e.g. self-doubt) and horrific (self-aggrandizing) fantasies. The chapters thereby open up a dimension of research activity that, to date, has been largely disregarded in reflexive and sophisticated discussions of methodology.

Hugh Willmott, Professor, Cardiff University, UK

RESEARCHING WITH FEELING

The emotional aspects of social and organizational research

Edited by
Caroline Clarke, Mike Broussine and
Linda Watts

FOREWORD BY

STEPHEN FINEMAN

Routledge
Taylor & Francis Group

LONDON AND NEW YORK

First published 2015
by Routledge
2 Park Square, Milton Park, Abingdon, Oxon OX14 4RN

Simultaneously published in the USA and Canada
by Routledge
711 Third Avenue, New York, NY 10017

Routledge is an imprint of the Taylor & Francis Group, an informa business

© 2015 Caroline Clarke, Mike Broussine and Linda Watts

The right of the editor to be identified as the author of the editorial material, and of the authors for their individual chapters, has been asserted in accordance with sections 77 and 78 of the Copyright, Designs and Patents Act 1988.

All rights reserved. No part of this book may be reprinted or reproduced or utilised in any form or by any electronic, mechanical, or other means, now known or hereafter invented, including photocopying and recording, or in any information storage or retrieval system, without permission in writing from the publishers.

Trademark notice: Product or corporate names may be trademarks or registered trademarks, and are used only for identification and explanation without intent to infringe.

British Library Cataloguing in Publication Data

A catalogue record for this book is available from the British Library

Library of Congress Cataloging-in-Publication Data

Researching with feeling : the emotional aspects of social and organizational research / edited by Caroline Clarke, Mike Broussine, Linda Watts. — First Edition.
    pages cm
 Includes bibliographical references and index.
 1. Emotions. 2. Social sciences—Research. 3. Organization—Research.
 I. Clarke, Caroline, editor of compilation.
  BF511.R47 2014
  001.401'9—dc23
  2014015478

ISBN: 978-0-415-64435-8 (hbk)
ISBN: 978-0-203-07957-7 (ebk)

Typeset in Bembo
by Apex CoVantage, LLC

Printed and bound by CPI Group (UK) Ltd, Croydon, CR0 4YY

CONTENTS

ACKNOWLEDGEMENTS

This book would not have been possible without the support and encouragement of several people. First, we acknowledge our debt to the many colleagues, students and researchers whom we can't name in the text, but who willingly shared their stories and experiences with us and our colleague authors. They know who they are! There is no doubt that their stories, which appear as vignettes throughout, have enlivened the book and will reassure researchers that their 'ups-and-downs' of doing social and organizational research are shared by many others. We have been reassured in this project, particularly in the early days of getting it off the ground, by the encouragement of many friends and colleagues who told us that this book was not such a mad idea.

Second, we have very much appreciated the support and patience of Jacqueline Curthoys, Commissioning Editor at Routledge Research, and Sinead Waldron, Editorial Assistant at Routledge. We also experienced our 'ups-and-downs' as we progressed with this project, and their timely episodes of warm encouragement made us feel that we were held safely throughout.

Caroline wants to single out the following special people:

Steve and David – with gratitude for your intellectual inspiration and friendship.
John Clinton – for your wisdom, care and belief in me all those years ago.
Andrew – for absolutely everything you are, and do.
And, my *family* (blended or otherwise), June, Claude, Peter, Terry, Di, Toby, Ben, Nigel, Christian, Florrie, Jemima, Tabitha, and Andrew (again) – for sharing with me the greatest of all emotions – love.

Linda thanks her husband Mike for his open-minded and generous support. She also wants to acknowledge the radicalising influence of Paul Hoggett's work on her approach to the personal and political in every facet of research.

And Mike wants to thank his wife Karen for seeing him through the 'ups-and-downs' he experienced in contributing to the book, and his daughters Claire and Sylvie who supported the project right from the start.

EDITORS

Dr. Caroline Clarke is a Senior Lecturer in Management with the Open University Business School. Prior to this, Caroline worked in the Bristol Business School and was a researcher for the Change Management Consortium, where she conducted extensive fieldwork in both the public and private sectors and within large (HMRC) and small organizations (Bausch and Lomb). Caroline describes her work as interpretive and critical in nature, with several research interests, including identity, power and politics, and change. However, her first love and strongest affiliation is around emotion in organizations. Caroline spent 13 years in corporate life before taking up an academic career, during which she became fascinated by the tensions between portraying an over-rational image of working, while simultaneously experiencing what it means to be a human being in the workplace. Caroline has published in *Human Relations, The Scandinavian Journal of Management, The International Journal of Human Resource Management* and *Organization Studies.* When not working, Caroline looks after her numerous children, runs a charity, and aspires to having a tidy house, which she never quite achieves.

Mike Broussine is a freelance organizational researcher and consultant. He provides consultancy and action research for client organizations, and his experience mostly lies in public services, especially local government. Until November 2007, Mike worked full-time at the University of the West of England and was Programme Director for UWE's M.Sc. Leadership and Organisation of Public Services, a two-year leadership development programme that promoted learning across the public, private and voluntary sectors. In parallel with his independent consultancy work, Mike continues his academic role as Visiting Research Fellow at UWE. His main research interests include emotions and power relations in organizations, gender issues and organizational research methods, as well as public services management and leadership. Mike's first book, *Creative Methods in Organizational Research*, was published by Sage in 2008.

Dr. Linda Watts has worked in corporate management and community development roles in local government for over thirty years, and she has seven years' experience in the voluntary sector, including three years as an action researcher making the case for a crash pad for young homeless people. She has recently retired and is actively involved in the voluntary sector in Bath. Her research interests reflect critical approaches to corporate management, bureaucratic 'rationality', managerial self-governance and organizational behaviour. Her doctoral thesis was based on an unusual reflexive and collaborative inquiry into her own governance role in a contended context, as demonstrated by a 'modernising manager' in local government – this was her own corporate role. She has a particular interest in ethnographic and psycho-social research methodologies that involve the use of multiple methodologies, to take forward in depth critical and reflexive inquiry.

CONTRIBUTORS

Professor Emma Bell is Professor of Management and Organisation Studies at Keele Management School, Keele University. She is interested in the critical study of management and organizational behaviour in a range of contexts, including her own. Her research is informed by a commitment to understanding cultures and focuses on the organization of learning and change and the role of spirituality and belief systems in management. She also teaches and writes about methods and methodologies of management research, including how management knowledge is created. She is the author of *Business Research Methods* (2011), with Alan Bryman, and *Reading Management and Organisation in Film* (2008).

Dr. Matthew J Brannan is a Senior Lecturer at Keele Management School, Keele University. He is interested in the development of the Service Economy and Service Work generally and has written about HR practice in the service sector, including recruitment and selection, and training and development. He has also published work on career development in service organizations and the role that gender plays in women's managerial careers. His most recent work focuses on the idea of Employee Branding; his research is characterised by extensive ethnographic immersion into working environments; and he is concerned to document the lived experience of workers and draw attention to organizational practices that produce and reproduce inequality. Drawing upon a broad background across the Social Sciences, he has been active in forging collaborative research projects with colleagues. Matthew has taken a primary role in the development of Internationalization at Keele University as Director of International Partnerships for the Management School.

Dr. Megan Crawford is a Reader at the University of Cambridge. She previously worked at the Institute of Education, London; Oxford Brookes University; Warwick

University; and the Open University. Her background is in primary schools, where she was a Deputy Head teacher. She is on the Executive of the British Educational Leadership, Management and Administration Society (BELMAS, www.belmas.org.uk), and was its Chair from 2009–11. She is a Graduate Associate of the University of New Brunswick, Canada, and was visiting Professor at the University of Calgary, Canada. Megan is very involved in Governing Schools, and was the Teaching Awards Governor of the Year, East of England, in 2009/10. She has been a governor of five schools, and is Chair of Governors at Oakgrove School, Milton Keynes. She was on the Board of Governors of the IOE, London, for three years. Her research encompasses principal preparation, teacher development, and emotion and leadership. Her book *Getting to the Heart of Leadership* was published by Sage in 2009. Her new book, *Developing as an Educational Leader and Manager,* will be published by Sage in 2014.

Dr. Louise Grisoni is Associate Dean Research and Knowledge Exchange in the Faculty of Business and Management at Oxford Brookes University. Her research is located in the field of organization studies with a specific interest in relational aspects of organization behaviour in times of change. Alongside this, she has developed a unique interdisciplinary approach to organizational inquiry which aims to understand deeper, emotional aspects of the research process using arts-based forms of inquiry such as poetry, making artefacts, singing and other art forms. Using an extended epistemology of knowing, she claims that the place where thought happens and new understandings occur is located in the boundaries between knowing and not knowing, experience, emotions and articulation in words.

Professor Chris James is the Professor of Educational Leadership and Management in the Department of Education at the University of Bath, a post he has held for the last eight years. Prior to his appointment, Chris was Professor of Educational Management at the University of Glamorgan. His main research interests are in the leadership and management in schools and colleges, the affective aspects of educational organizations, collaborative working in educational settings and school governing. During his career, Chris has directed a large number of educational research projects with a total value in excess of £1 million, and he has published over two hundred items, including six books. He has worked with a range of public, private and not-for-profit organizations, including numerous local authorities and schools. In the field of organizational psychodynamics Chris's current interests include affective containment educational organizations; archetypal behaviour in educational settings; defences against organizational change in schools and colleges; and attachment and educational leadership. He is married to Jane, and they have four grown-up children.

Professor David Knights is Professor of Organization Studies at Lancaster University and the Open University. His research interests can be divided into six principal areas, each of which have various degrees of overlap – Organization

Studies, Management Control, Power, Identity and Resistance; Gender and Diversity Studies; Financial Services Consumption, Education and Regulation; Information Communication Technology; Organizational Change and Innovation; Theory, Knowledge, Epistemology and Methodology. His current research has been on academics and business schools, the global financial crisis, the body and embodiment and, most recently, on veterinary surgeons. He jointly created and continues to edit *Gender, Work, and Organization* and is on the board of several other journals.

Dr. Stella Maile is a Senior Lecturer in Sociology and Criminology and convener of a public engagement initiative, Social Science in the City, University of the West of England. She draws on psycho-social research methodology to explore a range of social phenomena, from exploring the meaning of the British Honours System in everyday life, to investigating the social imaginaries and emotions people project onto cities. She has also written and published on managerial discourses in public sector restructuring, along with their gendered dimensions. Stella is interested in the submerged emotions of thought and action since these tell us something about the way in which social structure and culture is lived in the mind and actions of social agents.

Dr. Haneen Shoaib is an Assistant Professor of Organisation Studies and Strategy as Practice at the University of Business and Technology, Jeddah, Saudi Arabia. She did her PhD at Exeter University, School of Management. Her PhD research investigated dramaturgical aspects of the enactment of power within strategic interactions in Saudi Arabia, focusing on issues of gender, culture, religion and institutions. Her research interests lie in the area of organization studies with a focus on ethics, emotions and gender. Investigating issues of power and culture are very important to her on both academic and personal levels.

FIGURES

FOREWORD

Within the past twenty years or so, researchers from a clutch of social science disciplines – psychology, sociology, anthropology, management – have succeeded in bringing emotions out of the closet and into the foreground of social and organizational research. We now have a rich theoretical and empirical tradition to draw upon, challenging the old binary divide between heart and head, thinking and feeling, cognition and emotion. These operate together – interpenetrate – in complex ways to shape decisions, fuel doubts, drive quandaries, trigger conflicts, define loves, energise prejudices, kill ambitions and heighten joys. The interdisciplinarity of the research has lent a rounded feel to our understandings: that, for instance, biographical experiences cannot be discounted; that what we feel and what we express are often discordant and may 'need' to be; and that emotion is powerfully governed by gender, cultural and subcultural norms.

Yet, and ironically, rarely have these insights been turned back on the research process itself, or on to us as researchers. Formally, we are divorced from the very subject matter of our inquiries; it is about 'them', not 'us' as sentient beings. This is not difficult to comprehend. Objectification, looking outwards, is writ large in the canons of social research methodology, even for freewheeling ethnographies and qualitative inquiries. They may have replaced research 'subjects' with 'participants', or speak of 'negotiated arrangements' to the research methodology, but the researcher is still an anonymous figure in the background. Doctoral theses often pay lip service to the researcher's experience, but usually no more than a brief section at the back of the thesis. It is not what really counts or matters. The researcher's emotional life – fears, anxieties, blocks, conflicts, oppressions and joys – are private matters and are to remain in the closet.

Refreshingly, this book challenges this outlook, which is good for a number of reasons. First, once social research is defined exclusively as a cognitive/intellectual exercise, it marginalises what researchers, both novices and old hands, privately confess that they actually struggle with, and for which they seek support. Institutional arrangements for research students are often administratively driven, and it can be more chance than design that a supervisor is empathically tuned to the student's struggles and dilemmas. Indeed, as this book reveals, some supervisory settings are micro emotional-zones which proscribe the very feelings that should be shared and 'worked on' – because they frame the power balance and tone of the supervisory relationship.

A second reason is about honesty in social science. A discipline that claims truths as if they are separate from the inquirer is being disingenuous, or at least making an error of omission. Through an emotion lens we learn how research topics are attractive to particular researchers, not necessarily because they are intrinsically scientifically worthy, but because they are fashionable and could bring personal kudos; or because they chime with the researcher's own unresolved anxieties, stresses or relationship difficulties; or because they empower the researcher – the feeling of control of others as an 'expert'; or because of anger about a social injustice; or because they help the researcher subvert a social order they dislike; or because pleasing a supervisor or sponsor trumps all other considerations.

A third reason to 'come out' emotionally has less to do with the politics of topic choice and more with the doing of research – the fieldwork, the data analysis. Research in the interpretive tradition is typically ambiguous; doubts and anxieties mix with moments of delight and serendipity. In face-to-face fieldwork the researcher is, amongst other things, an emotional labourer, calibrating what to show of his or her feelings to participants who may be hostile, reluctant, domineering or disliked, or, conversely, attractive and seductive – they give the 'right' answers and flatter the researcher. Differences in age, gender or race can define the emotional subtexts of such encounters. These experiences are typically glossed over or sidelined after the event, but they should not be. They are germane to data interpretation and – on a different level – to the researcher's professional identity, confidence and sense of self.

A final consideration is the sink-or-swim ethos of the research publishing 'game'. This is a serious game with massively more losers than winners, and with rules that can be obscure, idiosyncratic and partial, yet on which an academic reputation hinges. Its vagaries shadowed the production of this very book, as the editors tell us with unusual candour. Few researchers remain untouched, even scarred, by their intense feelings of vulnerability when exposing their work, a part of their selves, to the scrutiny of their peers. Academic reviewers can live a Jekyll and Hyde existence – as friendly, understanding colleagues who, under the cloak of anonymity, transform into acerbic critics out to inflict maximum damage. In part this is an expression of a profession riddled with existential insecurities and self-doubt, and a need to 'prove' oneself. Deprecating the work and ideas of others is self-affirming, but feeds an ethos of ungenerosity at odds with academia's nobler aims – a healthy exchange of ideas and constructive debate. These can soon get lost in the scrabble for survival and recognition. Some of the answer lies in the employment and reward structures for researchers. Some rests with institutional arrangements for support.

But, arguably, these are but tinkerings around the edge of a deeper cultural problem within the research community.

This edited collection grapples with these issues, breaking the taboo that surrounds looking inwards at the researcher and research experience. Hopefully it will stimulate further discussion in the area and, in doing so, provide a platform for change where change is due.

Stephen Fineman
Professor Emeritus School of Management,
University of Bath

1

WHY SHOULD RESEARCHERS BE INTERESTED IN THEIR FEELINGS?

Mike Broussine, Linda Watts and Caroline Clarke

The loneliness of the long-distance researcher

> *The only noise is the tap tap tap of the pen on the desk. This activity is the only one in the room. I stare blankly, . . . the words do not come, stubbornly refusing to appear on my screen, unable to leave my head continuing to go round and round. . . . I want to scream, there is nobody to ask, nobody except me is doing this research; yes they ask me (bewildered) 'how is that research going?' But nobody understands, not even me.*

Researching can be a very lonely experience, and one that brings anxieties and insecurities to the fore. This intensely emotional vignette (which we return to in Chapter 9) explores feelings of guilt that are anchored to the dominant discourses constructed around research; it is an activity which must be tangible, observable and have a definite output within a defined time period. Yet doing research, and especially writing it up, is an inherently creative and potentially enjoyable process. It is an activity, in which words cannot be forced, where inspiration does not arrive by prior arrangement, and where there can be long periods of inactivity.

If you recognise some of these feelings as a researcher, and are sometimes anxious about them, then this book is for you. It will be relevant to master's dissertation students, doctoral students, academic researchers and research supervisors who are engaged in research within an academic or institutional setting. In addition we intend the book to appeal to any student or general academic reader who has an interest in learning more about emotions in social and organizational contexts and how to inquire into these. The text will appeal particularly to those researchers, whether staff or students, who are inclined to carry out research that requires a reflexive and critically self-aware form of engagement, and therefore most likely to be working within interpretivist socio-cultural and psycho-social paradigms. It is likely that such researchers might be using a range of qualitative methods including participative action research, action inquiry, collaborative inquiry, and auto-ethnographic and autobiographical approaches, involving direct interactions with research participants such as interviews, group work and creative workshops. The book will also be relevant to those who are engaged in a range of methodologies in a wide range of settings including organizations, communities and groups. It is likely also to be of interest to authors who come from various academic disciplines within the broad fields of sociology, psychoanalytic theory, systemic psychodynamic theory and psycho-social studies.

A concern with the emotions of carrying out organizational and social research appears to fly in the face of existing prescriptive models and books on 'how to research'. These readily offer up cognitive remedial advice for those researchers who may have gone 'off track'; but we argue that feeling 'off track' is part of the everyday struggle of being a researcher. Indeed, it is this very construction of the rational 'track' which both obfuscates the emotions of researching and renders them deviant from an idealised norm. Perhaps then, the activity of researching, in common with many other activities, is far more off track than on.

We believe that this book will act as a companion to the researcher who has embarked on her or his research journey, whether as a lonely research student, as an independent researcher or as part of a group of co-researchers. We hope also that, by illuminating the emotional *processes* of doing *social and organizational* research, this will inform practice by stimulating reflection in those responsible for managing research programmes and supervising researchers. Our contention is that exploring the implications of the emotional experience of researching will contribute to shaping and reshaping the theory and practice of organizational and social research.

In each chapter the authors discuss the emotions they experienced while researching in a variety of settings. Unusually, they make available to us, and interpret, the often intense feelings they experienced in undertaking their research – in research 'encounters' with research participants, stakeholders and 'power-holders' in a range of research contexts. Our colleagues offer several 'takes' on the topic, including power relations in organizations in which researchers may be working; psycho-social explanations of researcher emotions; feelings evoked in the process of researching by virtue of paradoxical relations with research participants, and the sometimes disturbing data that is gained; the emotional experience of research supervision; the politics of researching, and gender; and the intense feelings that may be generated in the aftermath of research – publishing, undergoing *vivas* and presenting at conferences. It will become clear to the reader, therefore, that chapter authors have exposed for us their anxieties, hopes and vulnerabilities in their stories, and we know that this has not always been an easy process for them (or us). As editors of this text, we very much appreciate and respect how much they have given of themselves in their writing for this book.

So, why should researchers be interested in their feelings?

> Our intention is to affirm this life, not to bring order out of chaos, nor to suggest improvements in creation, but simply to wake up to the very life we're living, which is so excellent once one gets one's mind and desires out of its way and lets it act of its own accord.
>
> (John Cage, Composer, 1912–92)

Our intention is to reflect on researchers' emotional journeys, so that together we may begin to increase our understanding of the feelings – positive or negative – that are, we believe, an inherent part of the experience of researching. We think that this text addresses an important area in the literature by focusing on the emotional aspects of research. Researchers' accounts of their experience and feelings (vignettes) are set alongside some theoretical considerations concerning emotion and how these are often downplayed in the existing research methodology literature.

We begin with the proposition that the relationship between researchers and their research is not straightforward, though researchers can sometimes feel under pressure to think otherwise, as the following vignette supplied by a colleague research supervisor illustrates.

> So, the three of us – the prospective PhD student, the Dean of the Faculty and me – sitting around the table in the Dean's office. This was the first time that the three of us had got together. As is to be expected on these occasions, we were struggling to choose a possible focus for the study. The student was a very busy senior manager in a complex public service organization, so it wasn't at all the case that her ideas were lacking in any way – it was just very complex, and we were trying to find a way through. It felt to me that this was an interesting and enjoyable exploration, and the student was enthusiastic about what we were doing. However, after an hour or so of this, the Dean apparently lost patience – was he trying to be helpful? I don't know. He got up and went to the white board in his office: 'Look, this is one of the easiest PhD's I've come across . . .', and proceeded to set down the ways in which the study could be conducted in 'five simple steps'. So, all the fascinating complexity that we had been talking about had been reduced to these bullet points. I glanced at the student, who met my eyes – she was clearly appalled, as I was. She pursued her studies at another university.

We contend that the primary focus and concern in much of the research methodology literature is the process of undertaking research as a 'task' with a number of steps; but the feelings that are experienced or provoked by the research process, and the possible reasons for these feelings, are downplayed, not explored in sufficient depth and often completely ignored. There are a few, and thankfully a growing number of, exceptions to this, and contributors point to some of these sources later.

So, why should we as researchers be interested in our own feelings and emotions as we carry out research? This hardly seems contentious since there is no human endeavour that escapes emotion; indeed, it is often our passion as well as our intellect that inspires us to devote time and energy to any piece of research. And this is as much the case in the natural as the social sciences, although we only tend to hear of this through inspired communicators of science such as Jacob Bronowski or Brian Cox. We could argue that feelings, emotions and passions are as important to human existence as the intellect, rationality and detached independence, but writing this way further fuels the idea that 'heart' and 'mind' can indeed be separated. Rather, we challenge (as many have) this Cartesian mind–body dualism. Indeed, throughout this book we explore how these ideas are inseparable in conducting research. After all, just as we find inhumanity unacceptable in everyday life, so the idea of 'inhuman research' is just as hard to countenance, particularly as this runs contrary to the experiences we have on a daily basis.

But, important as these ideas are philosophically, we need to go beyond this moral standpoint by suggesting that researchers who are reflexively and critically self-aware about their feelings, motives, values, biographies, ethics, prejudices, passions and ways of seeing are better equipped to conduct more insightful, deeper and richer research. Part of this insight comes from realising that we are always a part of what we are researching, no matter what kind of research we are engaged in and that this reflexive capacity brings both freedoms and responsibilities. The freedoms include allowing ourselves to pursue our commitments, to start the research in the first place and to follow our passions and avenues of inquiry in ways that challenge and fascinate us, but which also contribute to human knowledge. The accompanying responsibility is to be aware continually of our emotional and socio-political selves and to question, be in dialogue with and learn about who we are as people, and what are the conditions and consequences of our research practice for wider society, and not just for our own research careers. Therefore, a series of concerns or frames should be considered during our research as we try to reflect on our feelings and where they come from. Of course, it would be a tall order to achieve this completely, and we acknowledge that we can only ever be partially aware of all that we feel and the possible and multiple reasons why this may be so. But 'researching with feeling' may be facilitated and strengthened by at least some interrogation and exploration of these concerns or frames.

We set out to name some of the frames and influences in Figure 1.1. We are all too aware of the dangers that accompany 'models' that purport to provide universal explanations of phenomena, and therefore we are in no way making any objective claims surrounding our attempt. Instead the diagram and its component parts are offered both as an illustration of some of the core concerns of the book and as a way of enabling the reader to sense-make and explore the dynamics and complexities of researching 'with feeling'. These frames will be referred to throughout the book, but of course the 'worlds' involved in the relationship between researcher and research are infinitely complex and variable, and researchers' desires and fears may not be apparent, transparent or even known. We will explore the emotional

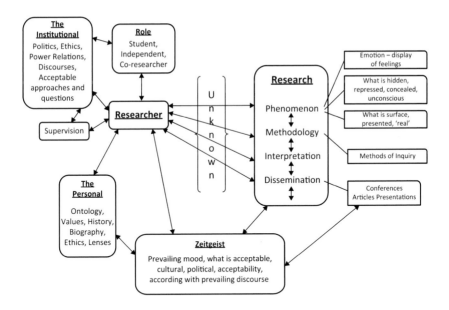

FIGURE 1.1   The dynamics and complexities of researching 'with feeling'

consequences for the researcher of the dynamic movement, complexity and interplay in the relationships – including power relationships – between the component
parts of the system of which the researcher is a part.

At the heart of the diagram, that which comes between the researcher and
the research, and permeates the experience of researching, is *what is unknown* or
unknowable, the root source of anxiety for any human being, but here we are specifically concerned with our anxiety as researchers. There are many reasons why we
have included what is unknown centrally in the diagram, for our sense of agency,
control and predictability are always partial, and the process of research is no different; will the researcher gain access to the research site? Does the researcher feel she
or he can do this? What will be thrown up in the data? Is the methodology going
to work? Is the research 'acceptable' to gatekeepers, stakeholders and the institution? How with it all turn out? At another level, Sturdy (2003) has argued that,
from certain perspectives (e.g. post-structuralism, social constructionism) *everything*
is unknowable, including our transient, private or disguised emotions, and it is these
views that have led either to the avoidance of the study of emotion in social systems or, alternatively, to attempts to objectify and/or commodify feelings (Fineman,
1993; 2000). The view argued in this book however is that the 'mist' that surrounds
the researcher/research relationship is central in understanding the anxiety, commitment, enjoyment, curiosity and frustration and a myriad of other feelings that
are possible in our quest to do good research.

In addition to the well-known complexities that are inherent in the research
process (as illustrated towards the right-hand side of the diagram), there is a range

of concerns and influences that impinge on the researcher, not the least of which is where the researcher is 'coming from' (*the personal*). Further, the critically self-aware researcher may come to realise that the emotional experience of researching may emerge, for good or ill, out of how his or her *role* is defined (or not), and what the expectations of *the institution* are (perhaps, in the case of research students, mediated or conveyed through the supervision process); these in turn originate in dominant discourses and the politics of the research enterprise. And all this is embedded within the social *zeitgeist* operating in the wider and outer reaches of any particular system.

Emotion is what it is to exist, to be human, and is present in every sphere of our lives. All activities are infused with emotion, even those that are constructed as 'rational', because rationality and emotionality are interpenetrated and entwined: in other words we are not *only* rational or *only* emotional, because all thinking is tinged with feeling, and all feeling is tinged with thinking (Fineman, 2000). However, rationality is constructed to depend upon 'the existence and absence of emotionality' (Putnam and Mumby, 1993: 42), and it is this rational discourse that smothers the 'natural' emotional state, with its 'triumph' lying in its ability to 'make itself appear so natural' (Hopfl and Linstead, 1997: 5). Yet if we support the notion that emotion is pervasive, interwoven and embedded in all that we do, it follows that it *should* feature in any literature on 'how to' research, as all research involves both a human researcher and/or a human participant. But when we read about 'how to research', where do we find support for this view? In common with many spheres of life, we find that emotions are all too often 'written out' of research accounts, 'written out' of the way we research, the way we feel about that research, and the overall experience of what it means to be a living, breathing social researcher.

Emotions are often ignored, suppressed and glossed over because they are seen 'to interfere with task performance,' and the 'visual display of emotion must be contained so that normal service can be resumed as soon as possible' (Fineman and Gabriel, 1996: 157). In this way, emotions, and particularly negative emotions, are kept backstage (Tracey, 2000), so the value of emotion is devalued since notions of logic and rationality underwrite many of our Western beliefs. Such beliefs, however, perpetuate a false discourse of rationality, as our experience tells us intuitively this is not 'how it is'. In this book we try to restore and reclaim the notion that research is eminently emotional, and we use a series of vignettes to illustrate and 'bring alive' these ideas. The etymology of *vignette* originates in the notion of 'decorative design', originally a design in the form of vine tendrils around the borders of a book page, from the French *vignette*, the Old French diminutive of *vigne* – vineyard. Vignettes occur throughout the book, however, not just as elegant presentational flourishes, but as a way for authors to offer their sometimes poignant and difficult stories, or those of colleagues and students who have shared experiences with them.

Social research is of course about relationships, and relationships are founded on feelings and ideas that we have about others and the way we interact with them. Emotions therefore are never something we 'own' privately but are rather to be found in 'relational' activity (Waldron, 2000) as our emotions are always about someone or something. Importantly, we argue that emotions are inextricably linked with other concepts such as power, politics, gender, class, race and voice. So, for example, in some of the vignettes included in subsequent chapters, we may see the gendered nature of certain institutions where masculine practices are privileged over feminine ones to form a particular kind of culture. These particular aspects of culture are often reproduced over time by those who enter them, or alternatively they may be reshaped or resisted.

Paradoxically, by writing any book about emotions there is a risk of falling into a trap – that, by focusing on emotions on their own, we are in danger of undermining the very notion which we argue for: that emotions are all pervasive. Worse, if we were to present emotion in isolation, and divorced from context, we might by implication suggest that our feelings exist in a vacuum, and that a focus solely on our feelings is self-indulgent. We keep this danger at bay in two ways: first, by using vignettes we will prevent emotions from becoming acontextual; second, we intend to link emotion where possible with other concepts, to illustrate the connections and links, and to show how emotions can never be absent, neutral or apolitical (as Figure 1.1 outlines). We also return to the potential trap of self-indulgence in Chapter 11. In the opening vignette we saw how doing research can be a lonely and isolating experience. In this next offering we show how, on this occasion, emotions, power and gender can be woven together:

> Ours was to be one of a series of workshops, held in a smaller room away from the main conference. We visited this room before the workshop start time, and found it easily because it was signed 'Women chief executives research'. The room was laid out in a formal fashion, but we were clear that we wanted the session to be participative, and so re-arranged chairs into a circle. Then we went back to hear the main speaker. When we returned, the room had been put back into its original layout – irritating, to say the least. Having recreated the circle, I went to the overhead projector to try it out. But there was something wrong: we got a very blurry image. I left it on while we talked about phoning for a replacement. Then we started to smell burning: a bit of newspaper had been inserted in the periscope of the projector, and the lens started to singe the paper. This turned out to be a page 3 'girlie' picture from that morning's Sun. This was scary! Someone had been in to sabotage our workshop! We already had an awareness of some of the messages we were getting from The System, and this added to our paranoia. We fantasized about who had done this – surely not anyone to do with our client? What if it was? What would this mean? Surely not. It must have been someone unconnected who wanted to take the piss. As our first participants came in, both of us held – shall we say – heightened emotions at that point, but we got amazing support from the participants when we told them what had happened. The workshop was a joy.

We believe strongly that feelings should be reclaimed and written into our accounts of researching, in order to reflect the experience of researchers who may feel puzzled or inadequate when reading cognitive 'step by step' books on how to research. Most researchers, we contend, will find that their own research activity has been far messier, complex and challenging than most methodology books prepare them for. In this next vignette we see how events do not always unfold in the ways in which we plan them, and how this can evoke heightened emotions for the researcher in unpredictable ways. 'How to' research books rarely prepare one for the unexpected.

> *I was presented with a misunderstanding by the manager about the purpose of the inquiry workshop. He introduced it as one in which I 'will give us feedback on his research so far, and bring us up-to-date on the latest thinking about the management of change'. In fact, I thought I'd made it clear that this event was part of the data-gathering phase, and wasn't a review of the project as he had thought. When I said that I did not see the workshop in the way he saw it, the manager became angry. While he grudgingly allowed me to proceed with the workshop as planned, the formerly co-operative relationship with participants was contaminated by the anxiety that this misunderstanding had provoked in everyone. I found myself trying to deal with this anxiety as well as the research task. The way I tried to manage this was to offer (too many) views and comments on what was being said, in a hesitant and hopeless attempt to appease the manager, e.g. stating how this compared with the other participating organizations, references to theory, etc. My losing the plot about my purpose, and my confused behaviour as a result of the surprise the manager had presented, led me to think at the time that this workshop was a disaster. But my re-reading of the transcript some weeks later – after the pain and embarrassment had subsided a bit – revealed some good data, but this wasn't an experience I wanted to repeat.*

Limited but growing literature on researchers' feelings

We have argued that the emotional experience of researchers has been at least underplayed in many methodology texts, in favour of 'rational' or positivist research approaches that somehow assume that the integrity of the research process is enhanced by excluding the researcher's emotional journey. This 'lacuna' represents an important void in the literature on research practice, and, critically, it also represents a significant gap in theoretical development.

Rigorous discussion of researcher emotion is not easy to find in the 'mainstream' qualitative research literature. For example, in the whole of the *Sage Handbook of Qualitative Research* (Denzin and Lincoln, 2005), the researcher's emotion is referred to infrequently or obliquely. This is not to be overly critical: the publication includes some working with emotion (though not named as such) among those authors who consider researcher *reflexivity*, e.g. Foley and Valenzuela (2005). References to the researcher's emotions that arise in the conduct of the studies, and how working with these can aid our understanding of social phenomena, are however few and far between. An exception was Kleinman and Copp (1993), who indeed called for a sociological approach to fieldwork that incorporated the validity of researcher's emotional experience. However, this interesting though short (eighty pages) text is now 21 years old, and our proposal widens the discussion from fieldwork to incorporate in its scope the personal, institutional and political contexts for research. More recently, of course, Stephen Fineman (1993; 2000) and colleagues have added substantially to our understanding about studying emotions in organizations, and the reader will notice that chapter authors have drawn on their work from time to time. However, Fineman's analyses have been less concerned with researchers' own emotions.

Indeed, Gilbert (2001) argued that the existing literature on qualitative research could be criticised for focusing on the emotions and feelings of the researched group (p.136), and commented that it was comparatively rare for researchers to include descriptions and analyses of intense emotions experienced in fieldwork. Although an important observation on the disembodied form that researcher's writing often takes, the implication in this text is that emotion is a potentially important 'add on' within ethnographic methodology, rather than being inherent to the research process. Campbell (2002) rejected the notion that the researcher's emotions may taint investigation, and she suggested that a reflective analysis of the researcher's emotions can provide additional theoretical insight.

A relatively large component of the academic writing on emotion in the research process is understandably drawn from, and geared to, research in health care or therapeutic settings, but it tends to focus on emotion as a research subject rather than 'researching with feeling'. These are accounts from established researchers, largely based in health care. Key themes include the 'emotion work' involved in doing research, the influence of the self and others on the research outcome, and issues of control. Emotion work emerges as being integral to the process of data gathering. Interestingly, acknowledgment is given to the emotional 'downside' of doing research in a way that implies a split or separation of emotion as a negative dimension. The term 'emotion work' is in itself rather revealing, as much of the material on research on emotion in a health context is concerned with managing and controlling emotion in interviews rather than 'holding' and exploring emotional expression (Hallowell, Lawton and Gregory, 2004).

The work of Ashkanasy, Hartel and Zerbe (2005) is worth noting in relation to researching emotion in organizations, but this takes a more cognitive approach – often advocating measurement and seeing different types of emotion as variables, and forming cause and effect explanations – and is not concerned with the emotions of the researcher. More often, relevant specific comment by academics is found in papers and articles rather than in the substantial methodology reference works. For instance, the paper by Hubbard *et al.* on working with emotion (Hubbard, Backett-Milburn and Kemmer, 2001) addresses the role of emotion in the qualitative research process and, in particular, the effects of emotional experiences on the researcher. Drawing briefly on the literature, they show the importance of

emotion for understanding the research process. But whilst this literature acknowledges the emotional risk for research respondents, there is little evidence providing
in-depth understanding of the researcher's emotions. They consider, theoretically
and empirically, the significance of emotion through the duration of a research
project. Using their own personal experiences in the field, they present a range of
emotional encounters that qualitative researchers may face and offer suggestions for
research teams who wish to develop strategies for 'managing' emotion. They conclude that unless emotion in research is acknowledged, not only will researchers be
left vulnerable, but our understandings of the social world will remain impoverished.

There is recent evidence that an academic interest in organizational and social
researchers' emotions is growing. Here are two examples. First, Koning and Ooi
(2013) suggest that researchers rarely present accounts of their awkward encounters
in ethnographies. But they argue 'awkwardness' does matter and affects the accounts
we write and our understanding of social situations. By explicitly exploring the
origins and natures of 'awkward encounters', we may improve our understanding
of organizational realities. Their paper discusses awkward ethnographic encounters
in the field, including encounters with evangelizing ethnic Chinese business people
in Indonesia. Based on analysing their awkwardness, Koning and Ooi make the
case for a more 'inclusive reflexivity'. Fieldworkers encounter awkward moments
when interacting with research, and, because ethnographic fieldwork is inherently
relational, it is also emotionally laden. However, the degree to which researchers
reveal or repress emotions, like awkwardness, in their writing is a marginalized topic
of discussion in ethnographic reflection – these are the 'untold stories of the field'
(2013: 17). In this book, we are attempting to tell a few such stories from the field.

Another example of a recent discussion about researchers' feelings is offered by
Angela Mazzetti (2013), who suggests, similarly to us, that much of the literature on
researcher emotion is situated within health and social sciences and is focused on
'sensitive' research with limited reference to the issue in management and organization studies. Her chapter draws on her own experience in researching occupational
stress through qualitative methodologies and suggests that qualitative research can
be challenging particularly when it involves the exploration of emotive issues such
as occupational stress. Her experiences hold a particular pertinence to this book.
Mazzetti suggests that, although research institutions provide ethical guidelines for
the protection and support of research participants, much less emphasis is placed on
the impact of such research on the researcher:

> In qualitative studies of occupational stress, participants often display a range
> of emotions to a researcher who is expected to be both empathetic and
> professional in his/her conduct. If qualitative researchers are inadequately
> prepared for the emotions they may experience in the field and poorly sup-
> ported through the research process, then they may lose confidence and
> eschew qualitative research in favor of quantitative work thereby maintaining
> the status quo in occupational stress research.
>
> *(Mazzetti, 2013: 287)*

Surfacing a major theme that we write about in Chapters 3 and 4 of this volume, Mazzetti also notes that researchers may encounter significant 'political' conflicts when they encounter organizational power imbalances which threaten to constrain or manipulate their research. Citing several sources, she reminds us that researchers are not always welcome in organizations and, in studies in which senior managers have granted access, participants may be suspicious of the intentions of the researcher. She concludes that the risks of such potential threats to researchers should be included explicitly in ethical approval processes.

Such welcome additions to the literature concerning researchers' experiences contribute to a sense that it is gradually becoming more legitimate to focus on and be concerned with researcher feelings more centrally in academic discourse. However, as the narratives and vignettes included in the following chapters demonstrate, the reader will get a sense that there is some way to go before there is a universally accepted view that a deep appreciation of researchers' feelings contributes to a richer and deeper understanding about what goes on in social and organizational systems and contexts.

The chapters to come

In this book, through our own writing and the work contributed by a range of interested researchers and authors, we hope to show how research is far more than a predictable process of linear cognitive events. At every stage of the research process, our experiences are marinated in all kinds of emotion: they are important, they are everywhere infusing everything we do, and to deny this obscures what it is to be human, and a living, breathing researcher.

Matthew Brannan's chapter – Chapter 2 – explores how emotions are avoided, overlooked, downplayed and even ignored within the context of social research, and he outlines the consequences of such strategies upon research outcomes. The author offers an auto-ethnographic account of how he sought to analyse the role that emotions played in the lives of research participants whilst marginalising or ignoring his own emotions during the conduct of fieldwork. While it is increasingly recognised that the separation of the act of research from its emotional experience is unsustainable, the account here demonstrates how such practices may remain strongly entrenched. For many, the first experience of fieldwork-based research is inextricably linked to the pursuit of a PhD qualification and peer-acceptance within the academic community. The contribution here is to argue that this institutional framework may encourage a certain inattention to issues of emotionality within the research context and this stands in stark contrast to the growth of research that takes as its object the emotions of others and wider trends toward reflexivity in research practice.

In Chapter 3, Caroline Clarke and David Knights discuss the relative 'status' of the researcher as well as the researched and argue that researching is intricately and intimately tied to our and others' gender, age, class, race, and sexuality and thus to links between power, politics and the personal. Identities are bound up inextricably with certain signifying 'characteristics' – commonly, our age, disability, ethnicity, gender and sexual preferences. There are other less physically visible (but equally important) signifiers of the self, such as religion and class, that influence the degree to which we are considered 'acceptable' in any given organization or community, depending on how difference/diversity is either celebrated or rejected by the members of a particular group. In many instances the researchers may be constructed as 'interlopers' into another environment. Researchers may then have to 'work' on their identities (through the performance of *identity work*) in order to create connections with other members, and suppress much of what they feel in line with any prevailing cultural rules. This chapter explores how researchers can feel marginalised because of their position, often as 'students', a traditional and therefore comparatively ambiguous identity. Researchers are often young and can readily be patronized by the people whose behaviour they are seeking to understand. In such circumstances, and as evidenced in Chapter 2, researchers may be the butt of jokes because they are seen as naïve and unworldly (Collinson, 1992). Other times, researchers may be co-opted into the culture and be in danger of 'going native'. This demonstrates how there is a fine line between the dispassionate and the over-empathetic research self.

Louise Grisoni and Mike Broussine recount the emotional experience of carrying out 'insider research' in Chapter 4, and this is based on their stories about conducting two action research projects that became 'politically and emotionally charged'. One of these involved a study carried out within one of the authors' institutions. The second researched the experience of senior women leaders within an organizational system. In the first example, they explore how researching in their own organization can lead to a range of tensions, conflicts and anxieties, and how these in turn influence the direction of the study itself, including methodological choices. As for the study of senior women leaders, they recall how the project provoked feelings in the author and his co-researcher following their negative encounters with the politics of the system – the voices of discouragement and disapproval that questioned the very need for the research. The chapter discusses how action researchers inevitably become part of a political system that is characterised by different actors holding different aspirations for possibly diverging research outcomes, and argues that not only do we need to listen to the range of voices that stakeholders represent but we also need to attend reflexively to our own emotions to assess their meanings and effects on the conduct of our research.

Anger is the focus of Chapter 5, in which Emma Bell and Haneen Shoaib argue that the formation of researcher identity is an embodied, emotional process based on socialisation into established cultural norms. Yet traditional research training encourages the suppression of embodied emotion, particularly if it threatens to disrupt formal learning. In this chapter the role of anger in research is explored by drawing on a study of gendered organizational power relations rooted in Saudi Arabian practices. The authors consider the role of powerful cultural norms in socialising researchers as gendered subjects and suggest that anger provides a resource through which identity threats may be resisted, reconfigured and reshaped. Using the notion of the research apprenticeship, they argue that anger can enable the construction of more caring research relationships.

Chapter 6 by Linda Watts draws from her own research to examine how psychology and its related disciplines, including psychoanalysis, approach the study of emotions and human experience. Psycho-social research aims to provide greater insight into the nature of identities, responses to social change, racial hatred and other significant contemporary concerns. They are concerned with the interrelation between individual subjectivities and the social and political domain. The argument is put forward that psycho-social forms of inquiry can make a significant contribution to our repertoire of qualitative and interpretive methodologies by accessing metaphorical and/or symbolic material. Psycho-social researchers are essentially reflexive researchers, committed to continuous self-reflection, including reflection on the emotional issues in their research processes and the implications of their own emotional engagement.

The emotional experience of research supervision is the subject of Chapter 7, in which Mike Broussine and Linda Watts explore researchers' emotional travails as they journey through their research process, and the role that research supervision can, does or does not play in facilitating this journey. An earlier collaborative inquiry with students and supervisors showed how major postgraduate research projects generate emotional experiences in researchers. As the student pursues his or her studies towards completion of a dissertation or thesis, the emotional highs and lows can be experienced over some years, and the research process may be life-changing. The authors explore the extent to which research supervision can provide a container for research students' feelings such as being in a cul-de-sac, isolation, distress, frustration, uncertainty and insecurity. However, in the role of supervisee, the student is likely to also experience complex power relations in the system, dependency, domination and gender dynamics. Tensions related to the demands for academic rigour may heighten anxiety significantly and foster 'the imposter syndrome'. This chapter is an experiential assessment of these fundamental yet relatively unacknowledged issues.

Stella Maile starts Chapter 8 by asking why is it so difficult to write about the feelings surrounding our studies and our research inquiries, or, more particularly, writing about *not* pursuing them. She suggests that some of the themes she explores in *not* researching where she grew up may be understood in terms of an emotional defence against the power-structures, practices and imaginaries of the past which may still live somewhere in and be enacted by us. Researchers might feel the embarrassment of self-indulgence and understand the risk of exposing an academic social taboo – not to speak of ourselves; or only to speak of ourselves in the service of understanding those who are 'worse' off than ourselves in some way; to focus on the emotions of others, the *researched*, as if they are entirely different from us. The use of our own subjectivity in research can, the author argues, quite rationally help us to think about our own experiences and questions in *relation with* others with whom we share something by virtue of being social and relational subjects – our histories, cultures and spaces.

In Chapter 9, Caroline Clarke takes us to the point when the researcher needs to write up and present his or her research, as a dissertation or thesis, or as a report, article and/or conference paper. For example, there can surely be few educational situations which provoke such anxiety as the *viva voce*, and she illustrates how the potential for anguish at this stage is deep and multi-faceted. Many if not most researchers report anxiety about writing up their research, especially from the point of view of 'going public' on something critical or radical. Feelings of self-doubt or the 'impostor syndrome' (Clance and Imes, 1978) are common, and these feelings can be reinforced by the experience of rejection (by supervisors, publishers, academia) or by the prospect of criticism and humiliation; others' vulnerabilities stem from wondering whether what they have produced is a 'proper' thesis or article. Researchers may also wonder whether they have done justice to the voices of those who participated in the study and/or whether they have projected their anxieties into their respondents. These situations provoke intense feelings, yet are rarely acknowledged in books about 'how to research' or even about the working lives of academics.

Chapter 10 asks an important question as we near our conclusion – how do we get interested by research generally and get fascinated by research with feelings specifically? Chris James and Megan Crawford draw attention to a very significant issue for researchers that lies at the heart of this book and adds to the fascination of the research: as they, and all the other authors, argue, the research process itself is imbued with feelings. Their fascination leads them to argue for an affective paradigm in social and organizational research that recognises, for example, the interplay between affection, cognition and volition and that aids interpretation of feelings-based practice and behaviour. The paradigm enables exploration of the 'problematics' of researching emotion. Furthermore, Chris James and Megan Crawford suggest that it aids understanding of the affective experience of *being a researcher*. Making sense of the affective experience of researching enables an understanding of how feelings influence our research practice and how to approach deeper personal understanding.

In Chapter 11 we offer the reader our concluding reflections. We begin by 'declaring our hands' (Watson, 1994) about the experience of writing and editing this book – which is, after all, a piece of research in itself – and discuss our 'backstage secrets' and awkward moments that show how this book has mirrored the content of itself at almost every stage. We felt it was important to revisit the origins of this book because they contain so much of our story, wrapped as it is in our passion, determination, feelings of potential surrender and ultimately the joys involved in working together and perhaps (we hope) producing something worthwhile. Being relatively new to the game of editing a book like this, we were taken aback by the self-doubts and setbacks that surfaced from time to time, even though these were precisely the experiences we were writing about as being 'normal'.

Finally we tackle the awkward question about whether a focus on our feelings as researchers is part of a self-indulgent exercise in narcissism and self-fascination. The possible accusation of self-indulgence may be a major inhibitor to our writing in the first person and may make us feel anxious about self-exposure (or showing our hands). However, these accounts of research experience may encourage researchers to develop their critical and reflexive self-awareness. We end by reassuring the researcher that he or she will undoubtedly experience an emotional journey, that this is to be expected and natural and that it can contribute to greater personal learning and new knowledge which is beneficial for research participants, communities and organizations.

References

Ashkanasy, N., Hartel, C., and Zerbe, W. (2005) *The Effect of Affect in Organizational Settings*, Oxford, UK: Elsevier.

Campbell, R. (2002) *Emotionally Involved – The Impact of Researching Rape*, London: Routledge.

Clance, P.R., and Imes, S. (1978) The Imposter Phenomenon in High Achieving Women: Dynamics and Therapeutic Intervention, *Psychotherapy Theory, Research and Practice*, (15)3: 241–47.

Collinson, D. (1992) *Managing the Shop Floor: Subjectivity, Masculinity and Workplace Culture*, Berlin: Walter De Gruyter.

Denzin, N.K., and Lincoln, Y.S. (eds) (2005) *The Sage Handbook of Qualitative Research*, London: Sage Publications.

Fineman, S. (1993) *Emotion in Organizations*, London: Sage Publications.

Fineman, S. (2000) *Emotion in Organizations* (2nd edn), London: Sage Publications.

Fineman, S., and Gabriel, Y. (1996) *Experiencing Organisations*, London: Sage Publications.

Foley, D., and Valenzuela, A. (2005) Critical Ethnography – The Politics of Collaboration, in Denzin, N.K., and Lincoln, Y.S. (eds) *The Sage Handbook of Qualitative Research*, London: Sage Publications, 217–34.

Gilbert, K.R. (ed.) (2001) *The Emotional Nature of Qualitative Research*, Boca Raton: CRC Press.

Hallowell, N., Lawton, J., and Gregory, S. (2004) *Reflections on Research: The Realities of Doing Research in the Social Sciences*, Buckingham, UK: Open University Press.

Hopfl, H., and Linstead, S. (1997) Introduction: Learning to Feel and Feeling to Learn: Emotion and Learning in Organizations, *Management Learning*, (28)1, 5–12.

Hubbard, G., Backett-Milburn, K., and Kemmer, D. (2001) Working with Emotion: Issues for the Researcher in Fieldwork and Teamwork, *International Journal of Social Research Methodology*, (4) 2, 119–37.

Kleinman, S., and Copp, M. (1993) *Emotions and Fieldwork: Qualitative Research Methods*, London: Sage Publications.

Koning, J., and Ooi, C-S. (2013) Awkward Encounters and Ethnography, *Qualitative Research in Organizations and Management: An International Journal*, (8) 1, 16–32.

Mazzetti, A. (2013) Occupational Stress Research: Considering the Emotional Impact for the Qualitative Researcher, in Perrewé, P.L., Rosen, C.C., and Halbesleben, J.R.B. (eds) *The Role of Emotion and Emotion Regulation in Job Stress and Well Being (Research in Occupational Stress and Well-being, Volume 11)*, Bingley: Emerald Group Publishing Limited, 283–310.

Putnam, L.L., and Mumby, D.K. (1993) Organizations, Emotion and the Myth of Rationality, in Fineman, S. (ed.) *Emotion in Organizations*, London: Sage Publications.

Sturdy, A. (2003) Knowing the Unknowable? A Discussion of Methodological and Theoretical Issues in Emotion Research and Organizational Studies, *Organization*, (10) 1, 81–105.

Tracy, S.J. (2000). Becoming a Character for Commerce: Emotion Labor, Self Subordination and Discursive Construction of Identity in a Total Institution. *Management Communication Quarterly*, (14) 1: 90–128.

Waldron, V.R. (2000) Relational Experiences and Emotion at Work, in Fineman, S. (ed.) *Emotion in Organizations* (2nd edn), London: Sage Publications.

Watson, T.J. (1994) Managing, Crafting and Researching: Words, Skill and Imagination in Shaping Management Research, *British Journal of Management*, (5) Issue Supplement S1, S77–S87.

2

RECOGNISING RESEARCH AS AN EMOTIONAL JOURNEY

Matthew J Brannan

Introduction

The focus of this chapter lies in exploring the emotional processes that are inevitably involved in conducting organizational research and the impact that they have upon research practice. Recognising the emotional aspects of research is important because, despite the recent 'reflexive turn', empirical research often seems to ignore the role of the researcher's emotion in the collection of data and the creation of textual representations. Here I want to explore the issue of how emotions are variously avoided, overlooked, downplayed and even ignored within the context of a specific research project and then to think through the potential impact of emotional avoidance on research outcomes. To do this I have drawn upon a personal account of how I sought to analyse the role that emotions played in the lives of the research participants whilst, at the same time, marginalising or ignoring my own.

Getting all emotional?

Part of the rationale for this book is a growing recognition of the importance of understanding the role that emotions play within research. This I think is necessary because there has been, up until now, insufficient attention paid to the role that emotions play. Understanding why this is the case provides an important context to this chapter.

The absence of emotion from many contemporary research accounts is puzzling given the explosion of interest in, and critical study of, emotion within workplace contexts. Much of this work stems from the publication of Arlie Hochschild's *The Managed Heart* (1983), a work that coined the term 'emotional labour'. Whilst the emotions of others has become *bone fide* intellectual territory, the emotions of researchers, despite increasing calls for and practices of reflexivity, remains noticeably absent.

A key task for Hochschild is to understand the nature of emotional labour in paid employment, and she achieves this by providing examples based upon observation and interviews (Hochschild, 1983: 14; Bryman and Bell, 2007: 409). Basic research tools as these clearly involve an emotional encounter between the researcher and the participant and occur in the context of growing empirical work into studies of emotion in society (Thoits, 1989), organizations (Fineman, 1993; 2000) and the workplace (Bolton, 2004) which are frequently based on qualitative research. It has been suggested that such styles of research necessarily involve the researcher in 'the management of feeling to create a publicly observable facial and bodily display' (ibid.: 7) and 'dealing with other people's emotions' (James, 1989: 15). The study of emotions in others is therefore clearly an emotional endeavour on a number of levels.

Given the growing interest in the emotions of others, it is therefore somewhat surprising that the emotions involved in the research process, and specifically those experienced by the researcher during fieldwork, have not come under more scrutiny (Dickson-Swift *et al.*, 2009). Whilst there are notable exceptions (see for example Lumsden, 2009), researchers' emotions are largely absent from research accounts, and this therefore might even be considered an 'alexithymic' tendency (Brannan and Priola, 2012): a term borrowed from psychiatry defined as 'the inability to find appropriate words to describe [one's] feelings' (Sifneos, 1973: 255).

In attempting to account for emotional absence or 'Alexithymia', Bellas notes that research is culturally often understood as a 'masculine activity', and hence any element of emotional labour (which has been historically associated with femininity) is 'typically minimised or overlooked' (1999: 97). Indeed, in the study of the history of sociology, Laslett argues 'cool-rationality' and 'un-feeling knowledge' provided 'a cultural space to which men could aspire without threat to their masculinity and provided a gate keeping mechanism that limited women's entry' (1990: 429). The marginalisation of emotions from research accounts therefore has much to do with the gendered assumptions surrounding the nature of emotional encounters, and research accounts that explicitly include emotional elements are less likely to conform to masculine ideals of what 'counts' as research. This approach however has important implications for the practice of research and research outcomes, as Jaggar (1989) argues, for example, the construction of emotions as 'epistemologically subversive' is a cultural blind spot in relation to emotions and their importance for the construction of knowledge.

Yet the systematic marginalisation of emotions from research accounts seems at odds with wider trends toward a 'reflexive movement' (Holland, 1999: 482) in social research, where researchers seek to acknowledge the active role they play in the co-construction of data and field relations. Etymologically deriving from the notion of 'bending back', from the perspective of social research, reflexivity means to bend knowledge back on itself, or as Pillow suggests, 'To be reflexive, . . . not only contributes to producing knowledge that aids in understanding and gaining insight into the workings of our social world but also provides insight on how this knowledge is produced' (2003: 178). Attention paid to the conditions of production of knowledge leads to a wide range of practices but, as Hardy *et al*. note, has led to a particular focus on 'the relationship between the research and the research subject ... and particularly the limitation of research in representing the subjects under study and their effect on the creation of 'knowledge' (2001: 532).

Given a context of increasing awareness of the importance of acknowledging the conditions in which accounts are produced, it is hard to comprehend the absence of systematic accounts of the way in which emotions in research play a key role in shaping research accounts. Indeed, a fully reflexive account of the research process would surely acknowledge the importance of emotional dynamics in understanding the relationship between the researched and the researcher.

Given this context and the aims of this book, by way of contribution this chapter explores the process of fieldwork as an 'emotional encounter' through the description of emotional interactions between the researcher and research participants. The chapter is organized as follows: first, the chapter starts by exploring recent developments in the understanding of empirical social research which position reflexivity at the heart of the research relationship. This location is argued to be important because it suggests sensitivity to the dynamics of the research relationship and renders problematic crude versions of empiricism that take the 'collection of data' as unproblematic processes. Furthermore, reflexivity calls for more attention to how researchers are implicated in various ways in the accounts that they produce. The original research aims, and their relation to the concept of emotional labour, are therefore established. The chapter then argues that this research and indeed most qualitative research efforts are inherently 'emotionally intensive' activities. Leading on from this, the chapter considers the specific process of negotiating access and gaining entry to the field and the establishment and development of relations with participants as a nexus that clearly involves emotional dimensions and interactions between participant and researcher. The process of building relations with research participants is explored together with the practical issues of conducting research whilst physically working in the research environment. The chapter concludes with a consideration how this might be usefully related to our understanding of fieldwork processes and the nature of conducting research within the institutional context of Higher Education.

The reflexive turn and emotional absence

The reflexive turn in empirical fieldwork often results in researchers paying more attention to their role in the shaping of the empirical data that they collect. It 'involves a shift in our understanding of data collection from something objective that is accomplished through detached scrutiny of 'what I know and how I know it' to recognising how we actively construct our knowledge' (Finlay, 2002: 532). Indeed it could be argued that reflexivity makes the notion that anything is 'collected at all' problematic; or put another way, "findings" are not *in* the data but created through the interaction of particular (either primary or secondary) researchers with particular respondents in particular locations and at particular historical junctures' (Mauthner *et al.*, 1998: 735 [emphasis added]).

Alvesson (2003: 14) suggests that reflexivity offers researchers two things: first, it removes the overly simplistic notion of the possibility that 'data reveals reality', and, second, it fosters a sensitivity to 'meaning' within the research process. Reflexive sensitivities, therefore, work to disrupt crude empirical notions that data can ever 'reveal' reality or the equally crude view that data can simply be read from participants. Suggestive of a move from the discussion of the hard concrete 'facts' to softer transient 'meanings' also, in many ways, seems to say something profound about the appropriateness of various instruments for research. If, for example, the object of research becomes something as ephemeral as 'meaning', how can researchers ever know their explanations 'capture' these meanings adequately? Questions of validity and reliability, more normally associated with more quantitative approaches, therefore still remain pertinent and important (Hertz, 1996; Creswell and Miller, 2000).

Lynch (2000) provides an open inventory of reflexivities, and this points to the variants and possibilities related to reflexive practice. Whilst this scope of practice is important, we might consider reflexivity to have two broad elements: epistemological reflexivity, which focuses on the impact of researchers' theories of knowledge, assumptions about the work and the impact that these have upon the data collected; and personal reflexivity, which involves an analysis of the research process and understanding of how the specific design and conduct of the research influences the kinds of data produced (Willig, 2001). In both of these domains, the noted absence of concerns and discussion in relation to researchers' emotions is problematic. It seems odd that personal reflexivity would exclude material that has an emotional component. What else could be more personal, yet have such an impact on how a researcher comes to think about fieldwork observations and corresponding construction of data, for example?

Yet reflexivity is not without its critiques and is far from a panacea for research practice. Critics of reflexivity for example argue that attention to researchers' emotions amounts to self-indulgence where areas of genuine research interest are foregone in favour of an egotistic focus on the researcher (Coffey, 1999). Similarly, a reading of Chia suggests that researchers invoke reflexivity as a strategy to authenticate their own research without turning reflexively back on themselves, so-called first-order reflectivity (1996: 44). Whilst it is almost certainly true that forms of reflexivity are deployed as capital to invest authority in the production of ethnographic texts, Brewer's argument locates reflexivity as key to a reconstruction of ethnographic authority (Brewer, 1994). Alternatively, reflexivity might assume the status of a virtue and therefore become a key marker of distinction and a form of capital to be leveraged in the battle between resources and status within the academic field (Lynch, 2000). Against this critique, Alvesson offers Pragmatic Reflexivity, which might be considered to work to balance 'endless reflexivity and radical scepticism with a sense of direction and accomplishment' (2003: 14).

This chapter starts from the observation that emotional accounts of research are seldom to be found in academic work, and, in the context of the recent 'reflexive turn' in fieldwork-based sociology, this is an artificial and unsustainable position. Empirical research often seems to ignore the role of the researchers' emotions in the field-led research, collection of data and the creation of textual representations. This chapter now presents an autoethnographic account in order to seek to provide a number of emotional vignettes drawn from extended ethnographic fieldwork to demonstrate how initial emotional responses act almost as anarchic impulses with little time given to reflection or a more sustained level of reflexivity in the field and wider research processes.

The case study context

Workplace ethnographies arguably provide a well-suited research methodology for attempting to comprehend the contemporary experience of work (Brannan et al., 2008) and equally a potentially rich and hitherto untapped source of insights into the emotional dimensions of fieldwork. Whilst such methods are well used within the field of industrial sociology, their implementation is far from unproblematic. In order to conduct ethnographic research I secured employment at CallCentreCo. between completing a master's degree and starting a PhD, during the summer of 1999. I was employed full time at the case study call centre for a period of thirteen months and engaged in all duties as required of a call centre employee. At the same time as learning the job of a customer service representative (CSR) and working full time at the call centre, I also started and maintained PhD study. I was therefore a full participant in the research setting in the fullest sense (Gold, 1958).

The fieldwork upon which this chapter is based was designed to explore issues surrounding the contemporary experience of work and employment. The context of telephone call centres was chosen as an archetypal form of interactive-based service work. Specifically, the research sought to explore the ways in which competing quality and quantity imperatives, as documented in existing call centre literature (see for example Taylor and Bain, 1999; Taylor et al., 2002), are managed by a small team of CSRs.

Emotional interactions lie at the very heart of CSRs' work routine; Taylor and Bain for example suggest that it is 'evident' that call centre work involves the performance of emotional labour (1999: 103), and key to this is an understanding of the relationship of the CSRs with customers who often require a range of emotional responses and managers increasingly utilising forms of neo-normative control (Fleming and Sturdy, 2011). The ascendancy in front-line service workers as *the* product (Macdonald and Sirianni, cited in Sturdy et al., 2001: 5) has profound effects, and Ashforth and Humphrey for example define emotional labour in service work as being about displaying 'appropriate' emotions (1993: 90) for corporate interests. In many call centre environments, emotional performances are so significant that often the processes through which such interactions are enacted are carefully and systematically regulated (Brannan and Priola, 2012).

Having located the chapter within the development of reflexive social research and situated the emotional focus and context of the research, the chapter now seeks to explore some of the emotional encounters that occurred during the pursuit of fieldwork. The purpose of this is to highlight the impact that such emotional encounters play within the research relationship and upon data collection and analysis. This will then provide the foundation for a conceptual discussion of the role of emotions in pursuit of fieldwork.

Understanding managerial misunderstanding

Full participation in the research setting offers a number of obvious benefits, and some authors writing on the experience of ethnographic research remark upon how the researcher must inhabit two worlds (Sherif, 2001). These might be termed the 'field world' and the researcher's normal 'everyday world'; the acknowledgement of the separations of these worlds however is automatically to acknowledge the distinction between the two and the work of negotiation that must take place to situate the researcher in either or both, a task which is made more complex by issues of temporality. On reflection it is clear that throughout the fieldwork I attempted to keep these worlds as separate as possible. I was reluctant for example to discuss my academic background and interests (wider than the research focus and background required for ethical disclosure) during work at the call centre, whilst at the same time being hesitant to talk about my experience of being a CSR outside of the call centre. Despite this artificial separation, on occasion these two separate worlds inevitably collided and eventually blurred (Leibing and MacLean, 2007). One example of such a collision was the formal institutionalised bureaucracy of conducting research as a PhD student and in particular the university's ethics committee and its requirement that all fieldwork be submitted for scrutiny to an ethics review board as part of the annual review process. This required a double disclosure: first, to the ethics committee, thus allowing the academic world remote access to the field world; and, second, discussing my research with call centre staff, thus allowing access to the academic world from the field.

Whilst all organizational research raises ethical issues for the researcher, and potential dangers for the researched, ethnographic investigation poses particular challenges and ones that are not readily solved by conventional approaches to ethical research (Bosk, 2004). Workplace ethnographies require the construction of an asymmetrical relationship where the researcher's primary aim, and reason for being in the environment, is to conduct sociological inquiry. This aim is, of course, divergent from other participants in the field and is operationalised by becoming a participant within the workplace. Following Murphy and Dingwall (2001), principles to guide ethnographic research can usefully be derived from notions of (a) non-maleficence and beneficence, (b) autonomy and self-determination for research participants and (c) justice. The maintenance of an ethical climate for the investigation was fostered through a discussion of the research, its interests and what the concept of 'data' might mean in an everyday call centre. This discussion took place with fellow team members and call centre managers, and explanations were given about the mode of data collection and how the data would be stored and used, and this included assurances regarding anonymity. The possible dangers or potential harm caused by ethnographic research for participants was explored and issues such as embarrassment, fear and uncertainty were discussed on a one-to-one basis.

Despite the desire to seek informed consent, the duration of the research meant that the establishment of my status as a researcher on entrance to the field might have become blurred over the course of the fieldwork. Indeed much ethnographic research is predicated upon this process of 'naturalisation', the idea that researchers' initial 'strangeness' *in situ* will become eroded over time.

As part of my initial introduction to the call centre, I had discussed with Amanda (the call centre manager) the possibility of conducting research within the call centre. Outlining a research interest in employee misbehaviour and monitoring, I also had discussions with peer employees that emphasised my interest in their daily routine. The construction of my 'frames of reference' were reflective of my pre-existing concerns to understand the lived experience of CSRs rather than a specific focus upon workplace resistance, which given the managerial consent which accompanied the project might have been interpreted as an official investigation of CSR misbehaviour. Despite the candour with which I believed I had articulated my interests, the research intent, especially at managerial levels, was constantly misinterpreted as being concerned with exploring the development of team working. This was indicated in informal discussions with various managers who openly discussed the project but framed the issues in relation to individual participation in teams and team working. Despite specifically highlighting my interest in workplace misbehaviour, the research was constantly misunderstood – as the following example from some seven months into the research demonstrates:

AMANDA: *Ooh Matthew, how's your project going, you finding out anything interesting?*
MATTHEW: *Well it's challenging but I'm enjoying it.*
AMANDA: *I read this article I think you'd be interested in it, it's about sharing knowledge in teams, and how software like 'Whiteboard' (a recent addition to the computers in the call centre) can help, I thought it would be right up your street?*
MATTHEW: *Yes in the company magazine . . . it's interesting . . . I read that, but you know that the project isn't really about knowledge management . . . it's more about workplace behaviour and new forms of working.*
AMANDA: *Yeah, but it's all the same thing really isn't it?*
> (discussion with call centre manager in staff kitchen, recorded in notebook, later transcribed in fieldwork journal)

Amanda's assertion that 'it's all the same thing really' demonstrates an ambivalence to the project and my particular concerns and is an example of a misunderstanding which is analytically significant, as Davies explains:

> The development of multifaceted relationships with some individuals in the field helps to sensitize ethnographers to the possibilities not simply for deliberate deception, but for mutual misunderstandings arising from cultural and sometimes personal differences. These latter may be among the most informative for analysis, particularly when the ethnographer and informants manage to uncover and move beyond them.
>
> *(1999: 83)*

I had expected to meet stiff resistance to research, but I sensed a tolerance in terms of what I wanted to do, or perhaps indifference. Although not actively encouraged, I was given clear instructions that I could carry on with my research as long as it did not interfere with any aspect of my work; in particular, any research should not impinge upon my time 'taking calls'! The gaining of managerial consent was somewhat surprising as, at the time (July 1999–August 2000), a number of high-profile stories of poor conditions in call centres had broken in the national news media, and reflecting on this I noted a sense that managers were keen to 'reveal another side of call centre work' (informal discussion with call centre manager), and from this perspective a researcher working as a CSR might be considered as a useful vehicle for a managerial public relations agenda. This highlights the potential for research participants to make use of, or attempt to make use of, research for their own ends. Indeed managerial consent to this project presented further challenges, as I was concerned that my interest in misbehaviour, together with managerial approval, might lead some CSRs to conclude that I was a management spy.

On reflection it has become increasingly clear that the confusion that surrounded my research was largely ignored. Feeling irritated that what I considered to be a straightforward research idea could be so misunderstood, my attempts to explain the research further were abandoned as I began to question the legitimacy and usefulness of the project that I was undertaking. Perhaps the research design was at fault? Maybe the research questions were mis-specified? Making sense of this contextually, I felt at the time that I was engaged in an intellectual struggle to define my research, specifically in relation to the literature and a particular historical approach to industrial sociology. Such a clear misunderstanding of my research intent made me feel threatened and vulnerable; after all, if I was unable to articulate my research to management, how was I ever going to satisfy a seemingly hostile academic community? Over time it has become more apparent that this struggle for identity clearly influenced how I sought to manage field relations. Yet a more prominent emotion came to dominate, that of fear, or the horror of having access terminated. This, perhaps more than any other influence, meant that misunderstandings were not corrected, yet, as a number of authors note, this ignoring of emotions is itself a form of emotion work (Reger, 2001).

Perhaps more importantly, so noted by Davis above, misunderstandings are analytically important and in fact a rich source of analytical data. This particular misunderstanding displays the cultural difference between myself as a researcher and myself as a call centre worker; the concept of a researcher clearly is an anathema to the call centre, to the extent that it hardly registers. The ambivalence of call centre managers speaks to the value and perception of academic work within the workplace – tolerated as a curiosity, an eccentricity perhaps, not facing open hostility but certainly treated with scepticism. The interaction also reaffirms the primacy of 'answering calls' to all other forms of activity within the domain of the call centre – the crude calculus of capital revealed from beneath the thinly veiled rhetoric of 'teamwork' and 'engagements'.

Sarcasm on the shop floor

In common with other CSRs, I was employed at CallCentreCo. in a standard shift pattern which lasted from 8:30 in the morning until 5:30 in the evening. Ethnographic observations were recorded in an extensive fieldwork journal, which took the form of a Microsoft Word document, accessed and updated via my desktop computer during quiet periods of the working day. As CSRs were frequently required to use Microsoft Word, I was able to record entries without attracting unwanted attention. In pursuit of the fieldwork I also participated in a number of social events and voluntary community work which CallCentreCo. organized and in which all members of staff were encouraged to participate. Observations from these events were recorded in a notebook and added to the fieldwork journal at a later time.

After I had completed my initial induction period and I had been assigned to the NewsCo. team, it became necessary to inform the members of the team about the research. Initially, the team members, like call centre managers, took little interest; the subject was not discussed in any depth, although I was aware that there were a number of issues about which the CSRs in the NewsCo. team were concerned. Occasionally, within the first month of employment, I would be asked, 'what is it that you're doing again?' (question from unknown team member, response not recorded). In contrast to the ambivalence of management, I noted the subject of worker resistance was raised spontaneously a number of times within the team; the following example is notable in particular:

VENKAT: *(directed to Jenny) Arrr, I'm telling Tina* (sarcastically) *you're late . . . Matthew did you get that? Jenny is seven minutes late from lunch, quick write that down!* (group laughter)
(observed team interaction, recorded in fieldwork journal)

The interaction demonstrates how – despite plans, preparations and research design – the flux of fieldwork is clearly hugely influenced by emotional responses to events, conversations and observations in the field. Despite having what I considered to be a clear research agenda, I felt embarrassed and undermined by Venkat's comments, the whole research endeavour rendered rather silly and inconsequential by this clever and 'knowing' comment. Such sentiments and expressions of disdain from the shop floor were not uncommon, and as a direct emotional response I began to adopt a more 'covert' approach in the sense of attempting to keep a lower profile than originally intended. The attempt at humour by Venkat shows a veiled awareness of the issues of interest within the research and also signals to the rest of the group that caution is required. Suspecting that the knowledge of my research agenda, in particular the focus upon workplace resistance, had impacted upon the behaviour of the CSRs in the team, I decided not to openly initiate a discussion based on themes of resistance within the team. Instead, I would allow the subject to arise in discussion from within the group and then ask questions to explore issues further if appropriate.

Whose side are you on anyway?

In order to become an active member of any team within the call centre, all new recruits were required to complete a period of training, which would notionally last for around four weeks. The training consisted of two elements. First, structured technical training was provided centrally within the call centre; this aimed to ensure that all new recruits were given the generic technical skills needed within the call centre to be able to operate the various systems and procedures such as the telephone system and the computer database. Second, more specific client training was provided in a decentralised fashion, and this training took place essentially within the team structure whilst 'live' on the phones.

Although many trainees expressed concerns about the degree to which they felt confident about the prospect of their ability to deal with the work as set out in procedures, very few CSRs reported problems learning how to operate the systems to the trainers. Despite having previous computing experience, and experience working in customer services, I found the need to use the computer at the same time as talking on the phone a demanding task. I also noted that the responses to the difficulty of training were distinctly gendered. Trainers often adopted a caring disposition to female CSRs; male CSRs who experienced difficulties seemed to adopt a more aggressive attitude reflecting the trainers who adopted a more 'macho' style when dealing with questions from male CSRs:

MATTHEW: *Marc, did you get all that?*
MARC: *You must be joking . . . all that* (database) *shit goes straight over my head.*
MATTHEW: *Yeah I know what you mean, it's difficult to take it all in, I find it very confusing. . . .*
MARC: *I'll just talk to them anyway* (interrupted)
MATTHEW: *What do you mean, 'talk to them', you mean the client?*
MARC: *Yeah you know . . . to buy yourself more time, keep them, y'know . . . talking, that'll give me more time.*
      (one-to-one discussion during training session, recorded in notebook edited and transferred to fieldwork journal)

MATTHEW: *You know what Liz, I really don't think I'm getting this at all.*

LIZ: (laughing) *I know, I was talking to the other Liz from the TrainCo. desk and she said you never really get to know everything, like what to do in all situations, I think a lot of 'em just make it up.*

MATTHEW: *I guess so . . .*

LIZ: *That's ok as long as you can get away with it though, I don't think I can, it worries me, what's it going to be like and all that. I'm dreading doin' it for real.*
(one-to-one discussion during training session, recorded in notebook, edited and transferred to fieldwork journal)

My fears and trepidation regarding being able to perform the job role were very real; as the quotes above indicate, I took the opportunity to discuss my fears with other CSRs. Korczynski (2003) notes how customer service workers turn to each other to cope with the emotional stress of the job role, and in relation to this a key concern for the trainees seemed to be the potential for having to deal with what was termed 'awkward' customers or clients. A number of stories had begun to circulate amongst the trainees about customer interactions that had included verbal abuse. Despite the clear angst of a number of the trainees on this issue, the trainers seemed unwilling or unable to discuss possible strategies in response to such calls.

HELEN: *I just wanted to ask what we should do if we get an awkward one?* (referring to a potential abusive client)

TRAINER: *Well, you should just try and be as helpful as possible, you know like get all the information you need and end the call as quickly as you can.*

JIM: *I've heard that sometimes you get an earful, is that right?*

TRAINER: *Well sometime people get upset, but it's not personal, don't let it affect you, just do your job.*
(CSR and trainer interaction, observed during training session, recorded in notebook and later transferred to fieldwork journal)

As a counter to the lack of clear support from trainers, the trainees resolved to offer support to each other if such circumstances arose. The following discussion took place away from the training room on a coffee break with most of the trainees present.

JIM: *I don't really think it's right that we should be expected to take calls if we're getting abuse.*

NICKY: *I don't think it's like that really, I mean when we start like, I've worked in other call centres and there is no way you'd have to put up with things like that, I think as long as the staff stick together we'll be ok . . . I don't think they* (referring to the trainers) *really know what it's like on the desks.*

Situated as both researcher and participant my position to comment on what was acceptable in the workplace was problematic. I felt angered by the fact that my colleagues felt that they had to put up with abuse from customers. On a number of occasions I felt constrained to offer advice and even in the ways in which I acted toward customers. Through informal discussions with colleagues I was able to ascertain that generally the initial period of employment within the call centre is considered the most demanding. I was told that often it was 'touch and go' (general discussion with Tina, recorded in fieldwork journal) as to whether new recruits would make it through their initial training period. In some respects this seems to explain why little attempt is generally made by established staff to get to know temporary staff. Furthermore I learnt that whilst other call centres were not considered as 'tough' in terms of becoming proficient, high turnover especially of new staff was common. I was able to discuss the transition from training to work with the call centre manager:

MATTHEW: *It seems that the transition from training to working can be really stressful.*
AMANDA: *Yeah I know, it is difficult to get the balance right but I do think that you really need to be a certain 'kind' of person to do the job well, you have to be fairly tough.*
MATTHEW: *To deal with difficult calls?*
AMANDA: *That's one aspect of the job, but it's better if staff find out early that the service centre is not for them, rather than later.*

The response from the call centre manager illustrates how the transition from training to working within the CallCentreCo. call centre effectively constitutes a continuing recruitment process. The initial 'shock' of being thrust into taking calls in the call centre can be somewhat overwhelming, and it appears that the call centre managers use this as a method for assessing the strength of new employees. Little is done to mitigate the stressfulness of this situation by the call centre management team.

Although, like Liz, I contemplated withdrawing from the call centre, I felt great support from my colleagues within the team. Although Liz reported that she also felt this support, I felt encouraged, and my mistakes and errors were supported by other team members who constantly reassured me that the situation would improve as I became more proficient and experienced; this reassurance was vitally important. The repetition and reinforcement of the daily call centre routine did mean that, like other new recruits, I was able to come to terms with the daily demands of working in the call centre. Although, even after a year of working on the same team, I never really felt totally proficient, and the 'randomness' of the calls at times meant that I felt unsure about the correct procedures to follow. I suspect that this was the same for many CSRs.

The limited nature of the training and the way in which new recruits were left to sink or swim made me feel hostile to many of the call centre managers. It also promoted a number of issues with respect to my role in the field. At the same time as the fieldwork was taking place, the Trades Union Congress (TUC) was running a high-profile campaign to recruit call centre workers. I was aware that CallCentreCo. did not have a recognised trade union and that the 'it's your call' campaign might be the perfect opportunity to establish one. Yet, despite this opportunity, I felt frozen into inaction, too concerned with maintaining my low profile, this dilemma and a sense of shame due to my inaction. I did engage in a number of more 'subversive' activities, in which I sought to encourage those around me to reflect on the logic of the call centre and its organization.

Within the call centre, the Automatic Call Distribution (ACD) software plays the role equivalent to the production line within a factory (Russell, 2002) and significantly is therefore a key way in which the relationship between Capital and Labour is managed. The effective dehumanisation of the control of the Labour process through technological apparatus effectively reduced tensions between CSRs and managers within the call centre and presented little scope or opportunity for CSRs to subvert the mechanics of the productive process. Pressure to answer calls as quickly as possible was exerted, not only by supervisors and problem managers, but also from other CSRs within the team. The unwritten rule within the call centre was that a ringing phone had to be answered, and indeed the expectation was often that this would be achieved before the second ring. Yet the asking of the question, and thus questioning of rule, therefore becomes a provocative and political act and prompted some CSRs to reflect upon some of the unquestioned assumptions of the daily life of the call centre:

VENKAT: *There is no reason not to answer calls quickly, I mean if a call comes through you must be on 'ready' status, that's what it means, you're ready! All you have to do is press a button and you're connected, you shouldn't really hear the phone ring to be honest, it should just be 'bang', call coming through and it's answered and you're away.*

(one-to-one discussion with problem manager, during team-based training, recorded in fieldwork journal)

MATTHEW: *Do you ever think like, 'sod it', I'm not answering this one?*
JENNY: *You can't do that, not here!*
MATTHEW: *What are you talking about? Of course you can, you just don't answer it!*
JENNY: *Oh yeah* (laughing) *what happens then, it's like ringing and ringing and you're sitting there with your arms folded.*
MATTHEW: *Well you just wait for it to go away, like a missed call.*
JENNY: *A missed call, that's really bad, it means that NewsCo. have tried to contact us and they couldn't get through, the whole thing would fall down, why would you pay for a service that you can't use? . . . And besides, listen* (motions to the rest of the call centre) *can you hear phones ringing and ringing?*
MATTHEW: *No, that's my point, all these phones and not much ringing there're all answered straight away.*
JENNY: *That's MY point, it would be totally out of character, it's just not what we do!* (derisory shake of the head)

(general discussion in quiet period, recorded in fieldwork journal)

As outlined above, the technological character of ACD within this call centre provided an effective shroud to the actual Labour processes involved, with CSRs seemingly assuming that the process was both inevitable and equitable. Moreover, on occasion, agents would express frustration against the structural arrangements of the call centre, and this would often be directed towards the ACD system. I witnessed the following expression of frustration vented toward the system:

RAJESH: (finishing a call) *Yeah ok, don't worry we'll get onto it right away, I'll get back . . . yeah I'll call you later. . .* (terminates call by selecting 'end call') . . . (phone immediately rings again whilst Rajesh is still entering data regarding previous call) . . . *fuckin' 'ell, give me a chance* . . . (phone continues to ring)

VENKAT: *Should 'ave gone in wrap-up, use your wrap-up!* . . . (phone continues to ring)

RAJESH: *Fuckin' piece of shite* . . . (bangs dial/answer button on phone unit with fist) . . . (reverts to composure) . . . *Good afternoon NewsCo. service desk, Rajesh speaking, how can I help you?*

      (observed customer/colleague interaction during busy period, recorded in fieldwork journal)

These leading questions constitute what perhaps might be 'guilty academic pleasures'; they involve provoking respondents' reflections on their own practice and are intentionally disruptive. Politically they move the ethnographer beyond being 'sympathetic storyteller' (Foley, 2002, 470) towards a potential source of instability and change within the working environment. They evoked a sense of pleasure at being able to question the assumptions of the call centre by encouraging my co-workers to do the same, but these instances also carried with them for me a sense of guilt at not overtly calling for change, and provide a further affirmation of the researcher as emotional labourer (Jarzabkowski, 2001). This emotional encounter also highlights the in-built emotional tension in ethnographic work, residing in the traditional bias in ethnographic research towards non-interference, or minimising the role of the researcher in the field. In the examples provided here, this led to an emotional conflict where deep fieldwork produced empathy and a sense of responsibility to those that I was researching. In this example the conflict is played out between raising what might be considered the political aspirations of those I worked with, and those traditional biases that are built upon the assumption of a researcher removed from, but participating in, the everyday life of those in the field. This highlights the way in which deep immersion within the field is always an emotional undertaking: we get close to, and form bonds with, other field participants. Disentangling these human feelings from the purposes of academic research is impossible and would actually run counter to the spirit of immersive studies.

Discussion and conclusion

In this final section I seek to draw out the implications of the example provided above and offer an analysis of the complexity of understanding and documenting the emotions of the research process.

This chapter provides a number of examples of what might be termed the unintended consequences of research activity. The example of how the intentions of the research were misunderstood by both the call centre manager and other participants works to question the assumption that disclosure of research intent can ever be equated to a claim that participants understand fully the nature of the research. Whilst this will hardly come as a surprise to those of a social constructivist persuasion, it does question the continued dominance of approaches to research ethics that are based on initial disclosure. Moreover, this example of confusion effectively shielded the true intent of the research, and, although the account documents how misconceptions were challenged, this confusion certainly seems to have been productive in facilitating ethnographic research in this instance. These misunderstandings are clearly therefore grist to the ethnographer's mill, unintended but highly valuable consequences that further underline the iterative nature of the research process.

On reflection, it seems clear how I attempted to separate the fieldwork world from the rest of my life as a PhD student. The moments of overlap between these worlds, such as my attempts to engage with ethical considerations, show how precarious this artificial divide is. This further underlines the point made by Sin (2005) that researchers who engage in extended forms of research cannot rely upon an initial disclosure to assuage ethical concerns over fieldwork. Rather, opportunities to restate the researcher's intent throughout the research need to be taken. Feminist scholars have long criticised the distinction between rational and emotional forms of knowing (see for example Hubbard *et al.*, 2001; and Reger, 2001) in the sense that traditional approaches to social science favour the former. In ethnographic research, despite its extensive links with feminist and outsider epistemologies, the rational/objectivist current remains strong. Whilst the omission of explicit consideration of the emotions of conducting research is a form of privileging the rational over the emotional, a rearticulation of the Cartesian mind–body dualism (Foley, 2002), this chapter demonstrates that it has also gravely impacted on the ways in which research is carried out, and how data is perceived, recorded and analysed. So in my own account, the misunderstanding of the research by call centre managers is ignored as an interesting and potentially revealing statement on the perception of call centre workers' misbehaviour. Furthermore, my irritation, embarrassment and insecurity caused by co-workers' jokes about my research and the implication this has for how workers think about their own workplace misbehaviour becomes secondary to my own sense of purpose and confidence in my research design. Part of this reaction is of course the contextual lack of emotional vocabularies to discuss emotional elements to the research, a situation that I hope this account with help, in small part, to redress.

This raises the possibility and importance of identifying a corrective for the alexithymic tendency in research. It is clear from the forgoing analysis that it is a mistake to understand emotions simply as attributive to individuals or their actions, and therefore it might be more fruitful to consider emotions as a property of social relationships (Emirbayer and Goldberg, 2005) rather than existing within an intra-personal domain. From this perspective we might move to consider the social context of emotional engagement and interactions, and this may provide a way to explore the full analytical importance of emotional responses as indexical to social relations and the logic of the social fields in which they are embedded and from which they emerge. One of the key challenges of this, however, is to move beyond understanding emotions as a property of individual relations, a difficult task when it is considered that much academic work, which claims to be reflexive, is predicated on individualised accounts of emotional interaction. Maton for example argues that what passes for reflexivity is mostly sociological, individual and narcissistic (Maton, 2003). In contrast, and drawing on Bourdieu, he calls for reflexivity that is *epistemological, collective and objective,* and in this sense the development of wider communities of researchers might open up spaces for an ongoing discussion of the social significance of emotional interactions in a way that is currently unavailable to many researchers beyond seminars and conference events. Similarly, Riach (2009) calls for 'reflexivity-in-practice' as part of the positioning of participants within an ethical research process – also recognising the role that all participants in the research process may play in the development of 'reflexive-spaces' (p.366). Such a collective response to these emotional dilemmas seems entirely in keeping with Brewer's (1994) argument for example that at heart reflexivity has a key role to play in the ascription of authority in research accounts.

Moreover, the researcher is always part of a wider academic community of practice, and it is this community of practice which exerts a greater influence over the way in which research is designed and undertaken, and provides the socialisation and the learnt emotion vocabularies (Thoits, 1989: 319) with which we engage in social research. The inextricable link for many young career researchers between demonstrating competence and intellectual rigour, and their conduct in the field, means that the researcher's emotions, which are seen as an unwanted consequence of fieldwork interactions, may well continue to be marginalised without a more careful and systematically designed social organization of research practice.

Note

This chapter is a version of a paper which first appeared in the *International Journal of Work, Organization and Emotion* (2011, 4[3]).

References

Alvesson, M. (2003). Beyond Neopositivists, Romantics, and Localists: A Reflexive Approach to Interviews in Organizational Research. *Academy of Management Review* 28(1): 13–33.

Ashforth, B. E., and Humphrey, R. H. (1993) Emotional Labour in Service Roles: The Influence of Identity. *Academy of Management Review* 18(1) 88–115.

Bellas, M. L. (1999) Emotional Labor in Academia: The Case of Professors. *The Annals of the American Academy of Political and Social Science* 561(1) 96–110.

Bolton, C. (2004) A Simple Matter of Control? NHS Hospital Nurses and New Management. *Journal of Management Studies* 41(2) 317–333.

Bosk, C. L. (2004) Bureaucracies of Mass Deception: Institutional Review Boards and the Ethics of Ethnographic Research. *The Annals of the American Academy of Political and Social Science* 595(1) 249–263.

Brannan, M. J., and Priola, V. (2012) 'Girls Who Do Boys Like They're Girls'? Exploring the Role of Gender in the Junior Management of Contemporary Service Work. *Gender Work and Organization* (19)2 119–141.

Brannan, M. J., Pearson, G., and Worthington, F. (2008) Ethnographies of Work and the Work of Ethnography. *Ethnography* 8(4) 395–402.

Brewer, J. D. (1994) The Ethnographic Critique of Ethnography: Sectarianism in the RUC. *Sociology* 43(3) 231–244.

Bryman, A., and Bell, E. (2007) *Business Research Methods*. Oxford: Oxford University Press.

Chia, R. (1996) The Problem of Reflexivity in Organizational Research: Towards a Post-modern Science of Organization. *Organization* 3(1) 31–59.

Coffey, A. (1999) *The Ethnographic Self*. London: Sage.

Creswell, J. W., and Miller, D. L. (2000) Determining Validity in Qualitative Inquiry. *Theory into Practice* 39(3) 125–130.

Davies, C. A. (1999) *Reflexive Ethnography: A Guide to Researching Selves and Others*. London: Routledge.

Dickson-Swift, V., *et al.* (2009) Researching Sensitive Topics: Qualitative Research as Emotion Work. *Qualitative Research* 9(1) 61–79.

Emirbayer, M., and Goldberg, C. A. (2005) Pragmatism, Bourdieu, and Collective Emotions in Contentious Politics. *Theory and Society* 34, 469–518.

Fineman, S. (1993) *Emotion in Organizations*. London: Sage.

Fineman, S. (Ed.). (2000) *Emotion in Organizations*. London: Sage.

Finlay, L (2002) "Outing" the Researcher: The Provenance, Process, and Practice of Reflexivity. *Qualitative Health Research* 12: 531–545.

Fleming, P., and Sturdy, A. (2011) Being Yourself in the Electronic Sweatshop: New Forms of Normative Control. *Human Relations* 64(2) 177–200.

Foley, D. E. (2002) Critical Ethnography: The Reflexive Turn. *Qualitative Studies in Education* 15(5) 469–490.

Gold, R. L. (1958) Roles in Sociological Field Observations. *Social Forces* 36(3) 217–223.

Hardy, C., Phillips, N., and Clegg, S. (2001) Reflexivity in Organization and Management Theory: A Study of the Production of the Research 'Subject'. *Human Relations* 54(5) 531–560.

Hertz, R. (1996) Introduction: Ethics, Reflexivity and Voice. *Qualitative Sociology* 19(1) 3–7.

Hochschild, A. R. (1983) *The Managed Heart: Commercialisation of Human Feeling*. London: University of California Press.

Holland, R. (1999) *Reflexivity, Human Relations* 52(4) 463–84.

Hubbard, G., Beckett-Milburn, K., and Kemmer, D. (2001) Working with Emotion: Issues for the Researcher in Fieldwork and Teamwork. *International Journal of Social Research Methodology* 4(2) 119–137.

Hutchinson, S., Purcell, J., and Kinnie, N. (2000) Evolving High Commitment Management. *Human Resource Management Journal* 10(1) 63–79.

Jaggar, A. M. (1989) Love and Knowledge: Emotion in Feminist Epistemology. *Inquiry: An Interdisciplinary Journal of Philosophy* 32(2) 151–176.

James, N. (1989) Emotional Labour: Skill and Work in the Social Regulation of Feelings. *Sociological Review* 37: 15–47.

Jarzabkowski, L. (2001) Emotional Labour in Educational Research. *Queensland Journal of Educational Research* 17(2) 123–137.

Kinnie, N., Hutchinson, S., and Purcell, J. (2000) "Fun and Surveillance": The Paradox of High Commitment Management in Call Centres. *International Journal of Human Resource Management* 11(5) 964–985.

Korczynski, M. (2003) Communities of Coping: Collective Emotional Labour in Service Work. *Organization* 10(1) 55–79.

Laslett, B. (1990) Unfeeling Knowledge: Emotion and Objectivity in the History of Sociology. *Sociological Forum* 5(3) 413–433.

Leibing, A., and McLean, A. (2007) "Learn to Value Your Shadow!" An Introduction to the Margins of Fieldwork. In A. McLean and A. Leibing (eds), *The Shadow Side of Fieldwork Exploring the Blurred Borders between Ethnography and Life*. Oxford: Blackwell.

Lumsden, K. (2009) "Don't Ask a Woman to Do Another Woman's Job": Gendered Interactions and the Emotional Ethnographer. *Sociology* 43(3) 497–513.

Lynch, M. (2000) Against Reflexivity as an Academic Virtue and Source of Privileged Knowledge. *Theory, Culture and Society* 17(3) 26–54.

Maton, K. (2003) Reflexivity, Relationism and Research: Pierre Bourdieu and the Epistemic Conditions of Social Scientific Knowledge. *Space and Culture* 6(1) 52–65.

Mauthner, N. S., Parry, O., and Backett-Milburn, K. (1998) The Data Are Out There, or Are They? Implication for Archiving and Revisiting Qualitative Data. *Sociology* 32(4) 733–745.

Murphy, E., and Dingwall, R. (2001) The Ethics of Ethnography. In P. Atkinson, A. Coffey, S. Delamont, J. Lofland, and L. Lofland (eds), *Handbook of Ethnography*. London: Sage, 339–351.

Pillow, W. (2003) Confession, Catharsis, or Cure? Rethinking the Uses of Reflexivity as Methodological Power in Qualitative Research. *Qualitative Studies in Education* 16(2) 175–196.

Reger, J. (2001) Emotions, Objectivity and Voice: An Analysis of a "Failed" Participant Observation. *Women's Studies International Forum* 24(5) 605–616.

Riach, K. (2009) Exploring Participant-Centred Reflexivity in the Research Interview. *Sociology* 43(2) 356–370.

Russell, B. (2002) The Talk Shop and Shop Talk: Employment and Work in a Call Centre Journal of Industrial Relations 44(4) 467–490.

Sherif, B. (2001) The Ambiguity of Boundaries in the Fieldwork Experience: Establishing Rapport and Negotiating Insider/Outsider Status. *Qualitative Inquiry* 7(4) 436–447.

Sifneos, P. E. (1973) The Prevalence of "Alexithymic" Characteristics in Psychosomatic Patients. *Psychotherapy and Psychosomatics* 22(2–6) 255–262.

Sin, C. H. (2005) Seeking Informed Consent: Reflections on Research Practice. *Sociology* 39(2) 277–294.

Skeggs, B. (2004) Exchange, Value and Affect: Bourdieu and 'the Self'. In L. Adkins and B. Skeggs (eds), *Feminism after Bourdieu*. Oxford: Blackwell.

Sturdy, A., Grugulis, I., and Willmott, H. (2001) *Customer Service Empowerment and Entrapment*. London: Palgrave.

Taylor, P., and Bain, P. (1999) "An Assembly Line in the Head": Work and Employee Relations in the Call Centre. *Industrial Relations Journal* 30(2) 101–117.

Taylor, P., Hyman, J., Mulvey, G., and Bain, P. (2002) Work Organization, Control and the Experience of Work in Call Centres. *Work, Employment and Society* 16(1) 133–150.

Taylor, S. (1998) Emotional Labour and the New Workplace. In P. Thompson and C. Warhurst (eds), *Workplaces of the Future*. Basinstoke: Macmillan.

Thoits, P. A. (1989) The Sociology of Emotions. *Annual Review of Sociology* 15, 317–342.

Willig, C. (2001) *Introducing Qualitative Research in Psychology: Adventures in Theory and Method*. Buckingham: Open University Press.

3

NEGOTIATING IDENTITIES

Fluidity, diversity and researcher emotion

Caroline Clarke and David Knights

In the introduction to this book, and in most other chapters, we have been at pains to point out how relationships between researchers and 'researched' are never straightforward. As well as cognition, logic and rationality, research is founded on relationships, and these are premised on emotions and the feelings that we have about others and ourselves, which are surfaced through our interactions. These feelings are often written out of conventional text books, whether of a general or specifically methodological nature, and yet they are critical to the research experience, the process, the 'success' of any study overall, and of course they are linked with the identities of the researcher themselves:

> the assumptions, interests and identity of the researcher influence, and will be reflected in, the selection and conceptualization of topics for enquiry, formulation of research questions, interactions between researcher and participants within the research context and subsequent analysis and representations of the research.
>
> *(Archer, 2002: 109)*

The comparative absence of references to identities, the body and emotion in 'methodological' texts is evident even in those that are qualitative 'despite the contingent, contextual and uncertain character of most research in organization and management, which is at least partly a function of the obduracy yet vulnerability of human bodies and emotions' (Knights and Thanem, 2011: 220). This is because the authority of masculine methodological conventions readily overrules the messy, contextual and contingent nature of events and experiences that researchers routinely encounter in the field (ibid.).

Insofar as most methodology texts generally only legitimise rational, linear logic and a series of systematic, mechanistic stages and technical procedures for the conduct of research, the organic, emotional and embodied aspects of the process are carefully and consistently concealed or denied in research reports and publications. Research encourages an under-reporting of the contingent, contextual, precarious and uncertain character of research in favour of often insipid, disembodied and depersonalised accounts of the accumulation of empirical data and the presentation of findings. Despite the numerous trials and tribulations, emotional upheavals, and 'failures' in conducting research, there is surprisingly little attention given to this in textbooks (Knights, 2011) or in the methodology and 'research literature' (Dickson-Swift *et al.*, 2009: 73). In this sense, the research community successfully avoids even the hint of a link between their own or respondents' 'private troubles and public issues' (Wright Mills, 2000), and there is considerable reluctance for researchers to fully 'reveal the hand of the puppeteer' (Watson, 1994: S86), reserving 'the messy and highly subjective nature of the researcher and researched . . . for university coffee bar conversations' (Bell, 1999: 18).

We need to challenge the tendency for current literature on messiness, emotion and the body to be 'dominated by the more mentalistic connotations of "emotional work"' (Wolkowitz, 2011). Here is an excerpt from a previous paper by the second author commenting on the tendency to write in a disembodied manner, on the part of ourselves as well as others:

> with some exceptions [esp. Sinclair, 2007; Thanem, 2011], few scholars have attempted to reflect about their own gendered embodiment. Not unlike conventional research in other areas, we tend to manage our emotions and bodies to maintain largely abstract prose, posing as if our own bodies are detached from the bodies we study.
>
> *(Thanem and Knights, 2012: 93)*

As Bell has pointed out however, the researcher's 'physical body image forms a negotiated part of identity work in the field' (1999: 26) since it is often observed and studied by those who themselves are being studied – it is simultaneously the instrument and the topic of study. Intimately linked to this, our chapter is about the relative 'status' of the researcher as well as the researched that we are interested in, as we argue that researching is inextricably and intimately tied to our and others' gender, age, class, race and sexuality and thus to links between power, politics and the personal (Hanisch, 1969). Our identities and the identity of the 'other' are fundamentally important in this respect – not only does it highlight an important question ('who do we think and feel we are?'), but it also raises the equally important question 'who do others think and feel we are?' For as Reay observes, we should reflect on 'uncovering/recognising the difference your differences make' (1996: 443).

This chapter explores some of these differences. We have to say 'some' because our vignettes are not inclusive with regard to the topic of diversity – they are primarily concerned with issues of gender, age and sexuality, whereas diversity ought to include something about disability, race and perhaps religion. We have felt uncomfortable about this but were also conscious that simply 'ticking all the boxes' of diversity smacked of tokenism and would appear laboured. Of course the sentiments of both appreciating diversity and experiencing it as potentially problematic have both similarities and differences across and within all marginalised groups. However, this separation of 'the self' in any form from the social is an analytical and therefore somewhat artificial binary since they are mutually embedded and inseparable; we only acquire a sense of who we are through our shared feelings and thoughts relating to one another, and these are in continual fluidity, flux and flow as they evolve, dissolve, shatter and shift.

Harris (2002) usefully suggests that institutions have a number of explicit and implicit 'feeling rules' dictating which emotions should be displayed, as some are acceptable, legitimised and rewarded, while others are discouraged and penalised. Harris suggests that these rules are rooted in occupational, organizational and societal norms and values, and in Chapter 4 you will read about how different aspects of these came to the fore during several research experiences. For example, the occupation of engineering displays heavy forms of male-dominated gendered job segregation (Cockburn, 1983; 1985), privileging masculine discourses in what is an often-tough 'macho' culture. However, while engineering and manufacturing more generally are highly masculinised workplaces, other areas of employment are not devoid of parallel discourses and cultures of control (see for example Chapter 4 and Chapter 5 of this book). Organizational cultures are of course a reflection of, and reproduced by, their members as they pursue their everyday discourses and practices in ways which tend to sustain a given set of norms and values that generate a sense of homogeneity. No better example of this can be found than in the homosociality and male bonding that has characterised the continuity of exceedingly obscene bankers' bonuses and salaries to managers who have blatantly failed during the recent global financial crisis (Knights and Tullberg, 2012). Even though the management practices and the organizational edifices surrounding them have been exposed as a sham, the demand to maintain the masculine accoutrements of material and symbolic success are invariably sustained.

Of course the intervention of any researcher (see Chapter 2) has the potential to disrupt occupational practices and working identities, and this may partly account for the difficulties of securing research access. Despite participants often enjoying the attention and the opportunity to express themselves through the research interview, prior to this experience the academic researcher can be seen as a threat – an outsider or informer who may gain trust only to later leak internal secrets (Goffman, 1959). Those who grant access may be concerned that the organization is potentially overexposed during such a process, and they may feel ill prepared for such scrutiny by non-members. In this vignette the first author shares her experience of (not) managing to secure access to a specific occupational group:

> *I was interested in researching traffic wardens since this group are so loathed and despised by the public that their 'dirty work' and 'tainted identities' were potentially fascinating to me and I am sure others. I wondered particularly how traffic wardens*

> *answer the question 'what do you do for a living?' when asked, and how they find meaning in their stigmatised work. I approached a number of authorities, who either did not reply or who expressed initial interest but then backed off because the unions did not like the idea of the research. I was starting to get downhearted when one authority replied to say they were very interested and I set up a meeting with them. James, the guy in charge was brilliant and really keen as he wanted to help those who worked for him, and felt the occupation received an overly bad press, as they were there to actually serve the public i.e. by keeping roads clear. The meeting lasted two and a half hours, and was followed by a flurry of emails regarding the number of sites that would be involved in the study, what questions I would ask etc. etc. Then out of the blue I got a sheepishly apologetic email from James saying that the regional director had told him 'not to touch this project with a barge pole as they had no control over the data'. It was hard to see how the reputation of traffic wardens could have been damaged further, but aside from that, the motives of my research had been utterly dismissed and rejected. I was guilty without being able to prove my innocence.*

In this vignette the managing director views academic work as similar to that of investigative journalism, anticipating that the data will be both derogatory and potentially dangerous to the identities of traffic wardens. Although this is 'partly a function of the public misunderstanding of much of our [academic] work' (Knights and Clarke, 2014: 346), it leaves the researchers with little scope for securing particular sites for study, or for demonstrating their own integrity.

One possible lesson to be taken from this is how important hierarchy is in securing research access. Some years ago, the second author secured access for himself and four other researchers to an insurance company that was sustained for over six years largely because it had been negotiated through a newly appointed chief executive who was seeking to 'shake up' the organization. He was convinced that being interviewed by academics would force his staff to reflect on their practices and thereby possibly improve how they performed their tasks. Whether or not our research questions had this 'intended' effect, it is one additional possible benefit that researchers can claim may derive from the research.

Gendered identity and emotion

While gender has increasingly become an issue deemed worthy of cross-disciplinary research (e.g. social science, feminism, organization studies, health and social care), the gender of the researcher has largely been ignored, or considered irrelevant in methods texts:

> Although gender is treated as an issue for the managers and workers who are the *subjects* of organizational research, an incorporation of management researchers *themselves* as gendered subjects within the research act would not seem to have been accomplished.
>
> *(Bell, 1999: 19; italics in the original)*

The following vignette from the first author's empirical work also describes the experience of visiting an organization for the first time, in an attempt to secure access for her research. It illustrates how the researchers can experience the emotional 'norms' and feeling rules of an organization as alien to them, thus provoking feelings of being interlopers or outsiders.

> *I enter the room with my research supervisor, a female professor. We are 45 minutes late, as we missed the boat to the Island. The room is very traditional, it has wood panelled walls (how many places still have wood panelled walls?) and there are artefacts of aircraft (engineers always call them aircraft, and never aeroplanes). The aircraft are omnipresent, in large scale models, photographs blown up to 6 feet by 4 feet, and hanging by wire from the ceiling. This is a man's world; boys and their toys. There are eight men sitting staring at us as we enter the room, arms folded, they have probably been sitting in this position for the past 45 minutes, waiting . . . for us, and the feeling is distinctly unwelcoming. My identity is of the 'other'. I am not a man, I am not an engineer, I am not a manager . . . I do not live on this island. The feelings I now have are of apprehension and trepidation – why had I not thought of this?*

> *[researching aerospace part one]*

We can see from this vignette how gendered practices can mean a sudden recasting of the researcher into the role of 'the other' which can disrupt our sense of ourselves and reshape our feelings about particular experiences. Assuming an identity, which is 'other' to those whom we are researching can be challenging, as the tendency to feel marginalised, disempowered or just not being taken seriously is potentially threatening and intimidating. However, there can also be benefits for both parties in the sense that researchers may bring an element of diversity into a homogenous population as illustrated in the second part of this vignette.

> *My identity as the 'other', rather than being the liability I expected from my initial experience actually became an absolute bonus. During my longitudinal research study, the engineers often admitted that they could confide in me precisely because I was not male, not a manager, not an engineer, and most importantly not an islander. In their view I was a safe pair of hands in whom they could divulge certain sentiments which were unacceptable in the somewhat parochial and intensely controlled macho context they inhabited. Although my study was focused on emotion during change in this organization, all public displays of feeling or emotion were frowned upon as tightly controlled feeling rules discouraged this, as evidenced by the continual use of the phrase 'pink and fluffy' to deride any remotely sympathetic behaviour. In contrast, the 'backstage' interviews were a chance for participants to reveal their inner anxieties and fears without being judged by those on the 'inside' of the organisation. During my third and final round of interviewing, several participants said how therapeutic it had been, and then asked if I could come back again – 'for a fee.'*

> *[researching aerospace, part two]*

This research context involved large numbers of engineers and was therefore a stereotypically masculine environment (Miller, 2002), where the assumptions that employees should be objective, analytical, strategic and tough (Clarke *et al.*, 2009: 342) were commonly accepted and rarely resisted. This vignette also illustrates how gender is still very pertinent in these relationships, although now perhaps the combination of being both youthful and female is advantageous to the researcher, helping to secure this high level of trust. Females are of course commonly constructed as a 'safe' audience (Archer, 2002), as being more receptive to listening, as caring and as 'empathetic', and as such these male engineers may also have perceived the researcher to be 'low risk' as a confidante. The status of 'other', however, should not be overlooked as it allowed participants to liberate themselves from the usual cultural norms in a way that did not pose a threat to their own identities. Finally, longitudinal research provides a rich source of opportunity for building trust, although this can of course also have adverse consequences. It is important to view the identi*ties* of researchers as relational and dynamic and 'highly negotiable' (Bell, 1999) rather than based on static assumptions relating to ascribed characteristics or preferences. Although ascriptions can dominate initially, this vignette shows how these assumptions can be broken down and reconfigured so what is initially constraining may instead become enabling. Of course this can also work in reverse.

Age and emotion

In the research context, youth can sometimes be perceived as a lack of experience and knowledge. In a professional context in particular, the young researcher may be dismissed quite readily, often on the basis of youth alone. In the following vignette, Ross, a newly minted university researcher, suffers from such a problem while working with an external organization with his colleague George:

> *I enjoyed working with George. He was industrially honed (lots of experience), and could connect in a pally sort of way with people (usually blokes) we researched 'on' in organizations. He was a good bit older than me and I was still fresh from my psychology PhD, but keen. We worked together assessment testing executives, along with coaching interviews, and we got some money for it. At the same time the data were just the job for my research publications on psychometrics and coaching.*
>
> *It seemed to be going very well. But one day I realised that appointments with the clients had dried up. I quizzed George about it, and he was evasive. I pushed him harder and he admitted that he was still doing the work, but now without me. I was aghast – why? What happened? He reddened a bit and pointed to his hair: 'You need a bit more grey stuff like me Ross; they're happy to keep me on but not you I'm afraid'.*
>
> *I was really confused. It felt like a humiliating slap in the face, and also a betrayal by a colleague. 'Why', I asked, 'didn't you say we were an item, both of us or none of us? That's what I would have said if they were going to cut you out and not me'. George, a practising Catholic, looked puzzled and quipped – 'It's just business Ross; don't get so upset about it'.*

> *But I was upset; a punch below the belt for my credibility and ego. But really, I felt an outsider, rejected because of my age and appearance. I didn't speak to George again for weeks.*

Here we can see how Ross's emotional reaction to the situation is a result of a threat to his identity as a competent researcher (as well perhaps to the pecuniary rewards which the research brought in). Ross's sense of identity is damaged by this rejection reportedly on the basis of his youthful image, although it is difficult to ascertain to what extent George has engineered the story, or the outcome. The vignette at best implies that George has taken the line of least resistance, and in a seemingly adept political move has severed his working relationship with Ross without notifying him. In a sense then, Ross receives a double assault on his identity, both from the client and from George, a previously trusted and perhaps admired colleague. The mention of George as a 'practising Catholic' appears to be an aspect of identity, which becomes more relevant to Ross (he does not mention it at the outset). Perhaps he associates his religion with an expectation of George being honest and less likely to lie. This vignette illustrates how Ross equates membership of a particular social category with predictable behaviour, although George's behaviour has called this faith into question on several levels.

The notion of a grey-haired male as the primary source of authority is of course deeply rooted in masculine images dominating Western society (although in certain contexts this can also be a disqualifier). George, in an effort to do some instant identity repair work, dismisses the episode by drawing on a masculine discourse of economic rationality – 'it's only business', i.e. not personal. George's attempt at 'splitting', or separating, the personal from business decisions is unsuccessful, for as feminist research shows (Hanisch, 1969) the personal cannot readily be separated from the political, although it is a classic way of legitimizing the view that business has nothing to do with ethics:

> There is one and only one responsibility of business – to use its resources and engage in activities designed to increase its profits so long as it stays within the rules of the game.
>
> *(Friedman, 1970)*

Returning to the vignette, by deploying the phrase 'don't get upset', George also attempts to relieve any sense of guilt by assigning Ross's feelings to the 'emotional dustbin'. Moreover, in indicating that those feelings are a sign of individual weakness and inappropriate in a business context, George is reinforcing the image of Ross as emotionally as well as physically immature.

Being a young researcher often brings with it a perception of inexperience or even naiveté, which can sometimes lead to the kinds of manipulation evidenced in this vignette. Within such relationships, errors and ill-informed decisions are more likely to result, and the next two vignettes illustrate this in similar yet different ways.

It is also important to understand the relational (Waldron, 2000) nature of emotion, since arguably both researchers are also unwittingly subject to unequal power relationships and agendas which have often already been set (Lukes, 1974). In this vignette Peter recounts a *faux pas* early in his research career when intimidated by the more experienced and higher status of the 'Other':

> *My research was about stress amongst engineers in the Sheffield coal mining industry. It involved confidential, candid, personal interviews with engineers, content analysed and a thematic report fed back to senior management with suggestions for organizational change.*
>
> *I was in the huge paneled office of the plant manager to summarise my findings. I hadn't done this before (early in my research career) and felt over-awed by the event and surroundings, out of place. The plant manager sat behind a huge teak desk, which added to my stress.*
>
> *I went through the findings and he seemed very receptive. He then asked more probing questions about one or two of his staff whom I had interviewed, so I took their transcripts out of my briefcase to find relevant passages to answer his questions. Looking at his watch he then said, 'I'll tell you what, let me have those and I'll keep them secure in my safe here. No one will know. OK?'*
>
> *'OK', I said, and handed them over.*
>
> *On the way back home the penny dropped about what I'd just done. I'd given him documents that were confidential to the interviewees and myself; I'd broken a cardinal rule of research ethics. Why on earth did I hand them over? It was too late to retrieve them I thought – I'd look even more stupid. I felt absolutely terrible and just hoped for the best.*

Peter experiences a tumult of emotion as a result of what is (presumably) conscious manipulation on the part of one of the managers. The characteristics of the researcher – his relative youth, experience and status – means he is firmly embedded within an unequal power relationship, which partly accounts for his being readily overwhelmed. Such displays of alternative political agendas are rarely found in the 'how to research' books, although a breach of anonymity of this kind is ethically very serious. Researchers are obliged to protect their participants' identities and to treat their responses confidentially, and ordinarily access is secured on the basis of these commitments. The value of the data is often directly correlated with the trust that a researcher is able to secure from participants, and any breach of the kind illustrated can undermine research relationships specifically and universally.

The second author of this chapter experienced something similar when conducting research for his PhD in a newspaper sales organization that prior to the research had been on strike because a third of its staff had been dismissed following a consultancy report.

> *My introduction to the company came through a personal friend who was a member of the sales team and I negotiated my research access through both the Father of the*

Chapel (shop steward) of the union and the sales director who had just reinstated the threatened sales staff as a result of the strike. While the sales director raised no objections to my research those staff that had previously been dismissed were suspicious that I was acting as a spy for senior management. For this reason, I spent as much time as possible with them to try and allay their suspicions. Once I had gained their trust, they allowed me to participate in a series of skives where social activities displaced all formal work commitments.

After several months, the Father of the Chapel with whom I had become very friendly persuaded me to write down a summary of where I was up to in the research and I thought this would provide helpful feedback but naïvely, in retrospect, because he passed it on to all the staff. My analysis was largely academic in terms of identity, power and responsibility [see Knights and Roberts, 1982] and I cast no blame for the stalemate on either staff or management but those who felt most vulnerable to redundancy engineered a campaign to have me removed from the site for fear that I would report the skives to management.

The lesson of this vignette is never to be naïve about the politics of organizations. However fair and equitable the analysis seemed to the researcher, it was interpreted in much more threatening ways by different staff and so should not have been released before the research was complete.

The next vignette draws attention to a different but parallel issue to the one above, in that it relates to suspicions that the researcher is acting clandestinely to spy on the workforce. Here again, the participant is strongly suspicious of the researcher's identity as an interloper with duplicitous intentions:

Looking back it seems obvious why he would not participate fully. I have done over 500 research interviews in my time, with this being the only person to refuse to be recorded. We were in a manufacturing plant, which made contact lenses. The management had employed a 'snowball' technique for the assembly workers whereby they briefed one person on the study who was then interviewed. After this, the participant went back to the assembly line and tapped someone else on the shoulder who was to be the next participant. We were researching for an academic-practitioner change consortium, and this organization had asked for help in understanding the employee relations in a heavily unionized plant. We had been given two rooms in order to conduct the interviews – both in the management suite. The ninth person to be tapped on the shoulder was a union rep. He had to walk for ten minutes from the assembly line to the management suite. He arrived dressed in a tracksuit and had no knowledge whatsoever as to what the study was about. For him, interviews taking place in the management suite represented only one thing – management getting information. Although I did my best to brief him he refused to consent to the tape recorder being used, and the interview consisted only of his monosyllabic replies.

We can see how the image and identity of the researcher is of paramount importance, particularly in terms of positioning the study appropriately. The union representative perceives the researcher not only as 'other' but also as an ally of management, and therefore this means that his responses are purposefully guarded and limited in terms of providing any meaningful data. Such resistance, though, provides in itself a form of highly useful data, first about the trust relations between the union and management, and also as a salutary lesson on how *not to* design your research. Your identity as a researcher is not so much about *your* idea of who you are but the potential myriad of interpretations and projections made by your audience.

Already it is clear to see that many aspects of researching and being a researcher are far more complex than most texts intimate. Some aspects of our identities (variously conceived) may present a significant challenge to the relationships, which are so fundamental to the process. This prompts us to ask why these accounts of researching are so often omitted from the literature, and why the potentially helpful experience of others are hidden away.

Sexuality – similarity and difference

In the following vignette we see that Mary's idea of herself as a researcher is initially founded on a fear of specific differences between her and her participants, which she predicts will be an obstacle. However, what she experiences instead is a particular connection through an alternative but specific similarity.

> *Prior to this first session with Jack (an individual with experience of homelessness), I was a little apprehensive that I might feel like the metaphorical fish out of water – an identity clash, feeling socially and culturally incongruous – a middle class English woman engaging with working-class Glaswegians who had had, or were managing, drug and alcohol problems and many of whom had been guests of Her Majesty's Service at some point in their lives. I was quite honestly anxious about how I might relate to individuals whose backgrounds were so radically different from my own and, perhaps, vice versa – how were they going to relate to me and to what extent might I be regarded with circumspect due to perceived socio-cultural differences. My fears were allayed since my concerns were perceived and never enacted or, at least, not communicated by any members of the group! Despite my initial concerns about managing difference, it later transpired that Jack and I shared an aspect of our identity that facilitated a connectedness and relatedness that served to override those initial differences.*
>
> *In the 'getting to know you' exercise Jack told me that when his Dad 'discovered' he was gay, he locked him in a cupboard for 3 days and then threw him out the house. He was 16 years old. I was unsurprisingly shocked, but the story resonated with me on a profoundly personal level. As a gay woman, I reflected on how vastly different our experiences were. My fears about 'coming out' were born out of the shame of being 'different' which I attribute to the divisive homophobic discourse circulating in society; Jack's story and actual fears resulted, primarily, from being a recipient of an abusive and homophobic father. This and similar experiences also brought to my awareness how my identity as a gay woman has provided me with the experiential and emotional knowledge of what it can feel like to be marginalised and stigmatised. I am aware that my identity has*

also driven, albeit subconsciously, my interest in and sensitivity towards researching the experiences of marginalised and socially excluded communities.

However, as a researcher, I am mindful of needing to avoid the trap of over-identification – assuming that one's experience may be similar to another by virtue of a shared identity. It is important to distinguish one's own experiential baggage/history/identity from that of the other but perhaps also recognising when those experiences may be similar. While Jack's background – his experience of coming out and his trajectory into homelessness – was very different from my own background, this understanding and our shared identity enabled me to feel more connected to my co-researcher and gave me greater insight into the stories of others.

Mary's experience supports the view that 'a participant's story may evoke strong reactions from the researcher because it reminds the researcher of their own personal experiences' (Dickson-Swift *et al.*, 2009: 65) and is also a good illustration of the multifaceted nature of our identities. In this chapter so far, and for the purpose of being explicit, we have ourselves broken down certain 'characteristics' of self, but it is important to remember that each of us has multiple, dynamic, overlapping and often contradictory identities. To isolate and reduce people to one aspect of their identity closes down other 'possible' or alternative selves (Markus and Nurius, 1986) and 'reflects the limitations of identity categories' (Kelemen and Rumens, 2008: 105). It is also precisely the reason why large sections of society experience marginalization. While in this context Mary is uneasy about her middle-class upbringing and blemish-free prison record, it is actually her sexuality that is unexpectedly given primacy in her relationship with the research participant. Of course, there will be numerous instances where this is also used as a disqualifier (Burrell and Hearn, 1989; Colgan and McKearney, 2012; Willis, 2012), but on this occasion it grants her an acceptance she was not expecting.

While this vignette demonstrates how sharing a parallel divergent sexual preference facilitated an empathetic dialogue between researcher and research participant, we return to the second author's research of the sales staff in a newspaper organization to illustrate how emotions surrounding a gender identity might result in concealing an important aspect of the research because it threatened that very identity. Only in retrospect several years later was the researcher able to disclose the emotional damage to his masculine identity:

The emotional trauma of having been 'thrown out' of the field rather than leaving voluntarily, resulted in my making no mention of it in any reports or publications that I developed from the research and it is only now that I am able to express my upset, embarrassment if not humiliation at being forced to leave. I would argue that it was my masculine pride of being reluctant to acknowledge any personal event that could be interpreted as failure that accounts for leaving out such emotional traumas from my research reports. However, it was also a function of cultural taboos within the social sciences and especially methodology texts to refrain from expressing subjective emotions when reporting on research.

Of course, the reluctance described in this vignette is supported by a whole range of rationales deriving from certain institutions that are inclined to describe such 'confessions' as self-indulgent. Indeed, as Kleinman and Copp argue,

> fieldworkers share a culture dominated by the ideology of professionalism or, more specifically the ideology of science. According to that ideology, emotions are suspect. They contaminate research by impeding objectivity, hence they should be removed.
>
> *(1993: 2)*

A major reason why so much of the human condition – much of which has major implications for the conditions, content and consequences of research – seems to be outlawed in any social science accounts or reports is because of the concern to emulate, so as to secure the same credibility and status as, the natural sciences. Both the view that the sciences are devoid of emotional content and the view that the social sciences can seek to suppress or even remove the human dimension (ontology) from its epistemology and methods are increasingly discredited in certain quarters (Kuhn, 1970; Foucault, 1973; Giddens, 1976). Despite this, there is still a degree of marginality or outsider status accorded to those who see an unbridgeable ontological discontinuity (Douglas, 1970) between the human and natural sciences because in the former both subjects (researchers) and 'objects' (the researched) are seen as active agents of interpretation and meaning construction in ways that is not the case for the objects of physical science.

The following vignette outlines a project involving the second author in experiences of an emotional nature. Inevitably these experiences were obliterated from reports on the research as if they had never happened.

> *One problem was that I had a different point of view than the funding agency and wanted to build this in to the research and this led to some disagreement with my research assistant who perhaps understandably because of financial dependence, was less concerned to challenge the funder's position. Later this disagreement developed into a major emotional conflict between the two of us that for me (David), and perhaps also for her, was damaging. This marked the partial demise of an intimate friendship that was extremely upsetting. It also disrupted the work in a number of ways but when publications were eventually produced, neither of these emotional tensions were even mentioned let alone analysed. However, from discussions with others it is clear that such conflicts are not uncommon in collaborative research projects and, in particular, between masters or doctoral students and their supervisors [see Chapter 7 by Broussine and Watts].*
>
> *It is only approximately 15 years ago when partly in response to such problems, universities introduced the practice of providing two supervisors for each doctoral student and although, in principle, this ensures that there is a fallback in the event of disputes, it is still no reason for methodology and other texts to leave such topics comparatively unexamined. Indeed, the provision of an additional supervisor can have the unintended consequence of adding to the complexity and dynamics of the supervisory relationship*

partly because of different views, ideas of who takes what responsibility, and sometimes, intense paradigmatic point scoring between the supervisors.

Conclusion

Many of the vignettes we have drawn upon can be seen partly to be the result of methodology being a legacy from epistemology as the representative of cognitive knowledge rather than ontology and its concern with what it is to *be* human. While logical positivism is simply one of a range of possible epistemological variants, there is a strong tendency in methodology texts for it to serve as the standard against which everything else is measured. As a result, numerous qualitative methodology texts (e.g. Yin, 1993; 1994; Denzin and Lincoln, 1994; Berg, 2008) defend their methods from a positivist standpoint rather than asserting an anti-positivist methodology and epistemology perhaps through reflecting more on the ontology of Cartesian mind–body and subject–object separation that lurks beneath many of these texts (Knights, 1996). Given such ontology it is not surprising that emotion, the body, difference and diversity are short-changed. Cognitive awareness of a phenomenon even when concerned with the body and emotion does not guarantee a change in consciousness or behaviour since our everyday practices are informed by heavily internalised norms and beliefs. Consequently, we may be cognitively aware of, for example, the legal importance of treating subjects equally regardless of age, sex or race and yet still act in discriminating ways because of deeply internalised prejudicial norms. Even writers such as Butler (1990) and Foucault (1973; 1979), who deconstruct the Cartesian binary that routinely elevates the mind and rationality over the body and emotion, have a tendency to produce texts that contain 'bloodless language [that] reinforces the very principle they critique . . . [and thus] . . . regulates and subjugates the very bodies they would liberate' (Stoller, 1997: xv). If this is so for authors who radically refuse the normative legacy of disciplines and discourse, it is much worse with respect to the social sciences more generally regardless of the focus of their studies. It is not then surprising to find research focused on emotions often taking a disembodied form, for the emotions become just another object (or variable) to capture and control, to organize and order, or to manage and manipulate. Examining the proliferating literature on emotional labour (Fineman, 2003; 2005; Dale, 2001; Witz *et al.*, 2003), Knights and Thanem (2011) criticised its tendency to provide a somewhat disembodied view of employees engaged in emotional labour.

Insofar as the majority of research methodology texts in the social sciences provide little or no licence for 'telling it like it really is', they offer little guidance or insight into the everyday realities of conducting and reporting on research. Instead, as has been articulated elsewhere in this book, these texts treat the research process as a unilinear, rational series of steps and stages culminating in an often anodyne and depersonalised account of various events, which only serve to further depress and alienate others trying to make sense of very different sets of experiences. Indeed it has been argued that the shaping of what constitutes knowledge in academia – by multiple stakeholders such as publishers, journal editors, funding committees etc. – encourages a deliberate 'suppression or omission of the emotional aspects of the work in order to get published' (Dickson-Swift *et al.*, 2009: 66); the fiction of the fully competent researcher must be maintained at all times.

In this chapter we have sought to depart from the conventional tendency to avoid discussing the disruptions and divergences, the cul-de-sacs and false trails, or the numerous feelings of despair and helplessness as researchers struggle often alone to make sense of a project that seems to be going nowhere, or going seriously awry. In doing so there has been no attempt to deny the body, conflicts, emotions, identities, diversity and contingent, messy, fluid and discontinuous nature of research. Rather than perceiving the disruptions and tensions of conducting research on human life as negative elements that must be denied, discounted or deleted, we suggest from our accounts that they can be turned into positive learning opportunities to render our research as rich and complex a tapestry as the world it seeks to describe and analyse.

References

Archer, L. (2002) It's Easier That You're a Girl and That You're Asian: Interactions of 'Race' and Gender between Researchers and Participants. *Feminist Review*, 72: 108–132.

Bell, E. (1999) The Negotiation of a Working Role in Organizational Ethnography, *International Journal of Social Research Methodology*, 2(1): 17–31.

Berg, B. L. (2008) *Qualitative Research Methods for the Social Sciences*. 7th ed. Boston: Allyn & Bacon.

Burrell, G., and Hearn J. (Eds.) (1989) *The Sexuality of Organization*. London: Sage.

Butler, J. (1990) *Gender Trouble: Feminism and the Subversion of Identity*. London: Routledge.

Clarke, C. A., Brown, A. D., and Hope Hailey, V. (2009) Working Identities? Antagonistic Discursive Resources and Managerial Identity. *Human Relations*, 62(3): 323–354.

Cockburn, C. (1983) *Brothers*. London: Pluto Press.

Cockburn, C. (1985) *The Machinery of Dominance: Women, Men and Technical Know-how*. London: Pluto Press.

Colgan, F., and McKearney, A. (2012) Visibility and Voice in Organisations: Lesbian, Gay, Bisexual and Transgendered Employee Networks. *Equality, Diversity and Inclusion: An International Journal*, 31 (4): 359–378.

Dale, K. (2001) *Anatomising Embodiment and Organisation Theory*. Basingstoke: Palgrave.

Denzin, N., and Lincoln, Y. (Eds.) (1994) *Handbook of Qualitative Research*. Thousand Oaks, CA: Sage.

Dickson-Swift, V., James, E., Kippen, S., and Liamputtong, P. (2009) Researching Sensitive Topics: Qualitative Research as Emotion Work. *Qualitative Research*, 9 (1): 61–79.

Douglas, J. D. (1970) *Understanding Everyday Life*. New York: Routledge.

Fineman, S. (2003) *Understanding Emotion at Work*. London: Sage.

Fineman, S. (2005) Appreciating Emotion at Work – Paradigm Tensions. *International Journal of Work, Organisation and Emotion*, 1 (1): 4–19.

Foucault, M. (1973) *The Birth of the Clinic*. London: Tavistock.

Foucault, M. (1979) *The History of Sexuality Vol. 1: An Introduction*. Harmondsworth: Penguin.

Friedman, M. (1970) The Social Responsibility of Business Is to Increase Its Profits. *The New York Times Magazine*, September 13.

Giddens, A. (1976) *New Rules of Sociological Method: A Positive Critique of interpretative Sociologies*. London: Hutchinson.

Goffman, E. (1959) *The Presentation of Self in Everyday Life*. Harmondsworth: Penguin.

Hanisch, C. (1969) The Personal Is Political, in S. Firestone and A. Koedt (Eds.), *Notes from the Second Year*. New York: Radical Women.

Harris, L. C. (2002) The Emotional Labour of Barristers: An Exploration of Emotional Labour by Status Professionals. *Journal of Management Studies*, 39 (4): 553–584.

Kelemen, M., and Rumens, N. (2008). *An Introduction to Critical Management Research*. London: Sage.

Kleinman, S., and Copp, M. A. (1993) *Emotions and Fieldwork*. Thousand Oaks, CA: Sage.

Knights, D. (1996) Refocusing the Case Study: The Politics of Research and Researching Politics in IT Management. *Technology Studies*, 2 (2): 230–284.

Knights, D. (2011) Body Matters: Breaking Gender Binaries in Social and Organizational Research, presented at Stockholm University Business School, Sept 15.

Knights, D., and Clarke, C. (2014) It's a Bittersweet Symphony, This Life: Fragile Academic Selves and Insecure Identities at Work. *Organization Studies*, 35 (3): 335–357.

Knights, D., and Roberts, J. (1982) The Power of Organisation or the Organisation of Power?: Management-Staff Relations in Sales. *Organisation Studies*, 3 (1): 47–63.

Knights, D., and Thanem, T. (2011) (Trans)gender Incorporations: Critically Embodied Reflections on the Gender Divide in Organization Studies. *International Journal of Work Organizations and Emotion*, 4 (3/4): 217–235.

Knights, D., and Tullberg, M. (2012) Managing Masculinity / Mismanaging the Corporation. *Organization*, 19 (4): 385–404.

Kuhn, T. S. (1970) The Structure of Scientific Revolutions. Chicago: University of Chicago Press.

Lukes, S. (1974) *Power: A Radical View*. London: Macmillan.

Markus, H., and Nurius, P. (1986). Possible Selves. *American Psychologist*, 41: 954–959.

Miller, G. E. (2002) The Frontier, Entrepreneurialism, and Engineers : Women Coping with a Web of Masculinities in an Organizational Culture. *Culture and Organization*, 8 (2): 145–160.

Reay, D. (1996) Dealing with Difficult Differences: Reflexivity and Social Class in Feminist Research. *Feminist Review*, 53: 57–73.

Sennett, R., and Cobb, J. (1977). *The Hidden Injuries of Class*. New York: Vintage Books.

Sinclair, A. (2007) Teaching Leadership Critically to MBAs: Experiences from Heaven and Hell. *Management Learning*, 38 (4): 458–472.

Stoller, P. (1997) *Sensuous Scholarship*. Philadelphia: University of Pennsylvania Press.

Thanem, T. (2011) *The Monstrous Organization*. Cheltenham: Edward Elgar.

Thanem, T., and Knights, D. (2012). Feeling and Speaking through Our Gendered Bodies: Embodied Self-reflection and Research Practice in Organization Studies. *International Journal of Work Organizations and Emotion*, 5 (1): 91–108.

Waldron, V. R. (2000) Relational Experiences and Emotion at Work, in S. Fineman (Ed.), *Emotion in Organizations*. 2nd ed. London: Sage.

Watson, T. J. (1994). Managing, Crafting and Researching: Words, Skill and Imagination in Shaping Management Research. *British Journal of Management*, 5 (2): S77–S87.

Willis, P. (2012) Witnesses on the Periphery: Young Lesbian, Gay, Bisexual and Queer Employees Witnessing Homophobic Exchanges in Australian Workplaces. *Human Relations* 65 (12): 1589–1610.

Witz, A., Warhurst, C., and Nickson, D. (2003) The Labour of Aesthetics and the Aesthetics of Organization. *Organization* 10 (1): 33–54.

Wolkowitz, C. (2011) The Organizational Contours of 'Body Work', in E. Jeanes, D. Knights and P. Yancey Martin (Eds.), *Handbook of Gender, Work and Organization*. London and New York: Wiley.

Wright Mills, C. (2000). *The Sociological Imagination*. New York: Oxford University Press.

Yin, R. K. (1993) *Applications of case study research. Applied Social Research Series, Vol. 34*. London: Sage.

Yin, R. K. (1994) *Case Study Research Design and Methods*. 2nd ed. Thousand Oaks, CA: Sage.

4

EMOTIONALLY CHARGED RESEARCH

Engaging with the politics of action research

Louise Grisoni and Mike Broussine

Entering different worlds

Like many of the authors contributing to this book, our experience leads us to argue that 'objective' action research does not exist – it is always political. Both of us have felt the 'political heat' of carrying out action research in organizations. This direct relationship between lived experience of the researcher and the wider research context connects back to references to 'the personal is political', a phrase originating in the women's liberation movement in the 1970s, and extends to questions of whether social research can ever be independent and objective. We would argue that research – in particular action research – is constituted by a political and emotional relationship between researcher, participants and the worlds they inhabit. Recent years therefore have seen a growing range of challenges to the idea that research should be governed by the principle of value neutrality. Critical, feminist, antiracist and postmodern analyses have argued that social research is intrinsically political. Hardy (1994) suggested that politics occurs as actors in the organization mobilise power, and that power is entrenched in the relationship between actors rather than being an attribute of a particular individual. The importance of such an analysis is to emphasise the systemic and relational nature of power – and, therefore, of politics – in organizations.

If we can agree that social research is political, what are the potential emotional effects on us as researchers? In this chapter we reflect on three themes that emerge through a discussion of our two action-research projects. The first theme relates to role conflict, power and the emotional impact these have on us as researchers. The second considers the influence of emotions on the direction that the research took and on choices and decisions made along the way. The third concerns the emotions experienced in the process of engaging in the research. We wish to bring to life some of the complexities of the research process when emotions are acknowledged and worked with as an integral part of a research inquiry, and our respective stories will be told partly by sharing vignettes (extracts from our research journals and recollections of experiences) which will illustrate some of the complexities of this process. As we discuss our stories and experiences later in this chapter, we will be writing on occasions in the first person, as Louise or Mike. Writing in this way can feel exposing and at times self-indulgent. It is our hope in highlighting the raw experiences of the politics and emotions of research that the reader is able to learn from our experience and relate this to his or her own research journey.

As action researchers working with and in organizations, we must concern ourselves – and prepare ourselves – not only with the nature of power exercised by individuals, but also in the relationship between those who have power and those who appear powerless, because these socio-political dynamics are represented in the groups and individuals with whom we might be working. Political and power relations are institutionalised and legitimised through language, symbol, structures, rules and regulations – a process which has been described as the 'management of meaning' (Pettigrew, 1977). We can see from our first vignette that those who hold power in the organization we are about to enter can, if we are not aware, begin to alter the 'meaning' of our research and indeed the methodology we propose to use:

> *'Congratulations', said the chief executive at our first meeting with the management team after being awarded the research contract. 'We're really looking forward to working with you both and the Business School. Now – where to start? I expect you'll need some help in getting your questionnaires out to staff?' Gulp! Our proposal had laid out our proposed methodology, and this didn't involve questionnaires at all. Instead we were going to interview people. So now, here was this powerful man at the top of the client organisation (by the way, a research chemist by background, as we found out afterwards) who had commissioned us: what to say? This provoked immense questions in that visceral moment – do I challenge or contradict? Acquiesce? In fact, somehow or other, we struggled through – God knows how! – and our proposal came out intact. But you couldn't help wondering whether this chief executive officer began to have misgivings about commissioning us, and this fear stayed with us for a while as we got into the project.*
>
> *(Mike's journal)*

So, here was an 'awkward moment' (Koning and Ooi, 2013). What if these researchers had acquiesced? Some of us can be seduced by, and can seek, the approval of powerful people in organizations, especially if they had a hand in commissioning the research in the first place. Like it or not, and even if we resist the potential for seduction, we suggest that the action researcher becomes part of the system, and just as there are 'organizations in the mind', so organizational members participating in the research hold a version of the 'researcher in the mind'. As soon as the researcher enters an organization and begins the action-research project, the system changes, and therefore the researcher's interventions – the conduct of his or her study – are inherently political. As Denzin and Lincoln (2005: 643) put it:

All observation involves participation in the world being studied. There is no pure, objective, detached observation; the effects of the observer's presence can never be erased. Furthermore, the colonial concept of the subject (the object of the observer's gaze) is no longer appropriate. Observers now function as collaborative participants in action inquiry settings. . . . [Observational interaction is] shaped by shifts in gendered identity as well as existing structures of power.

Questions always arise about who is representing the system (and truth) when the researcher enters a different world and begins to engage with people in it. Sometimes the structures and implicit rules of organizations do not always allow participants to verbalize experience and feelings, or they can only express them with a controlled and inauthentic voice. Marcic (2002), for example, has described the tendency of organizational leaders and managers to rely on self-presentation routines that are based in their competence and expertise. Self-aware action researchers – and researchers generally who conduct studies within, and/or for, organizational, community and governmental systems – soon come to realise that different actors in the system can hold different hopes for and anxieties about their research outcomes. As the following vignette illustrates, researchers need to learn – sometimes rapidly – about the organization they are seeking to access and to keep their 'political wits' about them.

I'd started my PhD at the age of 40, at the same time as running my consulting business and being a father to two young children. I was working flat out, without much spare time, feeling both energised by the PhD challenge, and often wondering whether I was 'up' to this. I needed to get ethics permission from a local National Health Service committee because two of my case studies were with staff working for the NHS. It was an important issue and part of my learning about ethics and access in practice. The preparation for my appointment with the local ethics committee body was difficult. I couldn't find anyone in my university who could give me useful advice on what to expect, and how to get my proposal 'through'. I'd heard some horror stories about people being turned down. It was very frustrating. My emailed requests for support brought nothing. No-one knew where our university expertise lay in dealing with these matters. I felt I was acting blind, was exposed, but had no option other than to proceed. The meeting was at 7:00 on a February evening. I sat outside the meeting room, waiting with other researchers, all seeking the same approval. There was a generalised, free-floating apprehension. My turn came and I was invited into the room. There were 12 people sitting at an oval table. Most didn't make eye contact, though the chairperson invited me to sit down next to him. I certainly felt like the outsider. They asked me questions: what is the research about? What methods would I use? How many people would I see? In what working circumstances? They didn't seem too pleased with my need to observe people in their real work, and to understand work processes in situ. I felt myself become more defensive and irritated as the meeting progressed, in a room full of powerful officials, unclear about the rules of engagement, unwittingly cut adrift by an institutional

lethargy. A week later I received a letter from the Committee Chair: 'Not approved . . .
intrusive observations . . . unable to comply . . . consider service evaluation'. It was a
low point in my whole PhD – without the access, this could mean seeking completely
different cases, which would take how long? . . . I was angry with my lack of support
from my university, disappointed and determined. I was also aware of the risk of me
stifling action by blaming a set of generalised others, when I might have prepared myself
better. I got stubbornly practical and asked for help again within the university. I found
two people who understood the NHS and gave me some advice: seek the permission
on the basis of doing a service evaluation: Don't call it research. I remember the Chair's
letter which had subtly implied the same course of action. I'd been too low to pay it
proper attention. I took the advice, resubmitted and gained the permission I needed!

(PhD student)

So far, we have discussed what might happen when the researcher, coming from
one kind of world, enters another. Recently, Koning and Ooi (2013) have noted
that, in ethnographic research in organization and management studies (and, we
would add, action research), discussions about emotions and awkwardness are still a
rarity. They mention that there are a few exceptions, for instance Down *et al.* (2006)
on 'fear and loathing' in the field, Whiteman (2010) on the 'burning pain of heart-
break' encountered in fieldwork, and Munkejord (2009) on emotional awareness
in the field: 'We concur with these authors that it is time to start taking "emotional
realities" seriously' (p.17).

A positivist view conceives researchers as people who are distanced from the
organization's political networks. Thus positioned, it is suggested, they are able to
inquire independently and neutrally. But social researchers (and, we would argue, in
particular action and ethnographic researchers) question such a view fundamentally.
We as researchers hold a set of beliefs, principles and commitments which drive
our actions and interventions. In other words, we are 'political'. As in every human
activity, our work as researchers is affected by, and in turn affects, our view of the
world. Morgan (1986) suggested that our practice can never be theory-free, because
it is always guided by an image of what we are trying to do, but,

The real issue is whether or not we are aware of the theory guiding our
action.

(p.336)

Politics includes personal relationships to the system being investigated. Both of us,
in our own ways, held particular attachments to the organizations we were working with, and we were aware, respectively, of our strong personal, professional and
political commitments to the institutions and people participating in our research.
There are of course some big advantages to such attachments, e.g. we had no difficulty securing access to data. However, we were aware that actors in our organizations did not necessarily hold neutral views about us, and, as we will see, we for our
part needed to remain aware continuously of the 'baggage' that we each brought

to our studies. Our own commitments and values meant that we both came to see our respective pieces of work that we discuss below as 'labours of love' (see Clarke *et al.*, 2012), appreciating that it might be hard to let it go on completion. This acknowledges the degree of personal investment and attachment to the research project as researchers. The project matters to us in terms of the relationships made with participants, the nature of the findings and the difference that the 'action' part of the research might make to the organizations involved. This connection has both emotional and political aspects.

The emotional impact on researchers: action research in your own organization

The focus of the first study that we reflect on here was concerned with student and staff experiences of teaching, learning and assessment (Grisoni, 2005). The research was conducted as part of my doctoral thesis. I (Louise) was interested in uncovering the range of espoused theories and theories in use that were associated with organizational strategy to highlight where practice-based improvements could be made. The ethical balance in this project was delicate, complicated by the decision to locate the study in an organization in which I held multiple role responsibilities – as a line manager, researcher and tutor – thus emphasising the need to be aware of and manage organizational politics and ethics (Coghlan and Brannick, 2010).

Being a manager also has an emotional and political dimension, and one member of staff who volunteered to take part in the study was someone I found challenging and difficult to manage. I felt this person's behaviour towards me was undermining and critical. This often left me feeling lacking in skills and incompetent even though I had considerable management experience from other organizations. Being new to the research journey through my doctoral studies meant I was a novice, learning about research process and nervous about doing things right. My concern about involving this particular member of the staff in the study was that this person might eat away at what little confidence I had. This person was always very clear that they knew the answer and could point out solutions, indicating weaknesses before anyone else. It is quite possible that this person thought they were well meaning, intending to be helpful – as this is how they qualified their interventions. Unfortunately this was not what I experienced. In terms of a research inquiry process, would I be able to hear what this person wanted to say without my own anxieties getting in the way? My supervisor was very helpful in getting me to think through the implications and impact this relationship had on the research choices I made in the study. My managerial role in relation to the teaching staff involved in the study needed sensitive handling. I recognised that certain data would need to be desensitised to protect the anonymity of participants, and I undertook this as part of the ethics requirements for the study.

Personal prejudices and opinions impact on data collection and analysis. Critical self-reflection and a personal journal help identify when and how this is happening concerning research participants. With my study, there was a potential problem in relation to power differences between staff and students, particularly if assessment of work occurred during the period of the study. Another question was how might students make use of interactions with an authority figure – they might not recognise it in managerial terms, but might there be some other use or effect on the interaction? For instance it was possible that students might wish to impress me with their comments in the hope that this would have a positive effect on their marks for the module. It therefore felt important to reassure student participants that there was no correlation between assessment and participation in the study where there might be hidden thoughts of preferential treatment as a consequence of involvement. A difficulty in this sort of research relates to participants providing answers and information they think you may want to hear. So students concerned to maximise their marks may want to participate in the research as a way of influencing this outcome (equally, staff may view their participation as a form of transaction).

The pressure students felt to achieve good final-year marks was expressed often, and it felt that by stating the importance of achieving a 2:1 degree to their future careers, somehow the responsibility for this was being transferred to me, in their minds a tutor. So it would become my responsibility, not theirs, to make sure they achieved good results. This insight became part of my findings around increased student dependency in final-year learning strategies. I brought attention to the importance of protecting the confidentiality of participants and sustaining a reflexive approach in my research diary in order to investigate the impact of multiple roles and inquiry into power differences between myself and research participants. In my research journal I noticed that at times some of my jottings were full of rant and irritation about colleagues and students especially when they seemed to be looking to me for solutions to the issues they were experiencing. I wondered why they were so needy. Why so demanding? What was I doing to elicit this sort of response? Was I too mothering in my approach, too assuring that I could provide answers to their problems and issues? I needed to work out whether it was me the researcher they wanted to take action, or me the tutor, or me the manager. Unravelling such questions helped me see where dependencies were placed and how much my preference for co-dependency and collaborative outcomes dominated my thinking.

The question of where the power rests is significant in the action-research process. Holian (2002), in her analysis of action research on ethical decision making in her own higher-education organization, highlighted the following factors: multiple roles and role conflict, the personal impact, learning from experience, sensibility of doing action research in your own organization and the value of doing research in your own organisation. Each of these factors was relevant to my study. I held multiple roles – namely, as a researcher in my own organization, as manager (Head of School), as teacher (with particular preferences for certain teaching and learning approaches) and as colleague to peers involved in the research. These roles involved tensions depending on the emerging findings, which impacted on my feelings during the research and on decisions I made about how to progress my study. A key learning point was how to deal with ethical considerations during the research process. Values held in relation to methodology, choices about the research process in terms of methods, varying emotions, decisions taken as the research progressed – all impacted on and were in turn influenced by various roles and relationships I held. What I found was that the research process for this study was in reality a complicated process. I developed figure 4.1 below to help me consider different elements as they affected issues of power and politics (Grisoni, 2004). It contained important clues as to where the 'hot spots' lay for me, concentrating around issues of emotion and power in relation to multiple roles. Reflections in my research diary provided the material for this review:

> *Sometimes my own nervousness and feelings of anxiety mean I shy away from asking follow up questions during an interview if I felt it wasn't going well or the participant wasn't very forthcoming . . . Sometimes if my day has been difficult prior to or I was anticipating a difficult meeting after a research interview, I might be tempted to hurry through the process or have difficulty switching into the role of researcher. Depending on how hassled I am feeling impacts on how relaxed I feel about the data I am gathering. I have learned to allocate complete days to research rather than try and squeeze interviews in between other activities. This decision helps me sustain my research focus, clarify my role as researcher, be sensitised to emotions arising from the research process, be alert to my value base and the subsequent choices I make regarding next steps in the process.*
>
> *(Louise's journal)*

The emotions that emerged in the research, combined with varying roles and relationships, influenced the choices and decisions I made throughout the study. The values I identified as important to research provided a baseline from which to make decisions in order to maintain an ethical position as I worked with participants and as the research process as a whole.

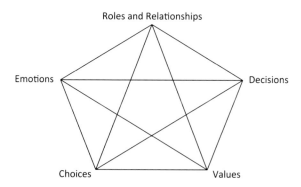

FIGURE 4.1 Power, politics and tensions in researching your own organization (Grisoni, 2004)

I found I was profoundly influenced by my mood as the research proceeded. There were times when I lost confidence and doubted that I was finding out anything useful, and there were other times when an insight, which led to combining ideas to create the models and develop theories, felt inspirational. I experienced the inevitable range of anxieties about whether I would be good enough as a researcher, whether the area I had chosen to investigate was worthwhile, whether I would be able to say anything new or different as a result of the study. I suspect that these feelings are very deep rooted and in my case not easily dismissed. My emotional state affected how much risk I took with decisions about different aspects of the research process such as data collection and presentation. When anxious I noticed that I adopted a more conservative approach, and at times when I had greater confidence I became more creative –

> *It's got to the point when I have to recognize that the research isn't going well. My management role is taking up too much of my time and I am getting frustrated with the rhetoric around a strategic approach that is being espoused. It contrasts with my understanding of the day to day experiences related to me by staff and students . . . On the one hand we were talking about developing independent learners and yet pressure of workload and marking makes staff adopt dependent strategies feeding students' desire to be spoon fed and instrumental in their approach to learning. I feel caught in the dilemma. I can bring these issues to the attention of staff but risk being placed in the position of someone not supporting or appearing to be critical of broader institutional strategy. At the same time I want students to be more engaged and active in their learning. Working with staff to achieve this creates increased pressure on already stretched workloads. I recognize the emotional strain this puts on my role as both manager and researcher. Whilst my research is able to highlight some clear areas for improvement of practice it is clear that it also creates tensions that need to be addressed. Taking action in one area impacts on my inquiry in terms of relationships with participants and in terms of data generated.*
>
> *(Louise's journal)*

I noticed parallels in my experience as a doctoral student with the focus on independent learning in the study drawn from undergraduate student experiences. I noticed that I looked for a level of dependence on my supervisor, evidenced in the importance I placed on feedback and supportive comments. Towards the end of supervision sessions I would seek reassurance from her expertise in terms of telling me whether what I had produced was good enough. I tended to be highly productive in the first few days after a supervision session, writing up data or searching for more references. This encouraged me to continue and have confidence that I would be capable of successfully completing the doctorate. I expected my supervisor to provide clear indications that I was working to an acceptable standard. In many ways this experience paralleled the issues I was researching among undergraduates – and led me to wonder whether there was a broader relevance to the study for postgraduate and doctoral-level students, in particular in terms of the research process and study experience. It would be usual to expect that working with your supervisor might help unravel the issues surrounding inquiry processes and analysis of data. However, this relationship is also subject to power relations in terms of satisfying the quality standards of what constitutes doctoral-level studies and may impact on how the research is conducted and written up. In my role as Head of School, I was also aware of delicate inter-institutional negotiations regarding potential collaboration as well as inter-professional relationships that affected what and who I felt I could discuss at my supervision sessions. (See Chapter 7 on supervision).

Being an insider researching my own organization had advantages of access and pre-understandings of the research setting, including the history, key events and jargon used. It also had implications for power relationships between participants and myself, and the emotional consequences of these, which I was sensitive to and have reflected on extensively in this chapter. Whilst the examples given are personal, hopefully they point to issues that others engaging research in their own organizations might be alerted to and find helpful.

The emotional impact on researchers: action research in a client system/organization

The second study (Fox and Broussine, 2001) aimed to investigate how women become local-authority chief executives; to explore their experiences of making it to the top, and the barriers they encountered; to understand more about their experiences of being chief executives in local government both in terms of how they see and carry out their responsibilities, and how others relate to them; to review how women's experiences are similar or different to those of their male colleagues and whether women have career and personal development needs that differ from those of men; and to assess training, development and policy implications given the rapidly changing role of local-authority chief executives. The sensitive political issue in this piece of action research was that stakeholders' commitment, indeed support, for the study varied considerably, from enthusiastic support through to hostility.

I (Mike) worked with a co-researcher (Pam) in designing and carrying out the study. It revealed a discomfiting picture of institutionalised sexism in local government in England and Wales. Our research uncovered some of the underlying factors that lead to the negative experiences of women. These factors were not to do with the 'deficiencies' of women themselves, but with cultural norms and often unconscious principles that underpin organizations. Clearly such findings were not universally welcomed in the local government system, though our report was well received in many quarters. Throughout, we were alert to the dangers that can be associated with studies of this nature. As we were starting the study, one woman chief executive told us that she did not wish to support our research. She argued that she did not want to be seen as a 'woman chief executive' but rather as a chief executive who happened to be a woman. Subsequently, in an item in the local government press, another woman chief executive was critical of how we presented our findings, arguing that we had differentiated too much between the experiences of men and women. These are important issues. Foster (1999) noted that the identification of 'womanhood' as a special issue could provoke anxiety in women. Because power holders in the system are predominantly men, the highlighting of women's issues may alienate those in power so that the study could be counter-productive. Such warnings served to remind us about the need for strong methodological awareness and rectitude, and to bear in mind two related issues as we proceeded: the danger of presenting 'essentialist' arguments (Martin, 1994); and the contention that a focus on women in organizations problematises women.

On some occasions we were discouraged by those who held reservations or who downplayed the potential importance of the study. It took us a long time to obtain funding from organizations that we regarded as obvious sources. We 'felt' the occasional covert disapproval coming from some of the power structures within the system, and, at times, it felt 'risky' to talk about the research. Not everybody was in favour of the research. Some of the more commonly expressed views included the following:

- There was no need for the study: women were being appointed in greater numbers, and, in fact, you were now more likely to be appointed if you were a woman;
- Such a study ran the risk of making women's experiences worse rather than better by replacing old stereotypes with new ones;
- Because the power holders in local authorities are largely male, the study could alienate them and produce a 'male backlash';
- The experience of women is not substantially different from that of their male counterparts, and therefore there were no issues to be studied.

At the time that we received these messages, I noted in my journal:

> *I am bloody furious. How dare they! I feel quite disconsolate and rejected, and don't want to go on with the study. Of course this is impossible, and I need to 'grow up'. I need to listen to others in the system who are more encouraging of us to keep at it, and Pam keeps reminding me about why we had embarked on this in the first place.*
> *(Mike's journal)*

The misgivings expressed by certain actors in local government began eventually to interest us (once we had calmed down). I admit my initial tendency was to reject and put them down to prejudice, to throw my toys out of the pram. In fact, as Pam and I talked it through, we found that they were useful in a number of ways, not the least of which was to learn how important it is to tell your co-researcher how you're feeling! What interests me in retrospect about the journal entry above is how I began at the time to self-censor my feelings ('I need to "grow up"') as if I was transgressing a self-imposed 'feelings rule' – that researchers had no place for emotions like being angry.

Through our own processes of working as a partnership of male and female researchers, we reflected that when we heard voices which were negatively disposed towards our research (and maybe towards us), we were experiencing some of the phenomena that we were studying. This became an important aspect of our research and, we believe, contributed to a development of our reflexive capacity. It was understandable that we would receive a mixture of expressions both of ardent support and of doubt and even hostility. For example, Pam was accused at one stage of being 'a bigoted old feminist', and I was sent an anonymous message that I had 'overstepped the mark'. However, the expressions of encouragement far outweighed instances of negativity (Broussine and Fox, 2003: 30).

The fact that one of the researchers was male and the other female was an important aspect of the research. We felt the fact of a man and woman working together on a study of women chief executives sent an important political message about the standing of the research. For example, those who might consider its findings uncomfortable could not simply write them off as being the imagination of an 'over-involved woman'. The mixed gender of the research team also had implications for the dynamic of the research. It meant that the research findings could be interpreted from different gender perspectives, and this sometimes led to some hot debates between us. However, our genders also presented difficulties. It took us aback somewhat when, despite the emphasis we placed on working together, it was assumed frequently that the project was being led by me. Pam was sometimes referred to as 'helping' with 'his' research. While we were irritated by such views, we came to see such responses as representative of the attitudes identified by many research participants as being detrimental to senior women managers, a kind of unconscious (or conscious) process of marginalisation.

If politics and values inhabit research, then what of 'truth'? As researchers, we were clear that we must be honest and non-manipulative, both of our research participants and of the data. A critical issue was the role of our own identities and political predispositions as we carried out the research. The study required us to be *reflective* (for example, about what was coming out of the data), but also to be *reflexive* – to be aware of ourselves individually and in relation to each other in the process of researching. Easterby-Smith and Malina (1999) thought that the starting point for understanding reflexivity was the idea that it is not possible for social researchers to be detached from what they are observing. Second, we learnt that to be reflexive required us to be critical of our own assumptions and feelings and to avoid making excessive claims to authority.

We were often affected emotionally by the stories we were told. For example, a major finding of our study concerned bullying in some of the participating organizations. Sometimes these stories resonated with certain personal experiences one or both of us had in our careers, with the result that we empathised considerably with our research participants. Our struggles with the experiences, assumptions and feelings evoked by the study became an important part of our way of working. While we were both equally committed to the study and agreed on our approaches to the research, we of course had our own biases and agendas. We had to work consciously and reflexively with our conflicts with each other and to access our respective underlying assumptions through dialogue. Sometimes this was hard and upsetting. Olesen (1998) suggests that such deliberate working with our biases as researchers may be regarded as a valuable resource which might create understanding of our interpretations and behaviours during the research. What is needed, she argues, is

> sufficient reflexivity to uncover what may be deep-seated but poorly recognized views on issues central to the research, and a full account of the researchers' views, thinking, and conduct.
>
> *(p.314)*

It will be clear from the narrative we have offered so far that powerful emotions were provoked in us as we began and conducted the study into the experience of women chief executives. However, in retrospect, we became aware that we were reluctant to let the study go, and we were at the time surprised by noticing the strong feelings that emerged after we had concluded and presented our findings. The normal view of finishing research is that reporting and presenting findings complete the process. This is a complex topic that is considered extensively in Chapter 9. For our part, we do not wish to quibble with the advice that is normally offered about the need to present findings effectively to appropriate audiences. Yet, given the depth of researcher commitment – our 'labour of love' – that was necessary to sustain our inquiry into complex organizational phenomena, the view that research ends with the presentation of the report seemed over-rational and abrupt. Our experience suggests that the mere (though crucial) process of reporting results should be seen as an important milestone in the process of change – it is not the end of the process if we believe transformation to be the primary purpose of action research.

When, therefore, does such research end? Is it possible for researchers to detach themselves from the changes that might be being implemented as a result of their study? What are our feelings as other actors in the system take responsibility (or not) to implement the study recommendations? These are some of the questions that occurred to us in the time period that followed the presentation of our report to a special conference. In the following recollection, we began to play metaphorically with the notion that our project was our 'child':

> *Why am I finding it so hard to let go? It feels like Pam and I have produced a child that needed to be nurtured and grown, and now it has grown into an adolescent and is about to leave home. I'm feeling sad, but there you go . . .*
>
> *(Mike's journal)*

As well as revealing a pretended stoicism about 'moving on', I was aware as I wrote this that it could play into the fantasy that Pam and I were romantically attached. There were times during our work when certain actors in the system we were studying hinted at such a fantasy, and on the few occasions that this happened, or we thought it had happened, I remember that this was profoundly irritating. But, again, we felt that this pointed to 'analytical clues' (Koning and Ooi, 2013) about the system we were inquiring into, and, we imagine, is an experience that will not be unknown to mixed-gender research or consultancy teams. James and Broussine (2007) subsequently wrote about experiences in working together as consultants in an organization and noted how

> the fantasies and projections of the group will have made us parents, a form of the basic assumption 'pairing' – just as also they might have made us a 'couple' in a romantic or sexual sense. Unconsciously, we guess we play into this fantasy at times.
>
> *(p.303)*

So even the conclusion of a piece of research to which we were highly committed, politically and professionally, provoked strong feelings – of irritation, loss, nostalgia and excitement. The period after presentation was characterised by anxiety, phases of exhilaration (such as when the Equal Opportunities Commission cited our study as it sought to influence government to address the under-representation of women in public life in the UK) and disappointment as the politics of the system became apparent in its reaction to the study. A special conference about the study was attended mostly by women senior managers, and few men participated. For a time, some of the relevant agencies and policy-making bodies avoided the issues highlighted by the study, and pointed the finger of responsibility at others to address the recommended changes. Yet other stakeholders were active 'behind the scenes' in exhorting stakeholders to pay attention to the research. This is not the place to discuss the outcomes from our study in depth. Our point is to reflect that what happens after the formal end of the research process gives critical insight into the politics of researching within systems. It will also be apparent that the study held considerable personal learning for us as researchers as we experienced the emotional roller coaster of our engagement. Our commitments and attachments have meant that it has been hard to 'let go' of the research, while paradoxically we felt encouraged as others took responsibility for the changes that might result. In fact, I am not sure that I have ever let our study go, and this continuing attachment manifests itself in the very act a few years later of contributing the story to this chapter.

Reflections

Our joint reflections from undertaking our respective studies include the importance of researchers identifying their values and strongly held political and other beliefs throughout the research process through noticing and developing self-reflective inquiry practices (Mason, 2002). In one case, Louise needed to achieve this through the supervision process (see Chapter 7), and, in Mike's and Pam's case, they needed to achieve this through a process of researcher co-supervision.

This discipline generates important data about the research questions and the interaction between researcher and participants, and between researchers themselves (if more than one). Our organizational inquiries were constructed to reflect an approach where the requirements of qualitative research included naturalistic settings, generating descriptive data, a concern with process and generating meaning inductively that enabled research of subjective topics (Bogdan and Biklen, 1998). Being 'insider researchers' brings particular challenges to the research process involving questions of ethics, confidentiality, power relations and the experience of sometimes intense feelings. Throughout our studies, we kept track of the development and implications of these issues through the use of a reflexive research diary or journals. Our underlying beliefs and values in relation to research needed to be surfaced as they influenced our approach to our studies and were articulated early in research journals and/or in discussions with co-researchers.

To return to Koning and Ooi (2013), we very much concur with their conclusions about the emotional experience of conducting research that is based in action inquiry and ethnography. First, they suggest that awkward encounters are intrinsic in the researcher's states of being and therefore should not be marginalized in the writing. We have both tried to demonstrate in this chapter that a focus on what we were feeling at various moments in our projects enabled us to gain insight into the organizations and systems which we inhabited. Koning and Ooi argue a strong case that an inclusive reflexivity is needed and can be attained by making room for emotions such as awkwardness and, we would add, the whole gamut of feelings that we experienced as we proceeded with our inquiries. Second, they suggest (p.29) that including and working with awkward encounters provides many 'analytical clues' and ethnographic insights, and that such moments can enrich our understanding of what we are studying and our own roles in this process. Our main learning has been to realise that we – our selves, our identities, our feelings – were part of what we were researching. We suggest that this gives researchers a set of freedoms, but also a set of responsibilities. The freedom enables us to pursue our interests and passions, to set the research going in the first place and to follow avenues of inquiry that challenge and fascinate us. The accompanying responsibility is to be continually aware of our biases and subjectivities, and to work reflexively and collaboratively with others. Being open about the political properties of our studies, and the feelings that these evoked, may give us the confidence to assert the value of our inferences and analyses, but also their limitations.

References

Bogdan, R., and Biklen, S. (1998) *Qualitative Research for Education*. Boston: Allyn and Bacon.

Broussine, M., and Fox, P. (2003) The Politics of Researching Gender in Organisations, *Management Research News*, (26) 8: 27–37.

Clarke, C., Knights, D., and Jarvis, C. (2012) A Labour of Love? Academics in Business Schools, *Scandinavian Journal of Management*, (28): 5–15.

Coghlan, D., and Brannick, T. (2010) *Doing Action Research in Your Own Organisation*. 3rd ed. London: Sage Publications.

Denzin, N. K., and Lincoln, Y. S. (Eds.) (2000) *Handbook of Qualitative Research*. 2nd ed. Thousand Oaks, CA: Sage.

Denzin, N. K., and Lincoln, Y. S. (Eds.) (2005) *The Sage Handbook of Qualitative Research*. 3rd ed. Thousand Oaks, CA: Sage.

Down, S., Garrety, K., and Badham, R. (2006) Fear and Loathing in the Field: Emotional Dissonance and Identity Work in Ethnographic Research, *M@n@gement*, (9) 3: 87–107.

Easterby-Smith, M., and Malina, D. (1999) Cross-Cultural Collaborative Research: Toward Reflexivity, *Academy of Management Journal*, (42) 1: 76–86.

Foster, J. (1999) *Women's Progress: Women Directors of Social Services 1997*. London: The Stationery Office.

Fox, P., and Broussine, M. (2001) *Room at the Top? A Study of Women Chief Executives in Local Government in England and Wales*. Bristol: University of the West of England.

Grisoni, L. (2004) *Issues of Power and Politics in Researching Your Own Organisation*. Paper presented at University of Bristol Doctoral student conference, September.

Grisoni, L. (2005) *The Boomerang Effect: A Qualitative Inquiry into the Implementation of a Teaching and Learning Strategy in a New University*. University of Bristol: Doctoral Thesis.

Hardy, C. (1994) *Managing Strategic Action – Mobilizing Change – Concepts, Readings and Cases*. London: Sage Publications.

Holian, R. (2002). Paper 3: Doing Research in My Own Organisation: Ethical Dilemmas, Hopes and Triumphs. *Action Research International*, 18.

James, J., and Broussine, M. (2007) A Reflexive Action Inquiry into the Experience of Working Together as Consultants, *Organisational and Social Dynamics*, (7) 2: 292–312.

Koning, J., and Ooi, C-S. (2013) Awkward Encounters and Ethnography, *Qualitative Research in Organizations and Management: An International Journal*, (8) 1: 16–32.

Marcic, D. (2002) Tuning into the Harmonics of Management, in Brown, T., and Brown, R. (Eds.), *The Encyclopaedia of Management*. London: Bloomsbury Publishing.

Martin, L. (1994) Power, Continuity and Change: Decoding Black and White Women Managers' Experience in Local Government, in Tanton, M. (Ed.), *Women in Management*. London: Routledge, chapter 7.

Mason, J. (2002) *Qualitative Researching*. 2nd ed. London: Sage Publications.

Morgan, G. (1986) *Images of Organization*. London: Sage Publications.

Munkejord, K. (2009) Methodological Emotional Reflexivity: The Role of Researcher Emotions in Grounded Theory Research, *Qualitative Research in Organizations and Management*, (4) 2: 151–167.

Olesen, V. (1998) Feminisms and Models of Qualitative Research, in Denzin, N. K., and Lincoln, Y. S. (Eds.), *The Landscape of Qualitative Research*. London: Sage Publications, chapter 9.

Pettigrew, A. M. (1977) Strategy Formulation as a Political Process, *International Studies of Management and Organizations*, (7) 2: 78–87.

Whiteman, G. (2010) Management Studies That Break Your Heart, *Journal of Management Inquiry*, (19) 4: 328–337.

5

THE NOT-SO-DARK SIDE OF EMOTIONS

Anger as a resource in research apprenticeship

Emma Bell and Haneen Shoaib

Introduction

It is often noted that doing social science research involves significant personal, emotional and identity work. As Coffey (1999: 1) observes, this 'occurs both during and after fieldwork. In writing, remembering and representing our fieldwork experiences we are involved in processes of self-presentation and identity construction.' Research can thus have an emotional impact, not just on research participants, but also on researchers themselves. The emotional aspects of doing research have the potential to change us in significant ways, and it is impossible to know in advance of undertaking a research study the emotional effects this will have on researchers (Hallowell, Lawton and Gregory, 2005). Identity issues can be particularly complex in situations involving insider research (Brannick and Coghlan, 2007), where the researchers are studying a culture in which they are a participant. In these situations, it is not so much that the researchers come to know a particular social setting through studying it, but that they come to know it rather differently.

In this chapter we treat the emotional aspects of fieldwork as 'epistemologically productive in the analysis of fieldwork and the fieldworker self' (Coffey, 1999: 6). We begin by reviewing the treatment of negative emotions in organizational life and in accounts of the organizational research process. Next we explore the role of anger in research by drawing on vignettes that arose from our experiences relating to a PhD study of gendered organizational power relations in Saudi Arabia. We consider the role of powerful cultural norms in socialising researchers as gendered subjects and argue that anger provides a resource through which such identity threats may be resisted, reconfigured and reshaped. Through this we reflect on what can be lost when negative emotions are suppressed and what can be gained when they are expressed. By applying the notion of a feminist ethics of care in the context of the research apprenticeship, we suggest that anger can be empowering through enabling relational understanding and enhancing reflexivity.

Anger in organizational research

The centrality of Hochschild's (1983) work in organization studies has encouraged a focus on the importance of emotional labour in managing an emotional front. This approach emphasises the importance of masking certain emotions during social interaction so as to maintain the social order (Goffman, 1969). It treats the management of emotions in social interactions as stage performances where actors display different emotions onstage and offstage. This can involve assuming an onstage emotional front that does not reflect the social actor's experienced emotions. In particular, negative emotions – including feelings of fear, anxiety, sadness and hate – are regarded as sources of disruption or destruction that need to be masked to ensure self-presentation accords with the social structure (Fineman, 2000; 2008). The social order is thereby maintained by sustaining a polite appearance of emotional harmony. This can easily be broken by a sudden expression of negative emotions, such as anger, including feelings of annoyance, displeasure or hostility. These emotional displays are detrimental because of their potential to disrupt social interaction. Hence they are sometimes referred to as negative or 'dark' (Kenny, 2008), because they do not accord with social expectations that generally promote the display of a positive emotional front.

Many researchers have focussed on the disjuncture that the requirement for emotional display in organizational contexts creates. For example, Bolton (2008) uses a dramaturgical lens to analyse nurses' emotional reactions in a hospital ward. She argues that real feelings are not expressed because nurses feel obliged to be 'nice' so as to maintain the social order. A further example, relating to negative rather than positive emotions, is provided by Rafaeli and Sutton (1991), who focus on emotional displays enacted by bill collectors and criminal interrogators. In this case, positive and negative displays of emotions are used to elicit a desired outcome from respondents. Such displays are interpolated through the body as the primary means through which emotions are enacted in situations of face-to-face interaction (Fineman, 2003). Gendered cultural norms also affect how emotions are displayed as this is linked to the way in which people are socialised in a culture and how they think others will judge them based on their emotions. This includes emotion scripts which 'define the ways people are able to talk about their feelings, within the social rules that govern those feelings' (Fineman, 2003: 20). The overarching power of social norms thus restricts the display of emotions, especially when 'change dislocate[s] comfortable routines and threatens our identity' (Fineman, 2003: 122).

Despite acknowledgement of the importance of emotion in shaping organizational life, there has been 'something of a silence' in relation to the emotional experiences of researchers doing organizational fieldwork (Kenny, 2008: 376). Recently, however, there have been calls for greater recognition of the importance of emotion in organizational research practice. As Brannan (2011) notes, doing organizational research is an emotionally intensive activity. Acknowledging felt emotions in fieldwork is therefore an important aspect of reflexivity which has the potential to generate insight (Kenny, 2008; Fleetwood, 2009). This applies in particular to negative, dark, uncomfortable or awkward feelings which researchers may be tempted to overlook or ignore (Kleinman and Copp, 1993). Negative or dark emotions are generally perceived as problematic, dangerous and volatile in the context of fieldwork (Kenny, 2008), as they can make participants less accepting of the researcher's presence and less inclined to talk to them. Koning and Ooi (2013) suggest the need to take emotion experienced in fieldwork seriously by focusing on 'awkward encounters' as a basis for emotionalised, embodied, rather than rational, cognitive reflexivity. This enables progression towards a more 'inclusive reflexivity' which recognises the anxieties of research participants and is more inclusive of emotions that 'we hesitate to publicly reveal' (Koning and Ooi, 2013: 17). This, they suggest, can enhance the trustworthiness of organizational ethnography.

Here we focus on the role of negative emotions such as anger in the research process. These emotions can arise because fieldwork constitutes a site of emotional labour wherein fieldworkers, especially female fieldworkers studying male-dominated settings, may be required to display an appropriate face, often as personable, usually young, women (Dingwall, 1980). We suggest that gendered requirements for emotional labour within fieldwork can be experienced as deeply alienating, giving rise to feelings of anger. We therefore propose an approach that involves creating a safe space in which to explore dark emotions by constructing caring research identities.

These ideas are based on our experience of dealing with anger in a fieldwork setting where negative emotions are regulated according to powerful gendered norms. Saudi Arabia is a context where strongly gendered social norms are used to regulate emotional self-expression in the public sphere, and men and women in Saudi Arabia are expected to act according to tightly defined emotional scripts. Social actors are expected to control their emotional front to demonstrate respect towards senior men in power (Shoaib, 2012). Politeness and pleasantness are normative requirements of display, and emotional displays of anger and displeasure are discouraged, particularly by women in the presence of men. In this context, emotions must be managed to conform to cultural expectations and maintain the social order. Negative emotions, especially anger, are rarely displayed publically since their expression is seen as potentially disruptive. These societal expectations are strongly gendered. For example, in organizational settings such as senior-level meetings, it is culturally acceptable for male managers to display anger but unacceptable for women managers to display similar emotions (Shoaib, 2012). Haneen's proximity to the culture she was studying meant that these practices affected her directly and deeply in the course of her research, prompting strong emotions and raising challenging questions about her identity.

In the section that follows we explore how these powerful cultural norms socialise researchers as gendered subjects and reflect on the role of anger as an emotional resource through which threats to researcher identity are encountered and resisted. We suggest that anger enables greater relational understanding between researchers, and potentially enhances researcher reflexivity, by encouraging consideration of uncomfortable feelings.

Haneen's story

Six years ago I moved from Saudi Arabia to the United Kingdom. Looking back, I realize I have changed significantly since my move. The timid, humble girl who meekly obeyed her parents' wishes has matured. I was taught to accept and never to question, to behave in accordance with expectations – especially religious expectations. I never believed that my thoughts mattered, and I never dared to imagine I could have thoughts of my own.

As a PhD student I quickly discovered that everything can be questioned and critically analysed. This mindset influenced many spheres of my life. I first questioned the educational system in Saudi Arabia, and the failure of my teachers and parents to teach me alternative ways of thinking. Perhaps it was easier for them to control children in a rigid system that condemned criticism? I then began to think about my identity as a woman in a traditional culture that places men first. I accepted a secondary role for most of my life; now that I have experienced an alternative way of life in the West, I can never return to my former identity.

Now, I am once again in Saudi Arabia. I am living in my parents' home, but I feel like a stranger. My father, a PhD-holder himself, supported my studies in the West. Although he is traditional in many ways, he has always respected my intellect. After visiting me several times in the United Kingdom, he learned to appreciate my new identity. My mother, however, feels that the West has ruined my identity. She accuses me of prioritising my personal needs over my cultural values. My mother constantly reminds me that my culture – and other people's opinions – are more important than my own identity. I try to build bridges, but religion and culture are powerful forces that stand between us. I understand that my mother's attitude is the result of her social upbringing; it cannot be changed easily.

Regardless of my mother's opinion, I cannot return to my former self. The past six years have changed me too much. After learning to think for myself, I can no longer unquestioningly conform to these social norms. For example, I am not willing to live with my parents indefinitely. In Saudi culture, unmarried women cannot live alone. I suggested to my parents that I should live in their apartment building but have my own flat. At first my father refused, but he eventually relented. My mother, on the other hand, categorically rejected my plan. She made it clear that if I even consider the option, I will lose her.

My current situation angers me. I have changed, but Saudi culture remains the same. I am frustrated by my decision to come back, but I feel that I owe it to myself to embody and enact the change I want to see in my society. I could escape and never look back, but amidst all this rage I feel a sense of accountability, first towards myself and then to my culture. If I am not courageous enough to voice my opinions, then I cannot think of myself as a fully-fledged scholar. In a culture that renders women powerless, I choose to be angry. Anger is a means by which I gain power.

Emma's story

When you first came into my office you were so quiet, so deferential to me as your supervisor. You sat on the edge of a chair nervously. I tried to listen and make a safe space where you could talk openly. I tried to imagine what it felt like to be you. After a few months, I started to read books about Saudi Arabia as a way of understanding more about your culture. Not so much as to appear intrusive, but enough to encourage the introspection that I knew you would need if you were to be able to question those things that you had always taken to be natural, inevitable or necessary. I knew your ability to do reflexive, qualitative research into your own culture, and to get a PhD, depended on this – especially as you were studying organizational strategy and power.

It sometimes felt a heavy responsibility. You told me about your life; sometimes you cried, often you were angry. I tried to respect and allow these emotions in the supervision space, to recognise and not to absolve them; to allow them to be a part of you. Was I being irresponsible in providing a space in which you could explore these difficult issues? What would the consequences of revealing these emotions be for you?

I was glad when you said you felt I was like a sister to you, contrasting this with the father/child analogy your previous supervisor had used to describe his supervision relationships. One day, you suggested I should visit Saudi Arabia. I knew then there was a limit to what I could learn just by listening and reading. You were asking me to put my identity at risk, just as I had encouraged you to do.

When I got off the plane I realised this was going to be unlike any other culture I had visited. You met me at the airport with your father. Even though this was an academic visit, I had come with my husband, as you had said this would be 'easier' for me. I quickly put the black abaya that you had brought with you over my clothes and covered my hair with the black scarf. At once I felt different. Sitting in the back of the car with its tinted glass windows to protect against the sun and prying eyes, I realised I looked more like you.

I hated my abaya. The crease-free man-made fabric that made me sweat, the full length robe that made it hard to get in and out of cars, and the sleeves that draped in my food. The way the desert wind blew my scarf from my hair, and tugged at the fastenings, threatening to reveal my own clothes underneath. I wanted to go for a swim but the hotel swimming pool was for men and boys only. You came with good news: there was an indoor swimming pool in the hotel, for ladies only! I put on my abaya and went out to find it on the seventh floor, but no matter how many times I pressed the button in the elevator, it wouldn't take me there. Eventually a hotel employee explained that access to the floor was restricted via a key, to ensure that men could not enter.

There were so many rules I did not understand. Things I did wrong without even realising. In the swimming pool changing room I was ushered into a cubicle and admonished for changing in the locker area. I felt my body was dangerous, a liability. When you came again to collect me from the hotel you could see from my face that I was furious. I wanted to swear and shout but instead I tried to remain composed. Is this why you had wanted me to visit your country, so that I would be angry too?

Haneen's story

Emma encouraged me to vocalise my thoughts and confront my anger. I said 'I will never go back' and she asked 'what are you trying to escape from?' In these moments, words failed me and the only solution seemed to be that Emma should see for herself what stirred my emotions so forcefully. I thought a lot about Emma coming to Saudi and seeing life there – life as I knew it. I did not expect her to agree to come. When she agreed, I was happy and scared at the same time. She was going to visit my home country, which was exciting. Then she would see what I was not able to express fully. Yet I wanted her to come and help me be stronger in a setting in which I felt very weak. When she arrived I felt she was on my side. 'Professor Emma Bell' is how I introduced her, and each time I said her name, I felt a sense of pride that my female supervisor was by my side. When we returned to UK I felt a deeper understanding between us. But still I feared my anger and preferred to block it out. I thought I could not do anything about it; she thought I had alternatives. I thought about my identity as an independent researcher and how to sustain it wherever I went. Thinking differently about who I am gradually diffused my anger.

I have decided to return to Saudi Arabia but I am determined to hold on to the person I have become. As a woman, I am no less capable than a man. My mother repeats the Saudi saying, 'women's wings are broken', all the time. I may not be able to drive in Saudi. I may not be able to go out for a run in the fresh air. But I will not forget the importance of these simple routines of life. As a researcher I have learned to argue for alternative ways of thinking. This language of absolutes has no place in my vocabulary. I would not have reached this point if it weren't for the anger, which has expanded the way I see my life. But I know I am not supposed to be angry. I wonder if anger will be directed towards me for thinking and saying these things? It is a risk I am willing to take.

Emma's story

When I got back to the UK I packed up my abaya and put it in the bottom of the wardrobe. For a few days everything felt strange. Before my visit I had felt respectful of women's choice to wear hijab. But now when I saw women dressed in this way, my Western sensibilities were tempered by a sense that we were not so different after all. My favourite photograph from the visit was of myself, Haneen and a female academic from the university we visited, walking away from the photographer – in our abayas it was very difficult to tell us apart. As a feminist writing from a critical, feminist perspective, I had thought of myself as sensitive to gendered power relations and had tried hard not to internalise these practices. Having gained a degree of insight into Haneen's lived experience it seemed that we shared something in common, most notably through our emotional responses to gendered power. When I told academic colleagues of my recent visit to Saudi Arabia, they were surprised – some even seemed shocked. If I spoke publically or even wrote about my experiences, would they be seen as a white Western woman professor's short, ethnocentric excursion into the field of the other before returning to her privileged social position in the West? I feared they would.

Anger as a reflexive resource in the research apprenticeship

The experiences described above arose in the context of a PhD supervision relationship. This process constitutes the primary mechanism through which junior researchers learn their research craft from those who are more senior, through a method of research apprenticeship (Bell and Thorpe, 2013). Apprenticeship involves learning how to do research through direct participation. The process can take several years and is based on the inculcation of skilled instincts, acquired through practical demonstration and observation. It involves acculturation into the norms, values and practices of the research culture. Apprenticeship highlights the situated nature of research learning, where knowledge is suggested to be contextualised and specific to the situations in which it occurs (Lave and Wenger, 1991). This is particularly relevant to ethnographic research due to its embodied and affective nature as a particular way of being in the world (Van Maanen and Kolb, 1985), one which is potentially disruptive (Lave, 2011).

However, the role of emotion in research apprenticeship tends not to be acknowledged or discussed. This is partly due to the Cartesian mind/body split which privileges the rational-intellectual aspects of research as the primary means through which successful academic careers are built (Hopwood and Paulson, 2012). Yet what it means to be a researcher is fundamentally reliant on understanding the bodily and emotional experiences through which research competence is achieved and demonstrated (Bell and King, 2010). Understanding our experiences, and the negative emotions they provoked, has therefore been important in building our research identities, as an ongoing recursive project. Our experience of anger in this research relationship was reciprocal; by establishing backstage spaces in which we were able to express and share our negative emotions, we were able to build a relational understanding of the gendered power relations that shaped our respective identities and identify ways of resisting them. The research apprenticeship is therefore understood as a felt and lived experience, as much as an intellectual one.

Although reflexivity is a standard component of fieldwork methodologies (Van Maanen, 1988), reflexive accounts are generally written in ways that preserve the norms of academic writing; this prioritises the academic, professional voice rather than a personal, sympathetic one (Kleinman and Copp, 1993). To explore the negative emotions involved in the PhD fieldwork process, we drew on the concept of disciplined reflexivity (Weick, 1999). This involves the researcher linking instrumentally to the past (by thinking, for example, about an event that occurred during fieldwork) and then looking forward by considering how processes come together in networks. According to Weick (1999), this can bring about better understanding of theory through focusing on matters relating to identity building and noting excluded voices in research. By treating our emotional experiences as an introspective-based data source, we sought to use it as a source of reflexivity after we had returned from the field, reflecting on what we had brought back and how it had changed us. Negative emotion thus formed part of a recursive redefinition of self in response to 'Othering' encounters (Prasad, 2014). Our shared feelings of anger and its expression in a safe environment was conducive to thinking about anger as a stimulus rather than something to be controlled or disregarded. Looking back at emotions felt in the field from the safety of this research space helped to alleviate feelings of powerlessness related to external factors beyond our control. This enabled us to connect feelings of anger to the empirical fieldwork context, which in turn helped us to become aware of power relations with research participants and between each other. By reflecting on our emotional performances in situations of face-to-face interaction, we were able to engage in reflexive analysis of these cultural power relations in a way which enabled a point of connection to be made in the course of the research apprenticeship. Anger was thereby constructed as an analytical resource, rather than something that needed to be suppressed or avoided.

However, the research apprenticeship is also located within culturally situated power relations that hierarchically differentiate and separate student from supervisor. Differences of power and cultural experience have implications for the learning relationship, especially when the supervisor has no direct experience of the cultural context in which the student's research learning arises. This apprenticeship took place in the context of relations between a white, Western woman who holds expert and structural power through her position as a university professor and supervisor in a UK university, and a female PhD student from Saudi Arabia. Such relations must be contextualised through the lens of postcolonial power relations as an identity project founded on definition of a superior West and an inferior non-West, emphasising the role of the former in civilising the latter (Metcalfe and Mimouni, 2011). This apprenticeship could therefore be critiqued as a project of seeking to liberate an Arabic woman from oppression and enable her enlightenment through the imposition of modernist values, whether or not such help is needed or wanted (Haddad and Esposito, 1998). While it is impossible to avoid these discourses and their effects, we sought to construct a research apprenticeship that was reciprocal, involving student and supervisor in embodied comprehension of activities, acquired through demonstration and observation in specific cultural contexts of study. Through this, it may be possible for white women to speak with, rather than for, Other women (Mohanty, 1991) by providing spaces within their embodied and emotionalised experiences that can be expressed and reflected upon without judgement. This involves acknowledging similarities in the forms of oppression that Western and non-Western women face, and the emotional responses that this stimulates.

We also sought to incorporate into our practice a feminist ethic of care that focused on attentiveness, trust, sensitivity, empathetic understanding and cultivating caring relations (Held, 2006; Noddings, 1984) as moral values to be understood and cultivated. This view approaches moral problems with a commitment to understand issues from different perspectives. It is based on relationality and respect for the interdependence of individuals in constituting a social group (Gilligan, 1982). Hence, care is not a virtuous disposition but a morality founded on respect for relations between persons. A feminist ethic of care also implies that ethical reason should not entail disregard for all that belongs to the emotion and the body. Through this we found that our feelings of anger were twofold. The first aspect was a reaction to personal experiences that formed part of the fieldwork and supervision process; this constituted anger on behalf of *ourselves* as researchers. The second was a felt response to a set of broader cultural experiences associated with the fieldwork setting where the research was conducted, and could be seen as anger on behalf of *others*. Anger for ourselves was individualised, whereas anger for others was shaped by cultural experiences and a broader desire for equality and justice. These two aspects of emotion were closely interrelated. By creating a safe space in the context of the research apprenticeship within which to explore anger for ourselves, we were able to locate our cultural fieldwork experiences in a broader context of anger for others. This emotional exploration offered a means of achieving interpretive depth, since it enabled us to better understand how we see and experience their world. Added to this, the dual status of PhD researcher as a cultural insider and a cultural analyst meant that her anger offered insight into both the research process and the culture under study.

Negative emotion in the research apprenticeship

This analysis has implications for understanding the research apprenticeship. Traditional models of doctoral supervision are based on notions of autonomy and independent scholarship (Johnson, Lee and Green, 2000). The role of the supervisor is to observe and monitor, while apparently encouraging the student to exercise free will and independence in the context of the authorised gaze of the established researcher. Normative control is achieved through the exercise of pastoral power, through which the disciplined selfhood of the researcher is formed. Traditional supervision thereby encourages the formation of a particular identity project for the modern, research-active academic. This model is associated with widespread isolation and abjection, particularly for PhD students who can feel marginalised by the dominant scholarly culture, including women and those who have ethnic, class and cultural identities that position them as subservient to the dominant academic norm. As such, the traditional model of doctoral supervision is fundamentally gendered, based on a masculine conception of the independent scholar that prioritises autonomy and reason and banishes embodiment and emotion. This can result in the identity formation of 'a hard-working, competitive and achievement oriented individual, a risk-averse workaholic who bases her self-worth on others' judgements and career progress, puts work first and has difficulty relaxing' (Brewis, 2004: 31). Scholarly identity work thus comes at significant personal and emotional cost.

In an effort to explore alternatives, we propose an approach to research apprenticeship that is more tolerant and supportive of the emotion work involved in doing research and becoming a researcher. Our view is that research entails a mutual responsibility of care between supervisor and student. Reflexivity is enhanced when it is shared and built upon through relationships that offer understanding and empathy. We have drawn on critical feminist work related to the ethics of care (Burton and Dunn, 1996; Held, 2006) to propose an alternative to the traditional model of the research training process which is more responsive to the identity risks and emotional challenges involved in doing research. Supervision based on an ethic of care is distinct from 'caring about', which can easily become paternalistic or patronising. It promotes the formation of researcher identities founded on relationality, rather than the autonomous individual. Supervision is based on the cultivation of caring relations between supervisor and student based on trust. This entails a move away from the position of supervisor as 'master' or 'father'. While this ethic is based on commitment to the practice and goals of caring for persons, caring is seen as a relation that involves both carer and cared-for who share an interest in their mutual well-being.

Yet developing emotionalised research apprenticeship practices is not without difficulty as expectations of the supervisor as the therapeutic listener who is continually receptive to student's difficulties can leave the supervisor emotionally exhausted and burnt out (Johnson, Lee and Green, 2000). There is also a danger of assuming that women have greater emotional competence and are more prone to exercise emotional sensitivity and responsiveness in the course of the supervision relationship. At the same time, emotion work in research apprenticeships need not necessarily be seen as a form of exploitation that involves the subordination of women's emotions. We suggest that emotionalised research apprenticeship provides an alternative to traditional research supervision models and encourages exploration of how gender, ethnicity and class influence the research learning relationship. Coming from different cultural backgrounds and holding different expectations about gendered power relations meant that we had to recognise and accept these differences. Emotionalised research apprenticeship practices also encourage greater collaboration and reciprocity and challenge academic norms about the formation of researcher subjectivity based on disciplining the emotional body in favour of the rational-intellectual mind.

Relations of learning and negative emotion in the research apprenticeship

The formation of researcher identity is an embodied, emotional process based on socialisation into established cultural norms (Bell and King, 2010). Traditional conceptions of research training take little account of these dynamics. Instead they encourage the suppression of embodied emotion, particularly if it threatens to disrupt hierarchical, formal learning. Here we have argued for the consideration of alternatives. Using the notion of the research apprenticeship, we have suggested that anger enables construction of alternative relations through drawing on an ethic of care. This has the potential to enable more situated, relational and culturally situated forms of knowledge to be built.

However, the expression of negative emotion in fieldwork should not just be seen as an aspect of teaching and learning relations, since it also has implications for the kind of knowledge that is generated through research. By distinguishing between anger for ourselves and anger for others, we have highlighted the potential use of anger as a resource that enables shared understanding of broader cultural issues of inequality and social justice. Acknowledging and exploring negative emotions and the power relations that provoke them forms a critical aspect of our ethnographic practice, through enabling us to understand culture as well as our-selves. Emotion thus has the potential to enable greater understanding of researcher identities and our relationships to the cultures we study. For the lone researcher, to confront these issues in isolation can be a demoralising and upsetting process. It therefore relies on establishing a safe and caring place in which to express negative emotions such as anger and deal with their consequences.

Yet the expression of dark emotions need not necessarily be confined to the backstage of the supervision relationship. This chapter has highlighted how poten-tially disruptive emotions like anger contravene the gendered feeling-rules that determine the appropriate conduct of researchers in fieldwork settings in cultural contexts where gendered emotion rules apply. We do not wish to suggest that emotions like anger, and in particular female anger, should always be masked in the front stage of fieldwork. Anger need not be seen as a dangerous emotion that must always be carefully controlled and managed within fieldwork settings. The conceal-ment of anger in fieldwork relationships is not a feeling rule that female, or male, researchers need always follow. Instead, by exploring the role of dark emotion in the formation of reflexive researcher identities, it may be possible for researchers to resist the requirement for positive emotional labour in fieldwork and to recognise the potential insights that can be gained from this.

Acknowledgement

An earlier version of this chapter was presented to the Standing Working Group on Organizational Ethnography at the European Group for Organizational Stud-ies Colloquium, Montreal, July 2013, and benefitted greatly from the comments of track organizers and participants. We are also grateful to the editors of this book for their helpful suggestions in dealing with these sensitive issues.

References

Bell, E., and King, D. (2010) 'The Elephant in the Room: Critical Management Studies Con-ferences as a Site of Body Pedagogics', *Management Learning*, 41(4): 429–442.
Bell, E., and Thorpe, R. (2013) *A Very Short, Fairly Interesting and Reasonably Cheap Book about Management Research*. London: Sage.
Bolton, S. C. (2008) 'The Hospital: Me, Morphine, and Humanity: Experiencing the Emo-tional Community on Ward 8'. In S. Fineman (Ed.), *The Emotional Organization: Passions and Power*. Oxford: Blackwell Publishers, pp. 15–26.
Brannan, M. J. (2011) 'Researching Emotions and the Emotions of Researching: The Strange Case of Alexithymia in Reflexive Research', *International Journal Work Organization and Emotion*, 4(3/4): 322–339.
Brannick, T., and Coghlan, D. (2007) 'In Defense of Being "Native": The Case for Insider Academic Research', *Organizational Research Methods*, 10(1): 59–74.
Brewis, J. (2004) 'Refusing to Be "Me"'. In R. Thomas, A. Mills and J. M. Mills (Eds.), *Identity Politics at Work: Resisting Gender, Gendering Resistance*. New York: Routledge, pp. 23–39.
Burton, B. K., and Dunn, C. P. (1996) 'Feminist Ethics as Moral Grounding for Stakeholder Theory', *Business Ethics Quarterly*, 6(2): 133–147.

Coffey, A. (1999). *The Ethnographic Self*. London: Sage.

Dingwall, R. (1980) 'Ethics and Ethnography', *Sociological Review*, 28(4): 871–891.

Fineman, S. (1999) 'Emotion and Organizing'. In S. R. Clegg and C. Hardy (Eds.), *Studying Organization: Theory and Method*. London: Sage, pp. 289–310.

Fineman, S. (2000) 'The Emotional Organization: Organizations as Emotional Arenas'. In S. Fineman (Ed.), *Emotions in Organizations* (2nd ed.). London: Sage, pp. 1–24.

Fineman, S. (2003) *Understanding Emotion at Work*. London: Sage.

Fineman, S. (2008) *The Emotional Organization: Passion and Power*. London: Blackwell.

Fleetwood, J. (2009) 'Emotional Work: Ethnographic Fieldwork in Prisons in Ecuador', eSharp, Special Issue: *Critical Issues in Researching Hidden Communities*, pp. 28–50.

Gilligan, C. (1982) *In a Different Voice*. Boston: Harvard University Press.

Goffman, E. (1969) *The Presentation of Self in Everyday Life*. London, Penguin.

Haddad, Y. Y., and Esposito, J. L. (1998). *Islam, Gender, and Social Change*. Oxford: Oxford University Press.

Hallowell, N., Lawton, J., and Gregory, S. (2005) *Reflections on Research: The Realities of Doing Research in the Social Sciences*. Maidenhead: Open University Press.

Held, V. (2006). *The Ethics of Care*. New York: Oxford University Press.

Hochschild, A. R. (1983) *The Managed Heart: Commercialization of Human Feeling*. Berkeley; London: University of California Press.

Hopwood, N., and Paulson, J. (2012) 'Bodies in Narratives of Doctoral Students' Learning and Experience', *Studies in Higher Education*, 37(6): 667–681.

Johnson, L., Lee, A., and Green, B. (2000) 'The PhD and the Autonomous Self: Gender, Rationality and Postgraduate Pedagogy', *Studies in Higher Education*, 25(2): 135–147.

Kenny, K. (2008) 'Aesthetics and Emotion in an Organizational Ethnography', *International Journal of Work, Organization and Emotion*, 2(4): 374–388.

Kleinman, S., and Copp, M. (1993) *Emotions and Fieldwork: Qualitative Research Methods*. London: Sage Publications.

Koning, J., and Ooi, C. (2013) 'Awkward Moments and Ethnography', *Qualitative Research in Organizations and Management*, 8(1): 16–32.

Lave, J. (2011) *Apprenticeship in Critical Ethnographic Practice*. Chicago: University of Chicago Press.

Lave, J., and Wenger, E. (1991) *Situated Learning: Legitimate Peripheral Participation*. Cambridge: Cambridge University Press.

Metcalfe, B. D., and Mimouni, F. (2011). 'Leadership, Social Development and Political Economy in the Middle East: An Introduction'. In B. D. Metcalfe and F. Mimouni (Eds.), *Leadership Development in the Middle East*. Cheltenham: Edward Elgar, pp. 1–60.

Mohanty, C. T. (1991). 'Under Western Eyes: Feminist Scholarship and Colonial Discourses'. In C. T. Mohanty, A. Russo and L. Torres (Eds.), *Third World Women and the Politics of Feminism*. Bloomington: Indiana University Press, pp. 51–80.

Noddings, N. (1984) *Caring: A Feminine Approach to Ethics and Moral Education*. Berkeley: University of California Press.

Prasad, A. (2014) 'You Can't Go Home Again: And Other Psychoanalytic Lessons from Crossing a Neo-colonial Border', *Human Relations*, 67(2): 233–257.

Rafaeli, A., and Sutton, R. I. (1991) 'Emotional Contrast Strategies as Means of Social Influence: Lessons from Criminal Interrogators and Bill Collectors', *Academy of Management Journal*, 34(4): 749–775.

Shoaib, H. (2012) *The Enactment of Power within Strategic Interactions: A Saudi Arabian Case Study*. Thesis (PhD). University of Exeter, Exeter.

Thomas, J. (1993) 'Implementing Critical Ethnography'. In J. Thomas (Ed.), *Doing Critical Ethnography*. London: Sage Publications, pp. 33–49.

Van Maanen, J. (1988) *Tales of the Field*. Chicago: University of Chicago Press.

Van Maanen, J., and Kolb, D. (1985). 'The Professional Apprentice: Observations on Field-work Roles in Two Organizational Settings', *Research in the Sociology of Organizations*, 4: 1–33.

Weick, K. (1999) 'Theory Construction as Disciplined Reflexivity: Tradeoffs of the 90's', *Academy of Management Review*, 24(4): 797–807.

6

A PSYCHOSOCIAL APPROACH TO RESEARCHING WITH FEELING

Linda Watts

Introduction

My own doctoral research took place in a public service context in the UK in a period when public services were being restructured yet again, with accompanying budget reductions and further privatisation. I experienced those changes as creating organisational upheaval and often painful disjuncture for individuals in a context where the rhetorical messages of corporate change appeared to have little relationship to reality. The predominant discourse was one where 'modernisation' had specific meanings including restructuring with reduction of resources allocated to services in tandem with increased performance measurement and control. 'Change' meant change that was compliant with that modernisation agenda within the controlling discourse of new public sector managerialism. The power of that discourse in some aspects of public services was such that it was not acceptable organisationally to criticise or deviate from the modernisation agenda. Thus personal public service values were suppressed.

My quandary was that my formal role at work was a role to disseminate the modernisation discourse, to be an agent of that particular change. My own values and history in participating in progressive social action over the previous twenty years were causing me to feel 'torn apart'. Many of my colleagues expected me to play a humanising, interpretive role in the face of organisational restructuring and the wider Blairite modernisation agenda, but my experience was that my role was becoming increasingly contentious in terms of my own values.

Hindsight informs me that I set out to use my in-depth research with fifteen managerial co-researcher colleagues as a form of personal catharsis. My intuition told me that a 'deep inquiry' into my role conflicts, personal history and the experience of my interviewees could generate rich and unusual research data and support us in contending with our work environment.

I felt from an early stage in my research programme that the politics of knowledge itself must be questioned. If we accept the notion that we have an 'inner politician', then our political self-awareness as researchers means building our understanding of how our political attitudes, commitments and emotional responses to issues have been affected psychologically by family, gender, sexual orientation, ethnicity, nationality and socio-economic status. Chapters 3 and 4 refer to the fact that research often involves significant personal, emotional and identity work.

Drawing on my own experience, I advocate that a researcher's emotional responses may be effectively reflected by using a psychosocial research framework, because the psychosocial is concerned with the essential inter-relation between individual subjectivities and the social and political domain. Psychosocial research essentially seeks to explore the relationship between social and psychological deep structure.

Research for a number of reasons, such as our early life experience, may inevitably generate intense emotional reactions for the researcher. Researchers may have had personal experience that resonates with that of their research participants. Personal experience includes early life experiences that have had a developmental impact at the level of the psyche, or unconscious. Inquiries may generate feelings of deep anger (explored in depth in Chapter 5) – about injustice and neglect – guilt, shame, denial, disapproval, empathy in relation to traumatic experience, and awe with regard to human agency in adversity, and generate a newfound drive to act by campaigning and raising awareness. I would argue that researchers' informal research goals are driven by human goals as broadly categorised by Jasper (2007): goals related to reputation, sensuality and connection impact on the world and curiosity.

> In my role at work I was striving to have an integrative role in a very fragmented, incoherent work environment. I had a deeply felt drive to make sense of the work context in my relations with colleagues.
>
> My interviewees reflected back to me that this attempt at integrative interpretation and sense making was highly valued by them. They were aware that they drew on my willingness to fulfil that role for them.
>
> Yet the role conflicts were literally 'doing my head in'. I felt increasingly that this continual attempt to humanise the role was unsustainable and I was highly stressed and emotionally exhausted.
>
> My research supervisors supported me in making links back to my own early life through autobiographical inquiry. I acknowledged that as a child I sought to have an integrative role within my family to create closer relationships between my stepsister and stepmother to my father and myself to create the idealised coherent family that I dreamed of. In childhood this search and striving for integration was stressful and exhausting.
>
> The increased self-understanding generated through the research process led me to be able to distance myself more consciously from work tensions that resonated subconsciously with my personal history.

This vignette is an example of research giving insights into the lasting effects of a subconscious fantasy.

Researchers' conscious and unconscious agendas

As I have illustrated above, the emotional journey of researchers is influenced by their own personal agendas. Stanley and Wise illuminated the dimension that 'self' brings to research: 'We see the presence of the researcher's self as central in all research. Ones' self can't be left behind, it can only be omitted from discussions and written accounts of the research process' (1993: 161). Reason and Marshall's argument is also pertinent, that 'researchers often choose (consciously or unconsciously) research topics which will restimulate old patterns of distress' (1987: 115), although the opposite may be the case as a researcher may avoid those painful research topics.

More specifically, Lea and West remark that research indicates that embarking upon higher education is to be seen as a way of seeking a new identity in which revising a self-narrative – the story one tells of oneself and one's personal history – is central to the process (1995: 177). Alternatively, researchers may select 'safer' topics in terms of their personal history and agendas, as Hubbard *et al.* (2001) suggest – researchers screen themselves out of dangerous research areas altogether.

In my own doctoral research I drafted an autobiographical reflection that unconsciously omitted my anger about difficulties and humiliating discrimination related to my lifelong experience of disability. Sensitive prompting from one of my supervisors led me to include that experience. A researcher may have an apparently conscious, confident view about a research topic, but it may also be a view that is in reality facilitated by avoidance or omission of contended issues. I avoided those issues because they were painful and messy in the context of an apparently rational research process.

Why use a psychosocial approach to include emotional experience?

Research themes are often highly emotive for researchers, and thus researchers' emotional experiences must be acknowledged, understood and documented as contributory data that has an intrinsic research value, although they are rarely seen as legitimate. A psychosocial perspective differs radically from positivist approaches and seeks to analyse and critique rationality, rather than complying with rationalist assumptions, including the assumption that researchers' emotional experiences and responses to their research process cannot be acknowledged and should be written out of a research process in order to maintain the fantasy of the objective researcher.

Most of our social experience based on the world is of authoritarianism, command and control systems, bureaucracies, narrow specialisations, separation of reflection and action, and sanctions against those who oppose these systems (Greenwood and Levin, 1998: 88). However, human beings are not fully defined by their social and economic circumstances. We have some capacity as human agents to be resilient, to exercise our will, question, resist, challenge and subvert. But our wilfulness and desire for self-determination may exaggerate this capacity and also deny its limitations. So psychosocial research methods may assist us to examine what is 'going on' in practice, including subconscious dynamics, to identify what interests or power bases are served by practice, to explore the real extent of human agency rather than fantasy and to identify possible means of resistance. For a researcher, emotional responses to such a testing and revealing research journey may range through anger, frustration, denial and shock and be accompanied by a sense of emotional exhaustion.

Research in the UK is necessarily undertaken within a socio-economic context that is neo-liberal in terms of national government and structurally patriarchal. Strikingly, in the UK there are inequalities of income and access to social benefits that are on many levels the most significant in Europe (Wilkinson and Pickett, 2009), as well as marked assumptions about social status and roles including the differences inherent in race, gender, disability and age. Research processes variously acknowledge, engage with or ignore the difficulties of exclusion evident in society. In that context, researchers' political awareness and values may be substantially challenged by even one single research encounter – in other words, psychosocial research in analysing social deep structure combined with openness to others' experiences of inequalities will be enough to force researchers out of their emotional comfort zones.

There are potentially rich rewards to be gained from using appropriate research methodologies to study 'difference and otherness' as discussed in Chapter 3, whether that difference derives from ethnicity, gender, sexuality, disability or socio/geographical identification etc. Difference and otherness is rooted in the development of our early sense of self and individuation, then socially perpetuated by psychic defence mechanisms such as racial hatred, misogyny, xenophobia and homophobia and structurally reflected in aspects of social policy and its implementation. Examples of such studies are to be found in the work of Clarke (2000; 2004). Research into issues such as racism may be deeply disturbing, saddening or enraging for researchers.

I have found that psychosocial research may fruitfully 'borrow' from feminist research methods not least because emotion is acknowledged by feminist researchers as part of the research experience. Feminist epistemological principles highlight the importance of a variety of aspects associated with the process of researching in terms of the following:

- the researcher–researched relationship
- emotion as a research experience
- the intellectual autobiography of researchers
- how to manage the differing 'realities' and understandings of researchers and researched
- the complex question of power in research and writing.

(Stanley and Wise, 1993: 22)

In relation to identities, examples of psychosocial approaches are to be found in the work of Frosh *et al.* (2001) on young masculinities, Reay (2008) on white middle-class identities and Segal (2007) on sexual identities. Again, for researchers, our construction of identities and life narratives may be challenged significantly through in-depth research encounters with others. This experience, albeit unsettling, is valuable research material that can be explored within a research framework that can facilitate the exploration of political affiliation, motivation and mobilisation, family and community affinities, tensions and schisms.

In the field of social welfare this research approach provides analysis and research tools that explore the major experiential impacts of the successive reconfigurations of welfare in the UK, for individual practitioners and communities. Institutional experience is often distressing and painful for care workers and patients or clients in relation to ill health or drug and alcohol dependency (Hoggett and Campling, 2000).

Researchers as emotive subjects

Feminist and psychosocial perspectives tell us that researchers are also the subject of the research rather than adopting an apparently objective 'neutral' stance based on an assumption that they can be detached from their personal history and that they are therefore value-free, unlimited in their ability to understand a research theme and unrestricted in their capacity to recognise what is significant in an interviewee's responses. An object/subject relationship between the researcher and the researched skews the ethos of the research towards the assumption of primarily intellectualised knowledge on the part of the researcher and 'here and now' knowledge held by the subject. In this relationship, reason and emotion are discrete, separate. Intellectualised knowledge rather than empirical knowledge derived from emotional response has traditionally been massively dominant and has had a high establishment value. As Postle (1993: 35) observes:

> This idealisation of intellect and action often seems to be in the very 'grain' of us as persons and because of this I have certainly been in danger of seeing it as given, as part of nature. I believe that this cultural bias in favour of the supremacy of intellect, coupled with the idealisation of practicality, too often acts to lock out from the generation of knowledge, the riches of the universe of feeling.

The level of discomfort for some researchers in dealing with research material that is contrary to deeply held values is not to be underestimated. An example is to be found in the work of Creek (2012), who reflects on the negotiation of fear, compassion and self-care in research. Mason (2002: 5) rightly describes the reflexive process as being very difficult, not least if it involves recognising and dealing with elements in your own assumptions which you would rather not face, but it is also a highly creative and exhilarating one. In my own research process I frequently felt vulnerable and therefore very defensive as my position as both a manager and a researcher felt risky. A useful concept for psychosocial researchers is that of the defended subject where both the researcher and the research participants are anxious subjects

whose mental boundaries are porous where unconscious material is concerned. This means that both will be subject to the projections and introjec-
tions of ideas and feelings coming from the other person. It also means that
the impressions that we have about each other are not derived simply from
the 'real' relationship, but that what we say and do in the interaction will be
mediated by internal fantasies which derive from our histories of significant
relationships.

(Hollway and Jefferson, 2000: 45)

Thus the psychosocial research process is inevitably a 'bumpy ride' rather than the
idealised linear progression that researchers may imagine at the outset, many examples of which you will find in textbooks. Periods of time may appear to be 'inert',
causing anxiety for a researcher in terms of drafting and cognitive thought, but
these inert phases in the research process may result in flows of intuitive understanding, rather like 'dominoes falling'. There are likely to be identifiable 'mega'
cycles within the research process with iterative cycles of intuition, reflection and
application as the research progresses – unless the research process is slowed or
halted in some phases.

Intersubjective interviewing

Interactive interviews are a research tool for drawing out the attitudes, the feelings
and some inner or unconscious processes of individuals participating in the research.
Such interviews contribute to our making sense of how we perceive, experience,
react to and thus play a part in framing and constituting our 'worlds'. Psychosocial
research typically includes expression of feelings by the researcher and research participants and mutual interpretive exploration:

the validity of the psycho social method to some extent hangs on the capacity of the researcher to share his or her thinking with the interviewees and
involve them in a joint process of sense making. This is an important methodological innovation given that psycho social approaches are sometimes criticised for being top-down.

(Hoggett et al., 2010: 173)

In intersubjective interviewing, both parties can create the capacity to generate
greater understanding through sharing interpretation. Capacity is a 'portmanteau'
term in that for us as researchers 'to hear the message' accurately requires the ability
to contain emotion, the ability to hold enough to be able to hold something for
another as well as for oneself (French, 2001). In other words, a psychosocial research
process may significantly develop researchers' capacity to 'hold' emotion while free-
ing up their expression of feelings about issues, where previously they might have
'rationally' managed their feelings.

Empathic researchers

My research interviewees' feedback made reference to their feeling that our interactive interviews were empathic. Empathy is underplayed in accounts of qualitative research methodology, but 'to a large extent the quality of the research experience (for all involved) and the quality of the research data, is dependent upon the formation of relationships and the development of an emotional connection to the field' (Coffey, 1999: 57). Our life experience develops our capacity as researchers to recognise and understand the manifestations of the unconscious mind: 'in the conscious thoughts, feelings, speech and behaviour of the people one is working with – and in oneself' (Menzies Lyth, 1989: 28). Interactive interviews do encompass a relatively higher degree of mutual recognition. We have a need for recognition, and we can recognise others in return, thus making mutual recognition possible (Benjamin, 1995). Research should generate an open-ended dialogue 'that can only be fully realised if its participants perceive each other as being of equal worth and moral significance' (Froggett, 2002: 4).

Therapeutic effects?

While myself and interviewees in the interactive interviews experienced those interviews as being 'therapeutic', the purpose and boundaries of a research process need to be carefully observed and respected, given the very different purpose and skills involved in identifiably therapeutic interactions. This therapeutic effect partly arises from the rare opportunity and 'contained space' created for us within a rational institutional context to give voice and to be emotionally expressive. There is a cultural association that correlates such a private, emotionally expressive exchange with manifestations of the 'therapeutic culture', especially as such an experience may be relatively rare for many of us.

My view is that a psychosocial perspective provides a fuller understanding of the less obvious dynamics that may take place in interactive research interviews where issues are explored in some depth over a sustained period. Emotions experienced by the researcher towards research participants and vice versa may originate from transference or countertransference. In a research context, transference can be defined as the process by which a research participant displaces on to the researcher feelings, ideas etc. which derive from previous figures in their life. Countertransference happens where researchers transfer their feelings onto a research participant. There may be some research topics, such as autobiographical exploration, where researchers' awareness of these dynamics could be particularly helpful during their reflection on interviews. As Fineman (1993: 24) indicated: 'We are all prisoners of our personal history. Repressed feelings do not disappear from the psyche, but are held in check through various mechanisms of defence which disguise the conscious presentation of the feelings'. The use of psychoanalytic ideas and theory in social research is discussed in the work of Clarke, Hoggett and Hahn (2008).

Hollway (2009) discusses the effective use of psychoanalytic methods in her research with mothers, describing two psychoanalytically informed research methods, a form of narrative interviewing and infant observation. She explores how, separately and together, they can go beyond a text-based method and conceptualise identities in ways that avoid reproducing assumptions of rational, unitary and discursive subjectivity.

In my own research interviews, I sought to adopt a person-centred approach borrowed from counselling. This approach involves an emphasis on tracking and sensing feelings of interviewees (Mearns and Thorne, 1999). My open questions promoted a mutual dialogue between myself as interviewer and the interviewee that included both of us in a reflective melee of challenge, contention, disclosure, contributing anecdotal experience and memory, pitching in ideas and leavening the discussion with humour. Wordplay, drawing, use of metaphor and ironical observations can be an expression of critical reflection, particularly in situations where interviewees experience themselves as being held by the bonds of formal language (Broussine, 2008).

Illustrating deep metaphor

Deep, or unconscious, metaphors emerge in the most frank and revealing exchanges, and they are often illustrated in drawings that are sketched as part of a research interview or workshop. Open questioning about such visual images is likely to generate vivid observations that can then be a form of raw research data. But this researcher found that the stark power of drawings was surprising and unsettling:

> Some time ago I used drawings to gauge managers' feelings about the changes that their organizations were going through. This experience, even a few years on, leaves me with powerful memories of how some of their drawings affected me at the time. The research uncovered a great deal of anxiety and distress among many of these managers, and while this didn't represent the whole picture (a minority of these managers were able to hold on to some optimism), the overall sense was that the situation was bleak for them. There were two facets to my feelings. One was the effect of certain drawings themselves on me: here are a couple of examples. (see Figures 6.1 and 6.2 next page).

> The second aspect I remember was an ethical question as well as an emotional one. I can sum this up as, "Who am I to unleash these feelings in these managers? Should I have?" Guilt I suppose. Then, "Can I do justice to their openness?" So, I was feeling that I was at the limits of my competence as a researcher; I can remember having an overwhelming sense of responsibility to my participants, and I wasn't always sure that I was up to this. By the way I had 86 participants in this study! In terms of the outcomes of the work for them and for me, would I do it again? Absolutely. But I'd go into it next time with my eyes more open about how I might be affected.

We must consider these sensitive issues, ethical considerations and ground rules during research design. These include how material contributed within interviews

FIGURE 6.1   Drawing 1, illustrating deep metaphor

FIGURE 6.2   Drawing 2, illustrating deep metaphor

will be attributed and whether the researcher will reflect back to the interviewee all of the emotions expressed such as deep anger and resentment. The researchers' own responses, contained by them in interviews, may warrant in-depth supervision support that also should be structured at the outset of the research programme. There are research settings where the ethical dimensions of the research process demand thorough preparation at the outset. Nicholls (2009) undertook research into the social defence mechanisms of occupational therapists in their everyday work in an acute hospital department, and she has described her concern not to expose research participants to the very telling, critical organisational analysis that was being undertaken as part of the research project.

Research focus on metaphor can also reveal why we have a deeper attachment to metaphorical images:

> *During the research process I explored more deeply my own ideogram/metaphor for a large organisation. I am conscious that I have held this metaphor for some considerable length of time. This is a city at night – a constellation of lights, blurred and obscured movements – a mosaic of dynamic activity and inertness/sleeping. Linking this back to my autobiography, on reflection, I had a powerful connection to the city that I was brought up in. In times of constraint or distress I would distance myself from family or other immediate surroundings by thinking of the city at night. To me, the city, especially the city centre, had a great life force. One of my interviewees also referred to a metaphor of the organisation as a constellation where the stars were individual people. The metaphor of lights or stars representing people has spiritual associations in the sense of light representing a spirit. On further reflection, perhaps I too had been looking over the years for the vibrant heart, or the spiritual light, in organisational life – to no avail. In the case of this interview, both myself and that interviewee had sought 'deeper meaning' from the organisation without consciously questioning why that meaning would necessarily be accessible to us from organisational experience.*

Keeping a reflective journal

My own reflective journal, maintained over some years, was 'raw data' for my inquiry, and it had intrinsic value for me as a research tool. The journal was a place of safekeeping, another 'container', where apparently diverse and disconnected events, feelings, dreams and insights could be held, to be subject to review at a later date. Over a sustained period of time, the totality of the journal illustrates a trajectory of emotional and cognitive development – not linear, but having its inner cycles, fallow periods and spurts of growth.

> *My research supervisors pressed me to include dreams in my reflective journal. I felt resistant to this idea as I saw the interpretation of dreams as being totally unique to an individual, rather than involving some of the common symbols or archetypes as defined by Freud or Jung. Also, many dreams appear to be incomprehensible. How could dreams be relevant in a research process?*
>
> *My research was exploring the deeper effects of role conflict and shortly after the discussion with my supervisors, I dreamed that I was walking along with great care and trepidation, as I was balancing a number of hats on my head, all stacked one on top of the other. It was imperative that I didn't cause the pile of hats to topple – quite a challenge as the mix of hats included a top hat and a flat cap etc. The dream, while seeming obvious in its representation of 'wearing too many hats' helped me to have a greater sense of the level of anxiety created by having multiple formal and informal roles and to respect the skill that I was using to maintain the balance of those roles. The writing up of the dream in the journal stimulated my reflective process.*

Another dream illustrated my experience of drafting my thesis. I dreamed that I was having a shower when the water from the shower was transformed into words – words were bouncing off my body and descending to the shower outlet. In the dream I felt an intense need to focus and identify as many words as possible but they were illusive and peripheral to my vision. But the feeling of the dream was not one of anxiety and frustration, but rather of curiosity and potential discovery and that feeling remained with me for some time – it was a sustaining emotion.

The keeping of a reflective journal gives a sustained opportunity and vehicle to include entries that explore an emotional reaction, a political slant or another interpretive perspective. This simple iterative process of note and reflection may be fruitful in generating numerous insights for a researcher, as if the reflection allows for another voice or interpretation to appear – an example of the creation of ambiguity in order to create an opportunity for looking at life from a critical perspective. So researchers are prompted by the journal to ask themselves why they felt anxious or angry. Their journal reflection is not intended to minimise or manage those feelings but rather to expose the underlying tensions or social issues. A reflective journal may thus liberate a researcher from writing in a disembodied, rational, linear fashion.

In my working life I was emotionally and intellectually drawn to the idea of integrity – what it meant in working practice and how integrity could be promoted – while I was also aware of the lack of cohesion of 'self' in the sense that our selves are fragmented and conflicting. In discussing the struggle for personal integrity in the face of incompleteness and irresolvable dilemmas, Miller identified that this internal struggle involves 'a debate about thought and feeling, desire and action, structure and agency, and the publicly concerned versus the privately concerned self' (1993: xiii).

Legitimisation

I was also very concerned to attain a level of integrity in my research inquiry that was faithful to the phenomenological spirit of the inquiry, while also being seen or 'judged' as being academically competent. A combination of interactive interviewing, the use of a reflective work journal and autobiographical inquiry proved to be an effective combination of methods to deliver in-depth qualitative data concerning 'self in role' as manifested in my specific working environment and political context (Watts, 2009).

During the last twenty years a much more explicitly acknowledged and validated relationship has been developed between social theory and social life (Seidman and Alexander, 2001: 2–3) that facilitates the type of analysis that is integral to psychosocial research inquiries. Essentially, psychosocial research approaches value the interrelated dynamics of subjectivity, social relations, and the impact of structural factors on social institutions and everyday life. Research topics necessarily incorporate emotional experience for the researcher and research participants.

A psychosocial perspective accords no hierarchy to either the personal or the political: 'The psychological cannot be reduced to the social and vice versa' (Hoggett, 2008: 379). We recognise the basic principle and 'importance of analysing personality development, everyday life, ideology and socio-historical processes as interdependent, rather than isolated, phenomena' (Sloan, 1996: vii).

There is now a body of work in terms of published research projects that inform ways in which this form of research can be validated. The challenge for psychosocial researchers is worth the trials and tribulations of the research journey. The gains – the legitimisation of the role of emotion in all research, the potential for personal insight and development and the contribution to understanding of the social nexus of the political and the personal – are substantial and, in many ways, life changing.

References

Benjamin, J. (1995) Recognition and Destruction: An Outline of Intersubjectivity, in *Like Subjects, Love Objects: Essays on Recognition and Sexual Difference*. New Haven, CT: Yale University Press.

Broussine, M. (ed.) (2008) *Creative Methods in Organizational Research*. London: Sage Publications.

Clarke, S. (2000) Psychoanalysis, Psycho-Existentialism and Racism, in *Psychoanalytic Studies* (2)4: 343–355.

Clarke, S. (2002) Learning from Experience: Psycho-Social Research Methods in the Social Sciences, in *Qualitative Research* (2)2: 173–194.

Clarke, S. (2004) The Concept of Envy: Primitive Drives, Social Encounters and Ressentiment, in *Psychoanalysis, Culture & Society* (9)1: 105–117.

Clarke, S., Hoggett, P., and Hahn, H. (2008) *Object Relations and Social Relations: The Implications of the Relational Turn in Psychoanalysis*. London: Karnac Books.

Coffey, A. (1999) *The Ethnographic Self*. London: Sage Publications.

Creek, S. (2012) A Personal Reflection on Negotiating Fear, Compassion and Self Care in Research, in *Social Movement Studies: Journal of Social, Cultural and Political Protest* (11)2: 273–277.

Fineman, S. (ed.) (1993) *Emotion in Organisations*. London: Sage Publications.

French, R. (2001) 'Negative Capability'': Managing the Confusing Uncertainties of Change', *Journal of Organizational Change Management* (14)5: 480–492.

Froggett, L. (2002) *Love, Hate and Welfare: Psychosocial Approaches to Policy and Practice*. Bristol: Policy Press.

Frosh, S., Phoenix, A., and Pattman, R. (2001) *Young Masculinities: Understanding Boys in Contemporary Society*. London: Palgrave Macmillan.

Greenwood, D., and Levin M. (1998) *Introduction to Action Research: Social Research for Social Change*. Thousand Oaks, CA: Sage Publications.

Hoggett, P. (2008) What's in a Hyphen? Reconstructing Psychosocial Studies, in *Psychoanalysis, Culture and Society* (13): 379–384.

Hoggett, P., Beedell, P., Jiminez, L., Mayo, M., and Miller, C. (2010) Working Psychosocially and Dialogically in Research, in *Psychoanalysis, Culture and Society* (15)2: 173–188.

Hoggett, P., and Campling, J. (2000) *Emotional Life and the Politics of Welfare*. Hampshire: Macmillan.

Hollway, W. (2009) Applying the 'Experience -Near' Principle to Research: Psychoanalytically Informed Methods, in *Journal of Social Work Practice* (23)4: 461–474.

Hollway, W., and Jefferson, T. (2000) *Doing Qualitative Research Differently: Free Association, Narrative and the Interview Method*. London: Sage Publications.

Hubbard, G., Backett-Milburn, K., and Kemmer, D. (2001) Working with Emotion: Issues for the Researcher in Fieldwork and Teamwork, in *International Journal of Social Research Methodology* (4)2: 119–137.

Jasper, J. (2007) Cultural Approaches in the Sociology of Social Movements, in Klandermans, B., and Roggeband, C. (eds.), *Social Movements across Disciplines*. New York: Springer.

Lea, M., and West, L.(1995) Motives, Mature Students, the Self and Narrative, in Swindells, J. (ed.), *The Uses of Autobiography*. London: Taylor and Francis.

Mason, J. (2002) *Qualitative Researching*. London: Sage Publications.

Mearns, D., and Thorne, B. (1999) *Person-Centred Counselling in Action*. London: Sage Publications.

Menzies Lyth, I. (1989) *The Dynamics of the Social*. London: Free Association Books.

Miller, T. (1993) *The Well – Tempered Self*. Chicago: Johns Hopkins University Press.

Nicholls, L. (2009) Seeing – Believing, Dreaming – Thinking: Some Methodological Mapping of Viewpoints, in Clarke, S., and Hoggett, P. (eds.), *Researching Beneath the Surface*. London: Karnac Books: 169–192.

Postle, D. (1993) Putting the Heart Back into Learning, in Boud, D., Cohen, D., and Walker, R. (eds.), *Using Experience for Learning*. Buckingham: Open University Press.

Reason, P., and Marshall, J. (1987) Research as Personal Process, in Boud, D., and Griffin, V. (eds.), *Appreciating Adult Learning*. London: Kogan: 113–125.

Reay, D. (2008) Psychosocial Aspects of White Middle-Class Identities: Desiring and Defending against the Class Ethnic 'Other' in Urban Multi-ethnic Schooling, in *Sociology* (42) 6: 1072–1088.

Segal, L. (2007) *Slow Motion: Changing Masculinities*. London: Palgrave Press.

Seidman, S., and Alexander J. (eds.) (2001) *The New Social Theory Reader*. London: Routledge.

Sloan, T. (1996) *Damaged Life: The Crisis of the Modern Psyche*. London: Routledge.

Stanley, L., and Wise, S. (1983) *Breaking Out: Feminist Consciousness and Feminist Research*. London: Routledge.

Stanley, L., and Wise, S. (1993) *Breaking Out Again: Feminist Ontology and Epistemology*. London: Routledge.

Watts, L. (2009) Managing Self in Role: Using Multiple Methodologies to Explore Self-Construction and Self-Governance, in Clarke, S., and Hoggett, P. (eds.), *Researching Beneath the Surface*. London: Karnac Books: 215–239.

Wilkinson, R., and Pickett, K. (2009) *The Spirit Level: Why More Equal Societies Always Do Better*. London: Allen Lane.

7

THE EMOTIONAL EXPERIENCE OF RESEARCH SUPERVISION

Mike Broussine and Linda Watts

Introduction

This chapter will explore researchers' emotional travails as they progress through their research and the role that research supervision can, does or does not play to facilitate this journey. Drawing on psychodynamic and psycho-social ideas for some of our analysis (see Chapter 6) and basing our arguments on the notion of critical pedagogy, we explore the extent to which research supervision can provide a 'container' for research students' feelings such as the experience of being in a cul-de-sac, isolation, distress, frustration, uncertainty and insecurity. We have found that the supervisee can experience complex power relations in the system, dependency, domination and gender dynamics and other issues of inequality (see Chapter 3). Tensions related to the demands for academic rigour may also heighten anxiety significantly and foster 'the imposter syndrome'. This chapter will form an experiential exploration of these fundamental yet relatively unacknowledged issues, after an initial brief commentary on discourse, social theory and relevant literature.

Our approach to exploring notions of good and problematic supervision and associated emotional experience was to set up, and participate ourselves, in a collaborative inquiry group (Broussine and Watts, 2009). The full story about this inquiry is told in Chapter 11. The group consisted of a mix of postgraduate research and doctoral students, and academic staff who were working in the social sciences and met periodically for eighteen months in 2007–2008. Exploration of the topic of supervision was not specifically mentioned at the outset as the main aim of the inquiry. What emerged, however, was that emotions provoked by reflections on the experiences of acting as a supervisor or as a supervisee formed a large component of what was experienced as an emotional 'roller-coaster' that some referred to in our inquiry. For this reason we decided to augment the data about supervision by beginning a second phase of the study. Colleagues (researchers and supervisors) from a range of UK universities were invited to be interviewed or to send email messages containing their reflections about the emotions involved in the supervision process. There were eight participants in the collaborative inquiry group (including ourselves, drawing on our own postgraduate research and supervision experiences), and we received views and reflections from twelve others from a range of universities in the second stage. We formed a general view about the inquiry – that participants (academic staff and students) found it worthwhile and reassuring to be involved in the inquiry because it added additional perspectives about their research: they found it useful to know that other supervisors and students held similar anxieties and hopes. A cause of concern was that the life of our inquiry was sustained because some participants reported that they felt they had nowhere to go in their institutions where they could access a similar space for critical reflection, emotional support and analytical perspective. Some said that their supervisor(s) were, ironically, the last people who might be able to meet such needs. The benefits of the collaborative inquiry group were captured in participants' reflective journal notes after one session as follows:

> We felt . . . our spirits had been lowered in this conversation, not because of the group, but because the group enabled us to get in touch with powerful feelings about research, and equally powerful feelings that there was a limited amount of what we could do about these. This has immense implications for "doing research", not the least of which is to ask ourselves why we bother to do it, and what sustains us. What was remarkable about this . . . [session] was the opening up of such reflections, and realising that we all needed a container for working with emotion, such as a good supervision process.

The need for such a container is important for both supervisors and students.

Academic supervision – origins and influences

Academic supervision has its origins in the medieval universities that based their supervision processes on the classical Greek master/pupil model. In this model the idealized master was regarded as all-knowing and supremely influential in shaping or propagating schools of thought. However, in modern educational practice, self-realization is more likely to be framed as being achieved by means of a more relational production-oriented discourse (Rowley and Sherman, 2004). But since the 1980s the pervasive discourse of performance-oriented managerialism, characterized by a low currency being given to emotion, has been on the ascendancy.

Our interpretation of discourse as we have used the term above derives from Foucauldian analysis:

> Discourse is a system of representation that regulates meaning so that certain ways of thinking, speaking and behaving become 'natural'. Discursive practices are used to present knowledge as 'true' and/or 'valid'.
>
> *(Best, 2002: 159)*

Supervision in public service contexts has also been influenced in recent decades by the development of models of supervision within the caring professions such as social work. These models are reflective and explore development needs in addition to being structured and providing guidance on how to deal with tasks.

Such notions of objectified knowledge as held and perpetuated to varying degrees by professional academics can represent an instrument of domination. 'Use of objectified knowledge permits the development of hierarchies of expertise, where those who know are able to judge the experiences and actions of those who don't know' (McKinlay and Starkey, 1998: 9). Objectified knowledge becomes enshrined in rule and regulation, and 'disciplinary power is most potent and efficient when it operates through administrative rules rather than *force majeure*' (McKinlay and Starkey, 1998: 9).

The effects of discourse in academic supervision provide a useful means of analysing conversation and text, but it is important to learn from theory. This was notably absent in the majority of the studies of supervision that we examined and in institutional guidance to prospective academic supervisors. A pertinent perspective is provided by critical pedagogy which the American cultural critic Henry Giroux defined as

> being guided by passion and principle, to help students develop consciousness of freedom, recognise authoritarian tendencies and connect knowledge to power and the ability to take constructive action.
>
> *(Giroux, 2010: B15–B16)*

His political analysis, focussing on the self-limitations of 'gated pedagogy' in the context of neo-liberalism, is cogent and persuasive with a transferable interpretation across to academic institutions in the UK and elsewhere:

> As is well known, higher education is increasingly being walled off from the discourse of public values and the ideals of a substantive democracy at a time when it is most imperative to defend the institution against an onslaught of forces that are as anti intellectual as they are anti democratic in nature'.
>
> *(Giroux, 2012: 1)*

Giroux and other critical theorists in this field have drawn on the radical principles advocated by Paulo Freire. The pedagogic and philosophical basis of these principles is an assumption that the creation of participatory and democratic learning environments, which encourage personal inquiry, provides people with the opportunity to overcome what Freire (1978) called the 'habit of submission' – the frame of mind that curtails someone from fully and critically engaging with and participating in their world, thus reducing their sense of personal agency and fulfilment through emotional expression. The argument is that – through participation in learning environments in which open, critical and democratic dialogue is fostered – people can develop increased self-confidence along with greater knowledge. In this context, debilitating anxiety in the learner is more likely to diminish. Freire pioneered an educational model that theorised the breakdown of the hierarchical teacher–learner relationship, thus promoting critical education in which the learner becomes an active participant in the appropriation of knowledge in relation to lived experience (Morrow and Torres, 2002). This active participation reflects a concern with a relatively democratic, dialogical and reflexive understanding of learning as well as a rebalancing of the power relationship.

Students' capacity for critical thinking and 'voice' is also a prominent theme in feminist pedagogy. The focus of bell hooks (1994) is the balance of power in student/teacher relationships and the potential to facilitate students' production of knowledge based on their differing realities and experience by breaking down traditional models of power in education. Practice goes beyond critical pedagogy by incorporating a caring dimension, and a concern for students' wellbeing (hooks, 1994: 15). Indeed, her work is striking in its attention to emotional wellbeing.

A critical stance towards postgraduate pedagogy is therefore key – Lee and Green (1995) make reference to adverse issues arising if rational 'science' models of research and supervision are adopted uncritically as normative across the academic-institutional setting but the means of monitoring research and supervision activity impose normative judgements.

We will address questions of supervisory practice towards the end of this chapter. At this point, however, having reviewed some of the philosophical and theoretical bases of the supervisory relationship, we turn to exploring the actual experiences that emerged from our inquiry as expressed by some students and supervisors. As with other chapters the voices of participants in describing their experiences and feelings in the shape of vignettes are included – in this case from the collaborative group sessions, email correspondence and interviews.

Research students' reflections

There's a risk about owning one's own idea, so the process seems to validate my own knowledge. I'm amazed at the confidence that grows in developing my own models.

(Research student A)

The process provides an opportunity for sense-making, puts it all into a context, and there's a lightening effect.

(Research student B)

The supervision process can represent a patriarchal performance measurement regime in the university.

(Research student C)

Research students reflected on a range of experiences and feelings generated by and from the supervision process. Because of their social science orientations, these reflections and critical analyses emerge from paradigmic views associated with these fields. We discuss researchers' experiences by reference to psychodynamic concepts where they are applicable. The range of issues that emerge from their reflections, and provided from the following cases, include the following:

- The potential for transference and counter-transference in the supervisory relationship
- Complex power relations
- Dependency
- Domination
- Gender dynamics
- 'Good' supervision

Transference and counter-transference

Yet another insight was that the dynamics within the research content itself may be re-enacted in the supervisory process. I shared my experience of a dynamic between me (a woman) and a female supervisor which was about her perception of me as a "corporate woman" – this was in fact a central theme in my research. She projected "corporate woman" on to me, coming from her anger, to some extent related to "corporate women" in [the university]. These social issues came right into my supervision and affected the supervision relationship for some time but as [and] when I had produced my critical analysis of self-construction in a corporate management context, this projection diminished.

(PhD student)

The analysis by this student is that the supervisor may have been playing out unconsciously a form of anger or resentment coming from her unsatisfactory relations with other more senior women in the university. The case shows that there can be unseen but powerful influences on the supervisory relationship that originate in our attitudes towards the things that are going on in our institutions. The supervisory situation is complicated by the fact that the process is surrounded by other important power-holders, as is illustrated in the next vignette from a different participant. (For more explanation of transference and counter-transference, see Chapter 6).

Dealing with complex power relations in the system

After a couple of years of excitement [with my PhD], I've not managed that after the progression exam. I've felt locked into a subservient position with [the Director of Studies] – I've needed to emotionally appease him rather than debate his points. It's created emotional disturbances. I've had emotional disturbances which reflected in my relationship with [my supervisor]. [She] has a stable, sensible, reassuring way of dealing with this roller-coaster. I feel that [the Director of Studies] has forced me into a more empirical way of doing things – for example he wants me to do 50 interviews, when actually the direction I want to go in is much more one of personal action inquiry – and I need [my supervisor]'s stability to stop me getting into depression and over-excitement – a form of 'manic depression' which is nothing like the rest of my life. But [my supervisor] comes in with a "steady on" reassurance so that my emotional dip can come back to normal. I seem blocked. It's not fear, but it's a lot of things: frustration, anger, etc. [the Director of Studies] seems to see the personal side of inquiry as an add-on rather than being a fundamental part of the thesis. But I'm sure he would engage in a counter-argument in a scholarly way – but I can't challenge him. I'm dependent on [my supervisor] to do so.

(PhD student)

This case reminds us that supervisory relationships are played out within a wider context than the tutor's office. The academic supervisor is accountable to and subject to the power relations that exist in the wider system dynamic, and this is characterised in this vignette by the sensitive relationship between both the student and supervisor – respectively and jointly – with the director of studies, as portrayed in Figure 7.1.

The student's hope that his supervisor can intercede with the director of studies on his behalf raises the pivotal question of dependency. He is quite clear that, in this situation, there exist severe limits to his capacity to exercise power vis-à-vis the director of studies, and he needs his supervisor to deal with this facet of the system. The inequalities in this power relationship are significant and can lead to students feeling that they are being infantilised.

Another student noticed:

One of my supervisors gave me some 'over-the-top' criticism, but actually he was communicating a message from 'the system' which at that time was tightening up on regulations.

In a similar vein, the following narrative describes a raw experience from a student who inadvertently is subject to and caught between the power plays that are enacted in the institution.

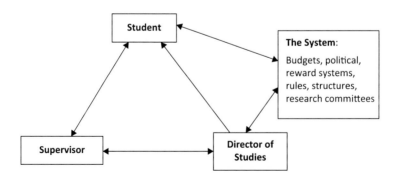

FIGURE 7.1 The 'tricky' student/supervisor and supervisor/supervisor relationships in the system

It was time for my yearly supervisory board. Naively, I asked what this was and was told it was just a review meeting with other lecturers in the department which is held every year. The purpose being to support my work – that I would attend with my supervisor. I was expected to write a 5000 word 'chapter' for this purpose. A few days before the meeting I heard that my supervisory board would be made up of the Head of Department and another Professor who I had heard of but never met, both of them men. When I asked exactly what this supervisory board was for I was told it was just something that they did every year and that it was intended to support me. On the day all four of us squeezed into a tiny room, the atmosphere was tense. I started to convince myself that what I had written had not been acceptable and that I was about to be confronted with this by these two strangers. But what ensued I can only describe as men posturing. This was not about me and my progress, it was men showing off, particularly my supervisor and 'the chair'. The session was not good, there had been an argument between my supervisor and 'the chair' about a particular perspective I was taking in my writing. They didn't ask me. I didn't get the support that I wanted and I left feeling again that I wasn't PhD material, that I couldn't do it. I was upset and . . . felt that I was embroiled in a political system that was bigger than me – to keep my head down. As I was leaving my supervisor came out of his room and commented to me that 'the chair' had never liked 'that line of thought' from anyone, but that he (my supervisor) was 'fighting' for me. I was irritated that these three men had not considered bringing another woman in – did they not realise that women feel supported with other women around – and that women think and behave differently to men.

Our observation about the behaviour described by this student is that there are masculine behaviours such as egotistical posturing, negative competition and 'fighting' that we recognise as being particular kinds of social behaviour – though of course they are not characteristic of all men. Some women may adopt similar behaviour, especially in competitive situations.

Dependency in the supervisory relationship

Students can be acutely sensitive to the potential disapproval or disappointment felt by, and expressed by, supervisors and other important actors in the research hierarchy, particularly through the use of competitive language. They can as a consequence be dependent on, and devote energy to, seeking their love and approval. This suggests that critically self-aware supervisors need to be able to take a reflexive turn with their students in order to manage potentially debilitating dependency relations or idealisation and to recognise the potential for 'the habit of submission' (Freire, 1978). They should seek to build supervisees' self-confidence to create a more agentic, inter-dependent relationship. The following case indicates what can happen if the relationship is not well managed in this respect.

I sometimes find that the supervision process makes me lose my voice and confidence. I need the space to help me to learn and develop, and don't want to have to pretend in supervision that I'm an expert. I struggle with dependence – I did have a supervisor who made our relationship feel quite interdependent: it was quite an equal relationship in many ways because he said that he was learning in the process as well. But some fellow students I know have been broken – they have great anxiety about every sentence they write in case it's not "right". With one of my current supervisors, it's not as bad as that, but I feel sometimes that he – his ideas, approaches – invade me like a virus.

(PhD student)

To be fair to supervisors, students can present (at least initially) as highly dependent subjects, having learnt the habit of submission earlier in their lives – at school and/ or even in earlier phases of their postgraduate studies that have led them to the dissertation or doctoral phase of the same course:

As subjects of the schooling process we are mainly required to be actively unquestioning. We are encouraged to be recipients of knowledge defined predominantly for us rather than with us. . . . Our schooling . . . affects us as learners by promoting a dependency on other people's knowledge.

(Vince, 1996: 113)

Supervisors should be careful to pick up on this issue and ensure that it does not exacerbate unequal power relationships.

Supervision as an exercise in domination

The deleterious effects of high dependency can be compounded by the supervisor's conscious or unconscious desire in supervision to impose and pursue his or her agendas through the student. We saw this to an extent in one of the supervisee's reflections earlier. Here is another vignette that reflects this tendency:

I often felt with my PhD supervisor at that time that I was undermined and unsupported. When I worked on my thesis I felt I had to please him all the time, and occasionally I also thought that he was in some form of competition with me, wanting to show that he was better and more knowledgeable than me. I like the fact that my current supervisor will have read . . . a draft chapter, whereas my previous one didn't always have the time to read it – and this added to a feeling of my being undervalued. Because I was a research student before, it seemed that he wanted to mould me towards his interests, but I didn't want to go there. He was impatient with my progress: I wasn't going quick enough for him. I have actually become a full-time member of staff now, and therefore my former supervisor is . . . a peer colleague. His attitude changed a bit, but in his mind I am a research student rather than being a colleague. Our relationship is quite tentative now. But I think the second supervisor coming on board and giving me the opportunity to have a voice was important as was the breakdown of the supervisory relationship with the first supervisor which was upsetting but also liberating – only the supervisor could have broken it off – I would never have done that however bad it got!!!!!!

The following PhD student also offered a narrative about her experiences with a dominating supervisor.

I had been pleased with my 6000 words, not particularly good academic writing (in fact when I look back on it, it was pretty poor), but I knew that something which I would need to improve on was this. I was hoping for some guidance. Instead I was heavily criticized for my writing and content, by what seemed like a very grumpy supervisor in front of me. I can remember thinking that I hadn't travelled all that way for this. I felt some relief when for a while he fell silent, I thought he was reading and that I was going to enter a useful discussion. As ever the paper was in front of his face. The silence became prolonged, I asked if 'he' was okay? He did not reply, I leaned to one side and noticed that he had closed his eyes still holding my paper up, I said again 'are you alright?', he jolted back as though he had dropped off to sleep, and without a word continued to pick holes in my writing. But then, as before that nugget of gold arrived, one small piece of wisdom from a man very experienced in his field as though I must be grateful for this. The suggested reading, a direction to think about these ideas, a new line of thought. . . . But I walked down the road in tears. Torn apart and wondering if I had made the right decision to pursue a PhD: had I bitten off more than I could chew?

These vignettes illustrate well the repressive emotional effects of domination and submission in practice and the consequent potentially damaging cycles of apprehension and resentment experienced by students.

Gender dynamics in supervision

My supervisors were supportive, but I sometimes had to keep them separate from each other – my supervisory team included two "big men", and so there was a gender dynamic. I ended up being the container of the dynamic between the two of them.

(PhD student)

At several points during our inquiry, students mentioned the effect of gender dynamics in the supervision process. The above represents one example, but the effect of same or different genders in supervision, and in the wider system, are explicitly narrated within some of the other reflections offered by dissertation or doctoral students. Interestingly, the majority of participants in our self-selected inquiry group were women. The issue of gender in research is sufficiently important for Wisker (2005) to devote a chapter (ch. 14) to the topic. Here she proposes that a number of gender-inflected issues might arise:

> If, for instance, the student wishes to carry out feminist research and the supervisor is not supportive or aware of this, there could be clashes between them. . . . There is also evidence that gender and power relations in the supervisor-student relationship can affects a woman's chance of succeeding in her research, particularly at doctoral level. . . . Gender and sexuality might affect success.
>
> *(Wisker, 2005: 213)*

Further – and to reinforce the earlier argument of how wider systemic dynamics and culture affect the supervisory relationship – Wisker suggests that the research process takes place in an environment of processes and expectations deriving from 'rigid, limiting versions of masculinity and masculine world views' (p.215). In 1998, Punch pointed to the 'patriarchal nature of academic life and the "research infrastructure"' (Punch, 1998: 161) and discussed how the powerful status of positivism tended to reside in such cultures. As may be seen from some of the reflections of students in the current inquiry, such views would be endorsed by a number of our participants.

The characteristics of 'good supervision'

It is possible to infer from much of the observation set out in this chapter that, frequently, 'things are not right' in the world of research supervision, and indeed some of the narratives that have emerged from this inquiry are disturbing. However, among the several cases of what may be regarded as 'poor supervision', there are also examples of experiences of good practice within interdependent student/supervisor relationships.

> *I had a long discussion with her [my supervisor] about what my new plans were, not to throw away all the work that I had done to date, but to take a new and different perspective. It had to be new in order to start again. She listened, offered her ideas, was excited and also challenging on some aspects of my thinking. I felt listened to, I felt she was trying to understand me and also steering me away from some common pitfalls. She explained to me the process that this School would require of me and my research. I had well over an hour and a half at this first session and I felt full – walking away with hope, intention and with my nuggets of gold as well. She believed in me and what I was doing, I could allow myself to feel stupid here and not be ashamed of that because I also felt validated.*
>
> *(PhD student)*

The above vignette is an illustration of a supervisor giving support, being challenging, advising and, vitally, enabling her student to feel sufficiently confident and optimistic to put new research plans into practice. Another research student added:

> *I have now had a number of supervision sessions with her, and have each time walked away feeling respected, like she is a friend to both me and my thesis. She respects me for the wisdom and experience I bring to it, I respect her for her wisdom and experience she brings to me. There are times when she has told me straight that something I have said is 'fluffy' or quite bluntly that I am going down a tricky alley on an issue!! I don't mind, I don't feel insulted, I feel we have enough trust to have built a good relationship where I can take tough feedback. And we can also take the time of day to talk about broader issues that we are both interested in. I still have a long way to go, but now I believe that I have what it takes to complete a PhD – I can do it and I am enjoying the journey.*

In this case, the human needs for mutual trust and respect are met, and the supervisory relationship is well founded. A third PhD student offered her view of 'good supervision':

> *Positive 'affirming' statements were made a number of times during my supervision. The inference is that the research student is essentially developing into being the expert in their field of research. So supervision involves an element where the research student is gathering and sharing knowledge with their supervisors, thus mediating the traditional hierarchical view of supervision where academic knowledge and experience is being passed one way to the student who is stereotypically a 'tabula rasa'.*

It is certainly the case, therefore, that some of our participants had satisfactory or positive experiences of the supervision process. However, our data also indicates that there can be highly problematic aspects in research supervision, and this finding is corroborated to an extent by other researchers. For instance, Morrison, Oladunjoye and Onyefulu (2007) found in their study that there was considerable dissatisfaction with aspects of supervisory practices. One issue raised by students in that study was that they found that supervisors could give good direction but were frequently unavailable. Ninety per cent of their respondents (n = 88) reported 'poor quality of supervision' although one factor may be students' idealization of the supervisory process. Another factor contributing to dissatisfaction may be consumerism, where a student considers that they have 'purchased' the right to a degree with an accompanying assumption of a successful outcome.

Our study concerned itself especially with the emotional and political experiences of both supervisors and students within the complex processes of supervision, and how the political system within academia can affect the relationship. It was our purpose to inquire into this essentially private encounter where there may be value conflicts between researcher and the supervisor, compounded by the politics and values of the academic institution or system that is the 'site' of supervision.

We know as experienced postgraduate teachers and researchers that supervision is critical in determining both the quality of the student's educational experience and the related emotional journey, and affects markedly the quality of the research outcome in the shape of a dissertation or thesis. Our experience also tells us – and this is reflected in some of the other quotes in this chapter – that supervision takes place in a national, international (see Chapter 5) and institutional context which affects the quality and nature of the dynamics between research student and supervisor. For instance, the economic pressures on academic institutions could have resulted in the restructuring and re-gearing of courses and research towards specific ends that comply with the more instrumental agendas of government and industry.

Supervisors' reflections

Our inquiry also generated a range of reflections and views from three academics about the emotional and political experience of acting as a research supervisor, and we present some examples here.

> *I am just embarking on my supervisory career, and I had a fantastic experience last year with a masters student; a really rewarding, friendly, intellectually enjoyable relationship which resulted in him getting a distinction. Now this year, I have been given 3 students to supervise (I keep getting them because I teach them research methods). After meeting one last week, I felt a strange conflict. He is pretty intelligent, has a good idea of what he wants to do but is really rather a dull person. That set me thinking . . . – how important is it to like our students? . . . I think the process of supervision is very anxiety provoking for most people – you wonder did I say the right thing? Or, did I give them too much information?*

A higher education lecturer shared this view about what enabled him to feel effective in the supervisory relationship with students, but also how 'negative' emotions can be experienced in the supervisory role:

> *I have felt good about supervising Paul. I steered the student towards a different and innovative path that made his study more useful to him and his organisation. I liked the way he reacted to my proposition – not just saying 'yes' (as some students do), but getting critically engaged with the ideas. I felt proud that I had helped to set him on a good journey. Sometimes students don't listen, though they pretend to, but with Paul I think we achieved a good dialogue between us when he and I engaged with the topic well. I think I get excited about supervising when it's about a topic that I'm interested in because I need some form of committed engagement on the part of the student if I am to supervise well. I see the purpose of supervision – the heart of it really – to be to develop the capacity of students to work critically with their topic. In contrast, what I find difficult are the students who are after satisfying the university requirements without a real commitment to the topic. As I get more experienced, you know, in my self-aware moments, I sometimes get frustrated with postgraduate students who come to us having finished their Masters up to the dissertation stage. Actually, I think the word is 'bored', particularly when they come along with set ideas about their methods*

without really having thought about it. The questionnaire is king you know! And then I catch myself trying to make their proposals more interesting – to get them to think about the use of other methods. I can say this is to extend their repertoire, but if I'm honest it's also about keeping my interest up.

These two supervisors' reflections begin to show us some of the dilemmas, tensions and joys of supervising. One theme that emerges is that the enjoyment of supervision is enhanced if either we 'like' the student concerned and/or the student can respond and develop in ways that suggest some personal agency rather than dependence. Another condition for a satisfactory relationship with students is suggested by the latter quote above, that there is a coincidence of interest in the topic between the supervisor and the student. Yet a further contributor to a 'good' supervisory relationship can be that of the nature of the student's commitment or engagement with his or her research and the topic. Thus a student who engages in a manner that may be described as instrumental (or conventional in the sense portrayed by the second supervisor's vignette), merely to survive the process or achieve the minimum in order to make the grade, may not encourage his or her supervisor's full commitment to the relationship. Responsibility for engendering effective relationships in the supervisory encounter is a two-way process.

So passionate students may be rewarded with passionate supervisors – but that is not always the case. A third colleague explained:

It's difficult integrating emotion into the project because it's just politically not acceptable. You can expect a bit of a backlash. There is a paradox though because in these days of a hunger for reflective space in learning, more and more students are coming from performance management environments. So how do you build up capacity in HE to work centrally with emotion in research? This isn't just a methodological point but a political one. Perhaps we can find ways of framing something and attach it to a recognised methodology – that might be OK.

This last vignette introduces the effects of what is seen to be politically acceptable within a particular institutional context. This staff member has the task of defending one of her students in the face of potential hostility from some powerful stakeholders in her department about the extent to which a large 'emotional' component in the student's work can be seen as legitimate research. As we see in some students' observations, the hegemony of beliefs and commitments to particular methodologies and/or what constitutes 'proper' research within the institution can have a marked effect upon students' hopes and emotional wellbeing, sometimes, as in this case, even where one's supervisor is interceding on behalf of his or her student vis-à-vis the system. So:

Academic institutions and research centres consist of staff and powerful actors (tutors, examiners, research committee members) who will hold a range of views about what constitutes good research. In many institutions, there is a creative tension between colleagues as they represent their paradigmic views. Such a climate can hold the prospect of respectful debate and learning, with the recognition that there is a need to listen to, and work with, different perspectives. However, in some other places, the opposite is true – there can be intolerance of the unorthodox and of the experimental, and to begin to think about suggesting dialogue, drama or drawings as the base of one's research will feel risky.

(Broussine, 2008: 18–19)

Supervisory practice

There is a growing literature on research supervision. Interestingly, many of these authors suggest that there are relatively few critical examinations of the research supervision process that acknowledge the research student's perspective. A very useful starting point is Gina Wisker's work (2005) that provides substantial guidance on effective supervision, both from the researcher's and the supervisor's points of view. She includes a suggested activity in which we are invited to draw up a list of six characteristics 'you think a good supervisor should possess' (p.42). Wisker goes on to suggest possible problem areas in the supervisor/student relationship, and groups several potential issues under 'personality factors' (e.g. neglect by the supervisor; clash of personalities; barriers to communication arising from differences in age, class, gender, race; and differences in approaches to work); professional factors (e.g. a misinformed supervisor; the supervisor having research interests which differ significantly from those of the student; the student holding unrealistic expectations of the supervisor); and organizational factors (e.g. the supervisor having too many students; inadequate support services; supervisors being too busy coping with other demands). She argues that the aim of a supervisory relationship should be to develop student autonomy based on sound knowledge of the research process and of the procedures and rules surrounding research, being clear about the research question, and being confident enough to get on with the task (p.62).

Armstrong, Allinson and Hayes (2004) explored the possibility that differences and similarities in the cognitive styles of students and their research supervisors might have a significant effect on socio-emotional aspects of their interpersonal working relationships and, ultimately, on performance outcomes. Their focus was on the nature of the student–supervisor relationship in undergraduate independent research projects. They suggest that the questionable quality of the supervision process has often been highlighted as one of the main reasons for problems such as non-completion, student drop-out, inordinate dissertation or thesis completion times and student dissatisfaction with the process. Armstrong *et al.* found that aspects of dissatisfaction included the absence of structure and direction; being allocated supervisors whose interests and knowledge do not match their own; and receiving insufficient guidance concerning planning, organizing and time-scaling. They found that levels of dissatisfaction rates were higher among social science students than in the natural sciences despite the fact that supervision itself was often regarded as 'the single most important variable affecting the success of the research process in the social sciences' (ESRC, 1991: 8). They note:

> Although there have been numerous testimonies to supervision's critical importance, there have also been reports of its exceptional difficulty (Acker *et al.*, 1994). It has been described as 'probably the most responsible task undertaken by an academic' (Burnett, 1977: 17), 'the most complex and subtle form of teaching in which we engage' (Brown & Atkins, 1988: 115), and 'the most advanced level of teaching in our education system' (Connell, 1985: 39). As several authors have pointed out, however, such observations seem curiously at odds with the general dearth of research on the detailed nature of supervision in the student–supervisor relationship in educational settings.
>
> *(Armstrong, Allinson and Hayes, 2004: 42)*

Malfroy has argued that more flexible models of supervision are needed – not necessarily a perpetuation of the dyadic relationship. She advocates a move, through the use of research seminars, to more collective models of supervision and collaborative knowledge-sharing environments (Malfroy, 2005).

Academic institutions normally have formal and comprehensive procedures, rules and guidance about postgraduate research generally, and supervision in particular. Typically such guidance and rules will insist on the training of supervisors and on the types of written records that need to be maintained both by the supervisors and by the students – e.g. what should take place at minimum in supervision sessions. These might appear along the following lines:

> *One member of the supervision team will be designated the Director of Studies. The Director of Studies is responsible for ensuring that the supervision is carried out in accordance with the University's Academic Regulations, and this Code of Practice.*
>
> *The Supervision team must ensure that the team meets with the student at appropriate intervals, and that the meetings are properly conducted and recorded.*
>
> *Meetings should, as a minimum, cover a discussion of the student's progress since the last meeting and should agree a set of actions resulting from a review of their project plan, publication plan and training and development needs.*

... and so on. Such procedures provide a formal framework within which supervision occurs, but typically offer little insight into the dynamics in the supervisory relationship, nor necessarily what constitutes 'good' supervision. Such guidance will structure expectations about supervision from task, performance, administrative and managerial orientations. These orientations may lead to misplaced notions that all is well with the research process because the required boxes have been ticked. Underlying assumptions about the nature of supervision itself are not explicitly examined – is it essentially facilitation of the research journey, task management, quality control, constructive criticism and empathic interpersonal exchange, or a balance of all of these? What does a 'good research student' look like? The expression of empathy in a dialogue may be more randomly covered (or not) in workshops for new supervisors.

Thus, students' anticipation of their emotional experience of the research 'journey' may be ignored, and the supervisory relationship may be initiated and shaped without the initial dialogue that defines mutual expectations. The work of Brockbank and McGill (2007) showed that supervisors and students had very differing expectations. Key policy features such as the identification of appropriate methodologies and the nature of the validation of findings can open up areas of substantial difference leading to tensions and distancing within the supervisory relationship .The typical supervisory pair are likely to draw on the supervisor's academic knowledge only, leaving the domains of affect and emotion untouched, so that the doing of research and the student's feelings about it are ignored (Brockbank and McGill, 2007: 303).

Despite this, what is clear from our inquiry is that it is quite normal for researchers to feel anxious from time to time, to doubt their capability to complete their studies (the 'imposter syndrome'), and to experience days when they feel they are achieving nothing. Moreover, to look at the other side of the coin, there seems to be little opportunity given for supervisors themselves to reflect on *their* anxieties, and we surmise that this dearth of 'emotional space' in an increasingly performative and task-focused institutional context may lead some staff to over-manage and dominate for reasons of expediency, with the potential consequence of diminishing their students. Indeed, the impact of the task focus as an underlying discourse for supervisors is indicated by a research study that found that supervisors interviewed 'supported their students intellectually, emotionally and structurally'. However, their task focus meant that they were not able to reflect on their supervisory capabilities and learn from these reflections (Vikinas, 2008: 297). Supervisors' potentially paradoxical roles have been elaborated by Anderson, Day and McLaughlin, who report on how supervisors saw themselves as having a gatekeeping role, a commitment to align student's work with academic standards, while at the same time having a personal commitment to enable students to pursue research topics that excited the students' interest and promoted the students' sense of agency (Anderson *et al.*, 2006).

Conclusions

The space in which the research supervision process takes place is an exceptionally private one in higher education. There are two (possibly three) people in a room, and anything might happen. It is striking that what goes on in student research supervision sessions is essentially a closed world in which there is immense potential for much development and learning (as reflected in some of our inquiry participants) but also for abuse and diminishment. We know as experienced teachers and researchers that supervision is critical in determining the quality of the student's educational experience, and this affects markedly the quality of the research outcome in the shape of a dissertation or thesis. Our experience also tells us – and this is also reported by others in this chapter – that supervision takes place in a politically and emotionally charged academic context which affects the quality and nature of the dynamics that take place between research student and supervisor.

This chapter demonstrates that supervision is a more complex and 'deep' relationship than is commonly acknowledged. Much of the written material about supervision is oriented understandably to the role of supervision in gearing academic effort towards the goals and standards of the relevant academic institution. Supervisors and students are both responsible in different ways for the research outcome – and differing pressures and concerns will be brought to bear. The supervision exchange involves coaching and counselling and essentially 'validation' – of our research and our selves. The validation of self inevitably generates vulnerability and a potentially painful emotional experience that an experienced supervisor will acknowledge. Sense making takes place in supervision – but in a context where validation delineates 'goodness' and 'rightness'. Thus, supervision is a very 'loaded' activity, ripe for transference and counter-transference to take place. There may be gender dynamics (and other equalities related dynamics) at play, and these dynamics within the research content itself may be re-enacted in the supervisory process. Thus we conclude that if research was acknowledged and understood more widely as a personal, emotional and political process, then a number of the adverse issues that are highlighted in this chapter would benefit from that understanding – in terms of the research student's 'process' and also the continuing 'process' of the supervisor/s.

In summary, a supervision model that is founded on the findings of our inquiry and informed by relevant literature would be a model in which the supervisor would adopt the position of facilitator rather than dictator (Wisker, 2005: 62), or in other words 'mentor rather than master' (Shannon, 1995: 12). This avoids the pervasive metaphor of the professional–client relationship as noted by Mackinnon. Instead, differentials of knowledge and power are respected but not exploited (Mackinnon, 2004: 395). Within this approach, supervision would be explicitly addressed as a meeting point for two or more agendas (Vehvilainen, 2009: 185).

hooks (1994) would envisage educators and students learning together after an initial exploration of the authority of the teacher or educator, in order to open up the discussion of power and authority in their relationship. In that context the emotional responses to major issues arising in the research journey would be acknowledged and explored in a context where those responses are understood to be significant and, in some cases, need to be incorporated as a dimension of research data.

Our inquiry participants offered us deep insights into the emotional experience of 'being supervised' together with critical insights that caused us to reflect fundamentally on our own practice as actual or potential dissertation or doctoral supervisors. We hope that this chapter provokes similar reflections in the reader, and that it has reassured research students that feelings – positive and/or negative – that emerge within or as a result of the supervision experience are 'normal' and can give valuable insights into their research and the context in which it takes place.

References

Acker, S., Hill, T., and Black, E. (1994) Thesis Supervision in the Social Sciences: Managed or Negotiated? *Higher Education*, (28)4: 483–498.

Anderson, C., Day, K., and McLaughlin, P. (2006) Mastering the Dissertation: Lecturer's Representations of the Purposes and Processes of Masters Level Supervision, *Studies in Higher Education*, (31)2: 149–168.

Armstrong, S.J., Allinson, C.W., and Hayes, J. (2004) The Effects of Cognitive Style on Research Supervision: A Study of Student–Supervisor Dyads in Management Education, *Academy of Management Learning and Education*, (3)1: 41–63.

Best, S. (2002) *A Beginner's Guide to Social Theory (Theory, Culture & Society,)* London: Sage.

Brockbank, A., and McGill, I. (2007) *Facilitating Reflective Learning in Higher Education*, Maidenhead: Open University Press/McGraw-Hill Education.

Broussine, M. (Ed.) (2008) *Creative Methods in Organizational Research*, London: Sage Publications.

Broussine, M., and Watts, L. (2009) *Reflections on the Research Supervision Process*, presented to British Academy of Management Research Methodology Special Interest Group Fourth Annual Workshop on *Teaching Research Methods to Business and Management Students*, University of Central Lancashire, 31st March.

Brown, G., and Atkins, M. (1988) *Effective Teaching in Higher Education*, London: Methuen.

Burnett Report (1977) Report of the Vice Chancellor's Committee on Research and Postgraduate Study, St Lucia: University of Queensland, in Moses, I. (1984) Supervision of Higher Degree Students – Problem Areas and Possible Solutions, *Higher Education Research and Development*, (32): 153–165.

Connell, R. (1985) How to supervise PhD's, *The Australian Universities' Review*, (28) 2: 38–41.

Economic and Social Research Council [ESRC] (1991) *Postgraduate Training: Guidelines on the Provision of Research Training for Postgraduate Research Students in the Social Sciences*, Swindon: ESRC.

Freire, P. (1978) *Education for Critical Consciousness*, New York: Seabury Press.

Giroux, H. (2012) Gated Intellectuals and Ignorance in Public Life: Toward a Borderless Pedagogy in the Occupy Movement, *Truth-out*.org., retrieved from http://truth-out. org/opinion/item/8009-gated-intellectuals-and-ignorance-in-political-life-toward-a-borderless-pedagogy-in-the-occupy-movement

Giroux, H.A. (2010) Lessons from Paulo Freire, *Chronicle of Higher Education*, (57): B15–B16.

hooks, b. (1994) *Teaching to Transgress: Education as the Practice of Freedom*, London: Routledge.

Lee, A., and Green, B. (1995) Introduction: Postgraduate Studies/Postgraduate Pedagogy, *The Australian Universities Review*, (38)2: 2–4.

Mackinnon, J. (2004) Academic Supervision: Seeking Models and Metaphors for Quality, *Journal of Further and Higher Education*, (28)4: 395–405.

Malfroy, J. (2005) Doctoral Supervision, Workplace Research and Changing Pedagogic Practices, *Higher Education Research and Development*, (24)2: 165–178.

McKinlay, A., and Starkey, K. (Eds.) (1998) *Foucault, Management and Organisation Theory*, London: Sage.

Morrison, J.L., Oladunjoye, G.T., and Onyefulu, C. (2007) An Assessment of Research Supervision: A Leadership Model Enhancing Current Practices in Business and Management, *Journal of Education for Business*, March/April: 212–219.

Morrow, R.A., and Torres, C.A. (2002) *Reading Freire and Habermas: Critical Pedagogy and Transformative Social Change*, New York: Teachers College Press, Columbia University.

Punch, M. (1998) Politics and Ethics in Qualitative Research, in Denzin, N.K., and Lincoln, Y.S. (Eds.) *The Landscape of Qualitative Research: Theories and Issues*, London: Sage Publications, 156–184.

Rowley, D.J., and Sherman, H. (2004) *Supervision in Colleges and Universities*, Lanham: University Press of America, Maryland.

Shannon, A. (1995) Research Degree Supervision: More Mentor than Master, *The Australian Universities Review*, (38)2: 12–15.

Vehvilainen, S. (2009) Problems in the Research Problem: Critical Feedback and Resistance in Academic Supervision, *Scandinavian Journal of Educational Research*, (53)2: 185–201.

Vikinas, T. (2008) An Exploratory Study of the Supervision of PhD/Research Students' Theses, *Innovative Higher Education*, (32)5: 297–311.

Vince, R. (1996) Experiential Management Education as the Practice of Change, in French, R., and Grey, C. (Eds.) *Rethinking Management Education*, London: Sage Publications, 111–131.

Wisker, G. (2005) *The Good Supervisor – Supervising Postgraduate and Undergraduate Research for Doctoral Theses and Dissertations*, Basingstoke: Palgrave Macmillan.

8

NOT RESEARCHING WHERE WE GREW UP

Stella Maile

In every voice, in every ban,
The mind-forg'd manacles I hear.

William Blake, 'London'
from *Songs of Innocence and Experience* (1789, 1794)

Why is it so difficult to write about the feelings surrounding our studies and our research inquiries, or, more particularly, what is the nature of the feelings that stop us pursuing our original topics of interest, in finding answers to the questions which somewhere we might have carried for years? Perhaps we are more emotionally involved in the projects we don't pursue than those we do because they are somewhere tied up with formative experiences? What has stopped me in my tracks in writing about such things is the anxiety of being self-indulgent. I am not the only one – colleagues have also spoken to me of their reluctance to pursue any personal writing because, although important on one level, it feels 'wince-making' on another. I know exactly what they mean. The first drafting of this chapter felt awkward, and the second drafting felt even worse – even though the comments were encouraging.

Not getting on with this chapter is a bit like some of the themes I will explore in not researching where we grew up (spatially, temporally and physically, as well as emotionally and discursively). The experience might be understood in terms of an emotional defence against the power-structures, practices and imaginaries of the past, which if not thought about with others may still live somewhere in and be enacted by us. The formative questions lurking behind our writing and our research are important because they re-connect us with our histories and the people who remain alive within and between us. We can do so much to take us away from where we started and might otherwise more interestingly begin.

To even feel the embarrassment of self-indulgence tells us something of what might be at stake: the risk of exposing a continuing academic social taboo; not to speak of ourselves, or only to speak of ourselves in the service of understanding those who are 'worse' off than ourselves in some way; to focus on the emotions of others, the *researched,* as if they are entirely different from us, because difference is after all everything, in these highly individualistic, neo-liberal times.

In spite of our more enlightened understanding of the interconnections of social and psychological structures, there may still be a suggestion that to speak personally is to speak only of individual concerns, and yet, as Bourdieu wrote,

> interpersonal relations are never, except in appearance, individual-to-individual relationships and that the truth of the interaction is never entirely contained in the interaction. . . . In fact it is their present and past positions in the social structure that biological individuals carry with them, at all times and in all places, in the form of dispositions which are so many marks of social positions and hence of the social distance between objective positions, . . . between social persons . . . so many reminders of this distance and of the conduct required in order to "keep one's distance. . . ."
>
> *(1977: 81, 82)*

'Keeping one's distance' has traditionally underpinned the authorisation of our 'scholarly' writing and our research. But, as an increasing number of ethnographic, auto-ethnographic, narrative and psycho-social researchers recognise, this distanced vantage point can mean that some interesting social realities and experiences are missed out.

The often sharp separation of 'scholarly' and impartial research from our own culturally laden, forgotten personal histories and emotions can force us to deny the selves, the situated subjectivities (Letherby *et al.*, 2013), we bring to our own research processes and questions. And so, the decisions we make in regard to our studies and our research can serve to keep some people and experiences at a distance, and we can be unconsciously involved in psycho-social processes of estrangement or alienation. In writing about the murkier emotions of research and her own involvements in research with community workers, Beedell (2009) made reference to a research colleague:

> From quite early days, even doing A levels, I was confronting arguments and data that seemed to help make sense of my own surroundings in ways that I didn't think were possible, or that I didn't think anyone bothered to do. . . . Here were some tools to make sense of my own past . . . kind of 'at last!' Here are some tools! actually, because there were a lot of things that still troubled me.
>
> *(Beedell, 2009: 109)*

The use Beedell's colleague made of psycho-social research tools for understanding the processes of research surrounding the negotiation of ethical dilemmas in contested communities was also being drawn upon to understand his own past experiences and the landscape in which they occurred. Beedell also helpfully reminds us of the immense emotional labour which is required to maintain the 'professional stance' of the researcher and the ways in which this performance draws on and perpetuates, unless carefully handled, underlying forms of knowledge and power dynamics. These are interesting to ponder when reflecting on the subliminal dimensions of our research choices. As I will attempt to show, exploring the emotions of research – or not researching where we grew up – also reminds us of the need for us to make sense of, with others, our formative surroundings, always those questions lurking behind our research choices and choices of study.

All of this represents a preamble to a discussion of some illustrative material regarding the involvement of some of the more difficult emotions surrounding our choices of study and/or our research. The examples I offer here draw attention to the landscapes and memories of our youth in an attempt to understand some of the more difficult or painful emotions surrounding a reluctance to pursue some subliminal emotionally loaded questions underpinning our research inquiries. The impact of not owning and staying with the emotions which frame our buried questions can potentially stunt our creativity and our research, even prevent us from pursuing our research. In the next section I will offer two vignettes to illustrate the ways in which our choices of study and research can function as distorted emotional inquiries; I later refer to this in terms of our chosen research topics sometimes veiling more authentic questions which derive from our formative experiences.

Research and study as displacement

A historian, Ken, told me that from the perspective of middle age he had come to realise that his choice of study represented both a flight from his (*own*) emotionally laden story as a young man struggling with formative experiences of poverty and feelings of disgrace and a movement *towards* understanding something about the impact of history on lives like his – even though he chose not, in the end, to study lives like his. It was actually much easier to study the lives of those whose history was formed by privilege, power and status, and these became the topics of his inquiry. A longing somewhere for those very things in childhood occurred in tandem with both a disavowal and a courting after the things that eluded him and his parents as they struggled together. His disgrace was to identify with those he could never be accepted by because of his social class; his desire was bound up with a boy's identification with and courting of those who would never know the shame of poverty:

> *History was a way of escaping where I came from . . . it was easier to look at the lives of others – lives lived centuries before and therefore at a distance from the life I was in and trying to escape from. It was so depressing the place I came from . . . bleak is the word really . . . why would I want to look at that . . . at one point we lived in a high rise tower-block where there was shit and urine in the stair wells and the lifts, graffiti*

everywhere, the couple next door beating each other up. . . . Interestingly, I flirted with the idea of becoming a sociologist — the funny thing is that the universities I applied to didn't think I was good enough for that. I suppose they saw that my interest in the subject was only half-baked. History seemed much more interesting and . . . comfortable.

Daniel's 'research story'

A sociologist, Daniel, had identified with the plight of refugees and later middle-class 'lifestyle' migrants. Both objects of inquiry were related to another question, close to Daniel's heart. He had initially pursued research on these topics with a passion which was short lived for reasons which should become clear in the recounting of his story. He told me:

> *I never felt I fitted in and I suppose I always related to other 'outsiders', it was fitting really that I studied the experiences of refugees and migrants. I had a lot of idealism in regard to the topic and then I realised that other researchers were not so idealistic and I became disillusioned with and possibly more self-aware that there was something in me that I wanted to articulate in some way . . . a sense of dispossession or a romantic sense of exile and then I became disillusioned or awake to that romanticised view of things. I suppose I was romanticising the experience of suffering really . . . I think something similar happened with some other research which I found initially interesting and then grew bored with and I put it aside . . . there was a sense of disillusion with the subject matter that . . . what once struck me as fascinating and interesting, no longer does. . . . I don't think that is boredom from familiarity but an active distaste in relation to something.*

When I asked for elaboration on the 'distasteful in relation to something', he replied:

> *It is probably to do with the fact that it didn't work; I didn't get what I wanted from it . . . it is not a neutral feeling . . . must have been let down by something . . . a bit like that. . . . Perhaps it is a distaste for a failed attempt to try to understand something and again, something I had idealised and then emotionally dis-invested from . . . something to do with a failure for it to supply answers, to really address what it is I might be interested in but it doesn't really give me the answers, or at least that is very limited. The answers to the questions I was asking felt elusive . . . and I am now scrambling around for something else to inspire me . . . if there isn't another object of study/research to get fascinated by, I get depressed.*

He went on to remark that his later research on middle-class migration to Europe had been a guarded interest because it related to his own experiences – experiences he would prefer not to look at for fear of appearing self-indulgent.

> *My mother had died, my work had finished and I had sold my flat and felt there was nothing for me in the UK and was interested in similar experiences of others but . . . I*

would avoid pursuing research with those whose experiences were too close to my own. One of my interviewees had also lost his mother and eventually, in growing recognition of the resonances of my research with my own experiences, I lost interest and avoided pursuing it.

Both types of research, research on refugees and research on middle-class migrants, had related to difficulties Daniel experienced growing up in lower-middle-class middle England in the 1950s. This included a feeling of a lack of 'being at home' in an atmosphere of culturally imbued and legitimised patriarchal and homophobic violence surrounding his mother's affair, father's depression and break-downs, other 'family secrets' (Smart, 2011) and shame of concealing the truth of his gay brother's sexuality and suicide attempts. As the youngest, Daniel felt exiled and excluded and not attended to by a mother who had limited emotional space, and a feeling that there was no place to feel safe or to have his own feelings recognised.

> *I was aware, somewhere, of those connections between my formative experiences and my research choices and when my mother died, funnily enough, I was no longer interested in the research. . . . My parents were, I think, attempting to contain their dissatisfied relationship and domestic situation and in some ways that was suffocating, and I was always fleeing from it and not feeling at home but at the same time – I wanted a home and to feel anchored – but couldn't. . . . There was in my youth always a strong feeling of not belonging and a strong desire to get away . . . even when I was very little, leaving with a little suitcase and my teddy, going down the road and being found and taken back again. I suppose all chintzy clutter they surrounded themselves with really amounted to touching attempts to anchor things . . . for them. . . . Even now, I still don't feel at home and would like to get a home somewhere else, it is not homely despite efforts to create nice interior spaces . . .*

There is much more that can be interpreted from the material given here, but it can be noted throughout that somewhere Daniel expressed the feelings of a 'homeless state of mind' and social exclusion (see Scanlon and Adlam, 2008) that initially inspired him to research the experience of refugees and migrants and then bored him on discovering the deeper emotions underlying his interest – feelings of displacement from a pressured 1950s household and a depressed mother. In some ways, Daniel's turning away from his research inquiry resonated with formative family experiences which advocated the avoidance of emotions.

In not speaking of ourselves, our own emotional involvements, including the more difficult feelings we reserve for those who may represent something we long for (overcoming displacement or dislocation, in Daniel's case; a longing to understand the feelings of esteem reserved historically for the upper classes in Ken's case), and our potentially more interesting research quests can become waylaid, stultified and faltering or in Daniel's case abandoned because of unanswered questions. Daniel would like to research and write about these deeper experiences, those that speak to a life-long wish to feel he belonged in what was a troubled home. He told me that it was much easier for someone else to write that – he wouldn't write about that himself – although he might give this dimension of his research more thought now.

As fellow travellers we can usefully reflect upon the subliminal feelings which connect us again with ourselves and the shared aspects of our social and human selves. Ironically, we might understand in psycho-social terms Daniel's boredom and reluctance to pursue his research as an enactment of the very problems surrounding the plight of the displaced, a refusal to really think about the socially excluding processes and sometimes violent repressions we are involved in. Such processes interweave the daily oppressive and repressive dimensions of family, community and national and international human and social relationships – the things we do not care to pay much attention to now signified for Daniel, and we might say all of us, by the refugee or lifestyle migrant. In this case, the haunting metaphor of the refugee, in particular, has somewhere come to signify an inquiry into all that can be rendered helpless and cruelly displaced. Through the displacement and projection of our own emotional experiences, a research project may be felt as futile, one bound up with the denials and defences against thought which are enacted in and through institutional and family life, for example.

In regard to the aims of this book, we might note the importance of allowing people the space to explore the subliminal emotions of their research because this can reawaken and enliven something which, if dulled, can become de-motivating. When, through our discussion of 'not researching where we grew up', we explored Daniel's feelings of boredom and located them in the psycho-social and culturally loaded dimensions of alienating social experiences of which social research is often itself immersed, Daniel conveyed interest, relief and a sense that actually reflecting upon his own unconscious emotional involvement in his research topic was interesting, useful and, actually, not self-indulgent at all. Daniel felt he could return to his research with renewed energy having felt that his experience has been thought about and made sense of.

Screen questions

Another way of thinking about the experiences relayed here is to liken the pursuit (or not) of a research question to a screen story, disguising an unconscious demand from the listener or the reader – to register something which cannot be more simply said or asked for by the readers of our research. In Daniel's case this could be seen as a plea to the reader to understand, on a more extreme level, the plight of the ultimate pain of homelessness – signified by the refugee, or the longing for social and public esteem in a decision to learn about the history of the nobility as in Ken's story.

In the context of a psychotherapeutic encounter, Phillips (1994) describes the function of a 'screen story', which conceals a plea to the listener to register something too painful to express directly and/or a question to ask for something more simply. It is because so much of what we remember or what preoccupies us conceals repressed experiences that the surface stories we tell ourselves and others may appear banal. They are less interesting than the feelings and experiences which they conceal and distort. The same might be said of our surface interests in our research questions and the things we write about.

Both Ken's and Daniel's choices of study and research can be thought about (once we register the subliminal feelings surrounding those choices) as functioning, emotionally, rather like screen stories which veil deeper emotional quests – in the case just described, the use of 'refugees' and middle-class migrants as, yes, real people, but also characters in a narrative who come, somewhere, to represent symbolically some experience of the researcher. In Daniel's case we might say the refugee offers a means of pursuing a deeper related question surrounding perhaps 'how to fit in, to gain the emotional and material needs for a safe home in its broader sense.' In this way, research quests are half pursued, the pursuit of questions relating only to someone else's experience, rather than to something shared, the aggressions and violence which surround excluding experiences in our own everyday lives.

Our inquiries into the lives of others, then, can also resonate with inquiries about our own lives. Why can't we simply acknowledge that and in so doing free ourselves to get on with the research and writing tasks we set ourselves?

Troubling research inquiries

The separation of research quests from our own more deeply held and fundamentally human inquiries are also associated with broader rationalising tendencies in which scholarly research, still enthralled by the positivist dimensions of the Enlightenment project, has been caught up.

Academically de-barred emotional and experiential material can be triggered, potentially, by our research choices, to return as elements of the repressed. Half-remembered experiences, feelings and fantasies may feel weird, unnerving, upsetting; boring, contemptible, hated; tantalising, desired – something reminiscent perhaps of our own formative landscapes. If we are somewhere unnerved by this, what might happen to that inquiry then? Do we stay with it or move away from it? Does it get jettisoned altogether or displaced? Or perhaps we pursue other strategies – those involving others, our very research participants/objects?

Psycho-socially, researchers as well as research subjects defend against anxieties relating to the embodied experiences of the kinds of things sociologists in particular like to inquire into, including inequality, poverty, sexuality, class, race and, inevitably, their associated feelings of stigma and shame (see Clarke and Hoggett, 2009; Hollway and Jefferson, 2000). One means of managing anxiety is to find suitable objects to project onto or, more powerfully, *into*. This is known as projective identification (Klein, 1946) and, unless thought about and processed, can make the person projected into re-enact some of the feelings that originated in another source. If there is no possibility that the projected-into receptacle of these emotions can reflect on or 'digest' the material to facilitate recognition and understanding, they remain raw and unprocessed and can continue to circulate between people and whole social systems (Hinshelwood and Skogstad, 2000; Menzies Lyth,

1960). As defended researchers ourselves, we are trained to be reflexive about our own backgrounds and experiences to better contain, think about and feed back, in more digestible form, the anxious emotion surrounding research as a psycho-social encounter. And this is extremely important and helpful to understanding.

But, we might ask, just as our research participants may be using *us* as containers of split-off anxious emotions, how are we using them? How might our research subjects and objects of inquiry be fulfilling an at least partly emotional function for us? Just as we might become the containers of our research participants' split-off emotions, so too might our research 'objects' become containers for ours, and I would argue that some of the stipulations to be 'dispassionate' can mean that this is more likely to occur. Through such processes, our research and research objects may be functioning not only as objects of sociological inquiry but as psycho-social containers of the parts of ourselves we might more usefully own and be curious about, rather involving ourselves in projects which surreptitiously express what we often, at least partially, if not wholly, share with others. This kind of splitting off – from our own emotional interests as these that are rooted in, say, our formative experiences and veiled by our research pursuits – can be debilitating and demotivating. Being in touch with ourselves in our research has the potential to bring our research and our writing back to life.

And yet we can balk at the possibility because sometimes it is easier to dress up our research as a quest to understand the experiences of *others* who appear to be far worse off than us. It is the dodgy thinking of the middle-class philanthropist – a ghostly spectre of the social researcher from days of yore. Our projects can then be obstructed by the more difficult to own feelings of pity, sadness, fear, disgust, contempt and irritation, and these feelings can tell something us of ourselves and the places in which we grew up. Social research is laced through with (small- and large-*p*) political interests, discourses, socially constructed phenomena and power inequalities and dynamics felt viscerally but rarely brought to the surface and discussed openly with others. Those things, places, concepts and people we think are interesting to research are usually the by-product of something else, in the desire to reach out and make life better – or, more troubling, unwittingly involving us in cruel and unjust political and social processes. As an unintentional, unconscious, dimension of our better motives, 'othered' people can become the objects of our scholarly research, as if they and all they represented were to be found outside ourselves. What arrogance then to pursue, instead, those apparently 'socially just inquiries' which can only speak of and to our liberality and kindness.

To recap, what and who we observe – what stands out as interesting for us, from the social landscapes that surround us – is bound up with the deeper questions we have about *our own as well as others' experiences*. In this we are interdependent, relational and fundamentally social; we draw on and use each other, sometimes without being aware – simply because it is easier to focus our attention on social problems we have put into others to contain, and then we can, rather outrageously, research them. Sometimes our research can falter or get stuck because of the unrecognised emotions underlying it.

Affective places

As we have seen in both Ken's and Daniel's stories, places too, the settings of our research and the settings of our own upbringings, carry in memory and in the present not thought about emotions or affects – which often float miasma-like in and around the people and places we frequent: 'waiting for a speaker or a thinker'. They might entice, repel, resonate – draw people together or separate or more positively, if policies and physical planning allow, provide space for people to go about their individual lives in creative ways (Winnicott, 1991), to play and work. They comprise the social relationships which dominate the meaning we invest in them as well as the experiences we take from them and express creatively (Bollas, 1992). In some ways they come to shape our characters and the nature of the infinite questions we ask (Bollas, 2009) and, we might also include here, our choices of study and our research questions. But there may be material forged from our psycho-social and material worlds which is sometimes too difficult to talk, research or write about – because of embarrassment, shame, fear and dread, all by-products of power processes and discourses which also include academia. Instead of questioning these processes, as Gordon writes, we can get caught up in haunting distractions. There is a tendency in academic research method to focus only on what can be rigidly tied down, categorised and measured – subjected to a series of methodological techniques which may distort further the often elusive, albeit very real, dimensions of social life. To illustrate the point, Gordon refers to Luce Irigaray's response to a question put to her about the social research methods she had chosen for her thesis; Irigaray replied:

> A delicate question. For isn't it the method, the path to knowledge, that has always also led us away, led us astray, by fraud and artifice
>
> *(Irigaray, 1985: 150; cited in Gordon, 2008: 39)*

As an at least partial distraction, Daniel's research inquiries had focused his attention on those who experienced dislocation, restlessness, homelessness, exile and then a bid to escape from false selves and repressed emotions which felt as if they vibrated in the streets and scenes of childhood:

> *. . . a suburban street, dull inter-war housing, set routines, father's car in the drive, two trees outside . . . darkness of the interior, the smell . . . something a bit cramped about it . . . my parents stuff . . . not particularly good furniture, attempts to make things solid, books, Robinson Crusoe, Jane Austen, not read . . . the drinks cabinet with chintzy glasses . . . mock cut glass that nobody drank out of . . .*

The memory may be a screen memory, as described by Phillips, but there is a bid in the memory, and its association with some sociological research, to learn of something else about a more fully embodied psycho-social experience.

Similarly, Ken's choice of study had been influenced somewhere by the experiences, feelings and memories of an uncared for and desecrated council flat, a 'shitty staircase and a broken down, urine filled lift' – memories and experiences Ken wanted to escape from through his own historical inquiries into other people's histories, including those who had historically acquired some sense of right to judge people like him.

For both, research and study choices represent a disguised, albeit creatively pursued, quest for understanding something which has not been thought about, understood or questioned.

Some unfinished research

Some years ago I was interested in pursuing research into the working-class culture of my youth, particularly the experiences surrounding the impact of the local economy, gendered labour markets, work-places, lack of work. There were practical considerations – time and money – and in order to pursue this work I would need to spend large amounts of time in the place of my formative years. But, when I refer to 'where I grew up', I am also talking about things I might observe in other areas which have drawn me to questions which have a basis in my earlier experience, but which somehow, unexpectedly and unconsciously, I have tended to move away from.

I had been particularly interested in the sociology of work because, somewhere, my experiences of work and labour markets and the cultures which had framed them had been painful to me as a young woman. Such experiences might be thought of as a facet of the 'un-thought known', the known but un-thought-about material which requires a thinker and someone to speak it (Bollas, 1989). Where I was brought up, this un-thought known included the difficulties of staying with, thinking about and understanding experiences of social injustice, inequality and poverty, and the feelings of systemic anger, felt in daily chauvinistic encounters, racial and homophobic prejudice and generalised misogyny of 1970s working-class culture, fuelled by authoritarian, conservative and unenlightened economic and educational policies of the area.

Not thinking about it but reacting to it, I took physical and emotional flight from the formative area of my youth and into a long string of tedious, low-paid jobs in different parts of the country, including London where I searched for answers to questions through other people and books. Eventually I joined various political causes before channelling my energies into night-school, university, research and teaching.

Luckily, there were people I found whom I could relate to – much better, whom I could connect with – people who also questioned the worlds around them; and theirs were the insights I gained from important scholarly research. Rather, like Beedell's (2009) colleague, I was given a language, concepts for thinking about what I came to understand as not unique to me, those experiences of estrangement and alienation – books critiquing capitalism, books based on research on gender and work. There was also was excitement in my reading of scholarly research which offered ideas to make sense of my surroundings.

Books, the outcome of rigorously pursued scholarly social research and intellectual inquiry, were powerful vehicles and containers for thinking about my
experiences, and my desire to teach and research was inspired by the ways in
which such inquiries could spark interest and take my thinking and experience
in a different direction, my own research, teaching to convey something of the
impact of inequality on people – the importance of social research for understanding the broader social dimension of experiences which, without that social
understanding, could only be experienced as personal. But, it also feels important
to note – through this writing process – just how much I have denied personal
experiences, believing, like Daniel, that to focus on such things would be self-
indulgent; and, a bit like Daniel, my curiosity in the formative experiences of
workplaces, and the questions which related to them, got overwhelmed by feelings
of boredom and impatience.

Uncontained and un-containing places (places of stress, of deprivation, of
neglect) often return the raw material as the experience of the uncanny (Freud,
1919) – experienced by people, unthinkingly, as haunting (Gordon, 2008), hysteri-
cally funny, psychotically busy, manically angry or downright depressing because
they partly reflect our own denied feelings and the feelings left by others, invested
in or disinvested in the material and things which make up a place. Stuff that gets
buried resides somewhere in a kind of collective unconscious.

As Bereswill *et al.* (2010) have indicated in their discussion of the work of Lorenzer, the feelings of unsymbolised scenic experience makes itself felt in the form of
somatised symptoms enactments, projective identifications, repetition compulsions
and so forth (Bereswill *et al.*, 2010). They demand 'to re-enter consciousness . . .
forms of life [*Lebensformen*], whose access to general consciousness has been barred'
(Lorenzer, 1986: 28).

Something I now understand was lurking behind these surface feelings of
boredom – were those which have been more difficult to bear, more akin to related
feelings of barely repressed rage in the ether of the area in which I grew up –
was signalled by the excessive number of speed cameras and surveillance systems
dominating the skyline – entities, I thought when I visited recently, reminiscent of
creatures from *War of the Worlds,* weirdly vibrating the un-thought, barely repressed,
manic rage signalled by high-speed, drunk driving.

My associations and the metaphors I am drawing on here also convey a message
about my movement away from an original interest in the rawer emotions underpinning an interest in the sociology of work, to what came to be the research of my
PhD and later publications – the sociology of management and management discourse – questions not so much about the experiences associated with low-skilled
work and reduced aspirations, more to do with the mechanisms by which some
of those experiences and emotions are managed rather than fully recognised and
thought through, and in so being managed are perpetuated. And so, somewhere,
my own emotions of formative work experiences and what might have been more
lively inquiries had somehow been overly managed in related, interesting but,

on some level, dulled and distracting research inquiries – those focused on management thought. Eventually I stopped writing about management thought and became interested in psychoanalysis and psycho-social inquiry.

Management thought acquires additional symbolic and emotional significance when thought about in the context of the containment of more difficult emotions surrounding my formative and gendered labour market experiences. Somewhere my own feelings of rage and my acts of rebellion got forgotten, channelled into research on management. It is not that I think this research was unimportant – but it was, in a way, fairly removed from the experiences that drew me towards an interest in the broader experiences and some of the emotions surrounding low-paid, monotonous work. While it was important for me to think about the mechanisms and dynamics surrounding management techniques and discourses, ironically, *management thought* (ambiguously referring also to my own thinking) may have played some role over the years in distracting me from being in touch with, hearing about and thinking about unjust social and economic policies impinging on everyday working lives and culture.

Finding another research voice

I am trying to say here that it is important to be in touch with the more difficult to own aspects of our situated emotional selves – yes, to register our better motives in our inquiries, but not to split off and deny feelings which are harder to express and which can stunt our intellectual and creative inquiries. It may be that, during those times we get stuck in our writing and research, there may be other related, distracting things which exhaust and then de-motivate us in our emotional struggles surrounding not attending to them. Not researching where we grew up may be a facet of some difficult truths, and our bids to inquire into other things through our research inquiries can be functioning, emotionally, as a screen or veil which, if we are brave enough to attempt to lift it, might reconnect us to our both shared and different practical, imagined, dreamed and embodied social endeavours.

Scholarly, dispassionate, research has an important part to play in developing conceptual tools for meaning-making, to think critically about experiences of those of us otherwise dominated by particular narratives and discourses. Research and writing can touch lives by providing a language to describe and analyse subjective and collectively held knowledge and in this sense has the potential to be educative. Being attentive to our emotional involvements can also tell us something of the repressed histories and power dynamics which get in the way of us asking more socially and politically difficult questions. In this way, the interweaving of subjectivity, including embodied experiences and the emotions of inequality, with the task of naming, conceptualising and theorising takes us away from solipsism towards shared understanding and critique. Something different is happening through the process of writing for this book – I am reconsidering my research inquiries and feeling again an interest in something put aside. I am reconnecting with the importance of publically engaged social research and practices which encourage linking up research, experience and emotions, because, like Daniel, I am reconnecting with the questions relating to where we grew up.

The mind-forg'd manacles I hear.

Conclusion

I believe that emotional knowledge we carry reflects some collective experiences which have sometimes been ignored, sidelined, dismissed and/or treated with contempt. Scholarly inquiry can function as an important container and vehicle for our more difficult emotional experiences but also, if too rigidly adhered to, can distract us from the very reasons we choose to research, or not, especially those social and political issues entwined in embodied, emotional experience. In other words, research can sometimes screen the more fundamental, embodied, questions which our more traditional 'scholarly' approaches only superficially touch upon. Being disconnected from our more emotionally laden (especially those that are most difficult to own) questions which derive from our humanity and connectedness can result in feelings of boredom, futility and de-motivation – perhaps because of the emotionally deadening and/or exhausting diversions into surface stories. This is partly to do with what we find difficult to contain within ourselves and those difficult to contain aspects of our culture – the things we are discouraged from talking about, researching, those aspects of cultural life which we are made to register as uniquely, sometimes pathologically, personal.

I regard writing for this book as containing space for thinking about a process which feels both deeply personal and socially important to rethink psycho-social processes surrounding our formative experiences and which may be struggling to find expression in our research choices and our choosing not to research them.

In this sense, it is important to draw attention to the unconscious plea which may lie beneath our narrations, and also our research questions. The plea behind Ken's choice of study was that people like him should be recognised and esteemed. The plea underlying Daniel's inquiry is related to a need to understand the pain of dislocation and exile from a world which was immersed in an oppressive home territory, now symbolically carried by the 'refugee'. My own inquiries have veiled a need for understanding of bewilderment and confusion and fear surrounding people's immersion in harsh working environments and cultures which vitiate thought and which I experienced as the pain of not being able to fit in and not knowing how to, or understanding why and how other people could. But in not pursuing my earlier interests, particularly those working experiences of my formative years and the culture surrounding them, I have, ironically, become immersed in dynamics which might represent a refusal to think – the very thing that led to me taking physical, emotional and intellectual flight.

Of course, there are likely to be far more complex processes involved, but it is interesting to begin to think about research choices themselves as playing the part of an emotional defence. Defences have an important part to play in our lives, and they can involve all kinds of creative pursuits. But they can also become rigid and counter-productive – the same might be applied as much to our research as to our more general emotional and private lives.

I have attempted to show here that in the subliminal, perhaps more simple, demands behind the research and study choices represented here is a plea to begin a process of dialogue about what we share and have shared, to reinstate ourselves into the experiences of confusion, exclusions, shame and denigrations underlying our research choices. If we can be a bit more in touch with the feelings behind those choices, we might be less inclined to objectify others and deaden our own inquiries.

There has been much written about the methodological benefits attaching to reflexivity, the importance, for example, of acknowledging potential biases within our research which obfuscate, limit and potentially undermine the pursuit of the truths – the class-infused objective structures, symbols and cultures – we attempt to capture in the very process of denying them. Attention to emotions surrounding and underlying our research can, if carefully considered, draw our attention to the symbolic violence in which we may sometimes unwittingly, unconsciously participate. Moreover, attention to the emotions surrounding our experience can also help us engage in meaningful inquiry into experiences of others which may resonate with, but also be different from, our own. The use of our own subjectivity in research can, quite rationally, help us think about our own experiences and questions in *relation with* others who we share something with by virtue of being social and relational subjects. We share histories, cultures, spaces – albeit in our different ways. As Letherby *et al.* (2013) have argued, appropriate attention to our own situated subjectivities can help bridge the false dichotomies set up between subjective and objective research. It is an approach which also allows us to register the fact that our research endeavours to capture truth are always in *process* – always the result of interpretation, meaning-making which comes from dialogue, rather than the end result, a claim of ultimate truth.

References

Beedell, P. (2009) Charting the clear waters and the murky depths, in Clarke, S., and Hoggett, P. (eds.) *Researching Beneath the Surface: Psycho-Social Research Methods in Practice*, London: Karnac.

Bereswill, M., Morgenroth, C., and Redman, P. (2010) Alfred Lorenzer and the depth-hermeneutic method, *Psychoanalysis, Culture & Society* 15: 221–250.

Bollas, C. (1989) *The Shadow of the Object: Psychoanalysis of the Unthought Known*, New York: Columbia University Press.

Bollas, C. (1992) *Being a Character: Psychoanalysis and Self-Experience*, London: Routledge.

Bollas, C. (2009) *The Infinite Question*, Sussex: Routledge.

Bourdieu, P. (1977) *Outline of a Theory of Practice*, Edinburgh: Cambridge University Press.

Clarke, S., and Hoggett, P. (eds.) (2009) *Researching Beneath the Surface: Psycho-Social Research Methods in Practice*, London: Karnac.

Freud, S. (2001). *The 'Uncanny'*. In *The Standard Edition of the Complete Psychological Works of Sigmund Freud, Volume XVII (1917–1919): An Infantile Neurosis and Other Works,* London: Vintage, 217–256.

Freud, S. (2001). *The 'Uncanny'*. In *The Standard Edition of the Complete Psychological Works of Sigmund Freud, Volume XVII (1917–1919): An Infantile Neurosis and Other Works,* London: Vintage: 217–256.

Gordon, A. (2008) *Ghostly Matters: Haunting and the Sociological Imagination*, London: University of Minnesota Press.

Hinshelwood, R., and Skogstad, W. (2000) *Observing Organisations: Anxiety, Defence and Culture in Healthcare*, London: Routledge.

Hollway, W., and Jefferson, T. (2000) *Doing Qualitative Research Differently: Free Association, Narrative and the Interview Method*, London: Sage Publications.

Irigaray, L. (1985) *The Sex Which Is Not One*. Ithaca: Cornell University Press.

Klein, M. (1946) Notes on some schizoid mechanisms, *International Journal of Psycho-Analysis*, 27: 99–110.

Letherby, G., Scott, J., and Williams, M. (2013) *Objectivity and Subjectivity in Social Research*, London: Sage.

Lorenzer, Alfred (1986) Tiefenhermeneutische Kulturanalyse [In-depth hermeneutic cultural analysis]. In Alfred Lorenzer (ed.) *KulturAnalysen: Psychoanalytische Studien zur Kultur*. Frankfurt: Fischer.

Menzies Lyth, E. (1960) Social systems as a defence against anxiety, reprinted in du Gay, P., Evans, J., and Redman, P. (eds.) (2000) *Identity: A Reader*, London: Sage: 163–182.

Phillips, A. (1994) *On Flirtation*, London: Faber and Faber.

Scanlon, C., and Adlam, J. (2008) Refusal, social exclusion and the cycle of rejection: A *cynical* analysis? *Critical Social Policy* 28(4): 529–549.

Smart, C. (2011) Families, secrets and memories, *Sociology* 45(4): 539–553.

Winnicott, D.W. (1991) *Playing and Reality*, London: Routledge.

9

TALES FROM POST-FIELD WORK

Writing up; vivas; conferences; and publications

Caroline Clarke

In this chapter we will look briefly at concepts of identity and emotion work, psychoanalytic defence mechanisms, and the existential meaning of what 'we do' to consider how these frameworks inform our understanding of the emotions experienced in the 'aftermath' of field work. As we have seen so far in the book, *doing* research can be fraught with difficulties and challenges, as well as delightful discoveries and encounters, but, once field work ends, it is perhaps just the start of another (equally) challenging series of experiences, for it must be analysed, written up, defended, presented and, if we are lucky, published. Of course these activities should come as no surprise (although they often do) since there is limited value in doing research if we are not going to share it, but the thought of doing so is often (but not necessarily) fraught with feelings of trepidation as well as excitement.

Although this chapter focuses on the 'aftermath' or final stage of research, it is of course part of the research process itself as, following months/years of life spent collecting data, something now has to be done with it, to translate it into some form of 'output'. However, this process provokes considerable feelings of insecurity and anxiety, not least because it invokes a number of questions which have to be confronted: 'is anybody interested in what I have done?'; 'am I saying anything worthwhile?'; and 'how on earth can I write this/present it in the format required?' All such deliberations form part of an attempt to secure our identities as 'competent' researchers, for it is argued that identities rather than 'given' are perpetually under construction, something to 'achieve if we are to have one at all, and ... must continue to achieve if we are to maintain it' (Schwartz, 1987: 328). I suggest that the 'work' we do on our identities is also bound up tightly with feelings of insecurity, self-doubt and uncertainty (Knights & Willmott, 1989) which is ultimately self-defeating since identity can never be secured in this way.

Part of establishing ourselves as competent researchers is perhaps to find meaning and success in what we 'do' all day, in order to provide some distraction from existential concerns and our own finitude (Sartre, 1943; Becker, 1971). Alongside this, we are experiencing research as a messy, unpredictable and emotional activity, and yet this is often at odds with the (Western) portrayal of a rational and linear process and a series of steps to be fulfilled for a satisfactory 'output'. Of course for some research and some researchers, these steps may well be how it goes, particularly in terms of conducting and writing up research that is highly structured – for example, when conducting quantitative and experimental work – although it is also likely to have its fair share of ambiguities. In any case, I think that if you are one of the people for whom research is incredibly straightforward, you are probably in the minority, and it is unlikely that you will be reading this book.

We now turn briefly to a more conceptual account of some of these ideas before drawing on some vignettes and specific experiences around research.

Conceptually speaking

As this book has already highlighted, and at the risk of being tediously repetitive, most research and methodology texts largely eschew or marginalize the emotional element of research, presenting and constructing it almost exclusively as a rational, masculine and cognitive enterprise. In common with many other activities, research is often written and spoken about in an emotionally 'anorexic' fashion (Fineman, 1993) with 'alexithymic' tendency (Brannan, 2011), as 'there remains something of a silence surrounding *researchers'* own emotional experiences' (Kenny, 2008: 376). This is the case particularly in methodology textbooks where the experience of researching seems to be almost entirely erased.

Research is intimately bound up with who we are and what we feel, so it may seem odd to suggest that we should have to 'work' on our identities or emotions while researching, because aren't these simply 'who we are'? But who are we exactly? Are we not different things to different people? Do I act or behave in the same way to a group of peers as I do to my children or my parents, or my dentist? However I act in front of these different audiences, it is unlikely to be totally consistent or predictable, yet consistency and predictability are the cornerstones of *personality* profiling, the measuring and boxing in of emotions within efficient labelling systems: introvert, 'thinker', 'feeler' – and yet somehow it all seems a bit too neat. *Identity* studies on the other hand are less inclined to assign personality traits or enduring non-physical attributes (these are labelled *essentialist* properties) to people. Instead identity studies frame particular ways of acting as part of a role (social psychology), or they construct identity as a fleeting and dynamic performance that can only ever be 'a matter of claims, not character; persona, not personality; and presentation, not self' (Ybema *et al.*, 2009: 306). Similarly a growing body of emotion theory argues that emotions are more of an 'outside-in' affair than 'inside-out' (Clarke & Fineman, 2009) as they are always relational (Waldron, 2000) – so relative to some*one* or some*thing*. Emotions, then, are not just inside us all waiting to be unleashed or discovered, but are dynamically embedded in relationships:

> emotions are not 'things' internal to the individual and their biological construction, but are to do with the social relations and interdependencies between people.
>
> *(Burkitt, 1997: 52)*

Whether certain emotions are universal is a topic of debate, although some scholars claim that there are 'basic' or primary emotions such as anger, envy, guilt, love, for example (Ekman, 1992). However, in this chapter I see the meaning and interpretation of any biological component of emotion as socially constructed so they are always shaped, guided, influenced, expressed (and disguised) through a social sieve of 'display' (Rafaeli & Sutton, 1987) or 'feeling' (Fineman, 1993; 2000) rules or cultural norms. For example, cultural norms such as masculinity determine the legitimacy of displaying particular emotions so that in an advertising house or acting school emotions are likely to be looser and less prescriptive than those in more formal arenas like an accountancy firm. In short, the kind of emotions we can express or must suppress will vary by and within certain segments of society, culture and country.

Emotion work is 'the effort we put into ensuring that our private feelings are suppressed or represented to be in tune with socially accepted norms – such as looking happy and enthusiastic at a friend's party when we actually feel tired or bored' (Fineman, 1993: 3). The commercial version – expressing or showing emotions that we don't necessarily 'feel' for a wage – is called emotional labour; for example, Hochschild's study (1983) looked at how cabin crew had to smile and look jolly for long periods of time to give customers the impression of enjoying their work while 'on stage'. Much of what we 'show' in public is the result of both identity and emotion work, as we seek to present ourselves in ways which might disguise what we (or others) might regard as *ugly truths*. In his seminal work *The Presentation of Self in Everyday Life,* Goffman (1959) writes at length about these ideas and the intricate rules bound up with the public presentation of the self. Here is an example of a researcher carrying out emotional labour to present a 'professional' self for the audience:

> *I was due to do my third set of interviews for my PhD when I got a call to say the dog had died. I was sad, and sadder that I wasn't there to tell the kids, or be with them when they found out. My participants didn't know me, and I was pretty sure they didn't want to hear about a dead dog as it would have just been uncomfortable for us all. Instead I put on a warm welcoming smile and entered the interview room. I am sure that the interview appeared to be just like any other, and they did not suspect that I was partially absent.*

Goffman's dramaturgical theory proposes that the notion of a successful performance is where the audience finds it believable in a way that is intended by the actors and without any noticeable disruption. Secrets must therefore be hidden, and the actor must be careful to 'accentuate certain matters and conceal others' (Goffman, 1959: 74) to maintain the performance.

With these ideas in mind, I want to explore some of the experiences which present themselves after our field work is over, and this work is presented under a number of different headings: the trouble with writing; that's me in the spotlight; the show must go on; and publish or perish?

The trouble with writing

> Every writer I know has trouble writing.
>
> Joseph Heller

Does it help to realize that we are not alone with feelings of inadequacy or of being overwhelmed? Recent research by Knights and Clarke (2014) explored how academics felt about their jobs in terms of the meanings they attached to work, and how competent they felt they were. Reassuringly, or perhaps disturbingly, the study found that most academics from lecturers through to well-established professors were insecure about many elements of their work, including whether their work was really good enough. Here are a couple of excerpts from their study about the difficulties experienced when writing, and the fear of ones' writing being inadequate:

> I have this sense of not writing anything that's worth reading . . . I read stuff and think 'bloody hell. I can't write like that'. . . .
>
> *(Senior Lecturer)*

> I feel that somebody's going to wake up and say 'oh, it's her', you-know, 'how come she's doing that? I remember her – she was rubbish'. So I think there is an element of doubt sometimes in everything.
>
> *(Senior Lecturer)*

One idea Knights and Clarke used in their work on academics was *the imposter syndrome* (Clance, 1985) – a belief that one is not as capable or adequate as others may perceive them to be. Aside from feelings of intellectual phoniness, imposter syndrome also includes thoughts that any success is down to luck. High-achieving individuals are said to be prone to this syndrome, which also includes a fear that one's incompetence will soon be discovered (September *et al.*, 2001). Knights and Clarke (2014) found that imposter beliefs were rife in academia, as were feelings of inadequacy, insecurity and self-doubt. Unlike much of the work on imposter syndrome though, they argued that these feelings are not a deviance from the norm, or a pathological problem, but merely a result of what Freud (1914) termed *ego ideals*: the idealised images we hold associated with perfection and which inform and guide our aspirations. I suspect that an honest account of most occupations and activities would produce similar findings and emotions, so it is important to remember that feelings of inferiority in tackling a big (or small) piece of writing are all too common, and appear to be perfectly 'normal'. After all, our research becomes very precious to us and therefore can soon feel like 'high stakes' because it is the fruit of much labour, blood, sweat and tears, and can never live up to our ideals.

The process of writing can seem devilishly intimidating at the outset, as Woody Allen is alleged to have said, 'Ninety per cent of the success of writing depends on getting started and finishing on time'. Perhaps this advice resonates with most of us since procrastination is an effective technique in never getting started, or finished. Undoubtedly this is an example of an unconscious *defence mechanism* (Freud) in the sense that denial is a protection of the self against judgement. Of course, 'rationally' there is no reason why we should not want to get started except, as Dawson suggests,

> not beginning protects you from the disappointment – no shame – of reading what you have written and finding it rubbish. . . . Success or failure can both be avoided by never starting at all – this then is the spell that procrastination casts.
>
> *(2012: 4)*

Such experiences, however, are too commonly eschewed in the 'on track' and rational/logical 'how to' research books. Consider the following (somewhat unpalatable) advice in this excerpt from the chapter 'writing up the research':

> Writing up often presents the greatest challenge to research students, but it is made somewhat easier if you have been writing notes and rough drafts throughout the period of the research. If you are a Ph.D. student and have put off writing until your final year, you are likely to encounter major difficulties or even failure.
>
> *(Collis & Hussey, 2003: 281)*

Such advice is of course not reassuring if you have put off your writing, but in contrast to this view, a major thread in this book is the idea that feeling 'off-track' rather than 'on track' is perhaps a far more common experience (even if you have been making rough drafts). Our view here of the 'point' of writing can sometimes also be mechanistic and narrow, as Richardson observes,

> I consider writing as a method of inquiry, a way of finding out about yourself and your topic. Although we usually think about writing as a mode of 'telling' about the social world, writing is not just a mopping-up activity at the end of a research project. Writing is also a way of 'knowing' – a method of discovery and analysis. By writing in different ways, we discover new aspects of our topic and relationship to it.
>
> *(1998: 345)*

This point is illustrated by the next vignette, which comes from a doctoral student who carried out a critical inquiry into her role of senior manager. The study was deeply reflexive, using methods including autobiographical inquiry and the use of a reflective work journal. The inquiry led to a 'deconstruction' of self in role at work and the value conflicts and pragmatic compromises inherent in self-governance. It was thus an exploration of identity that was quite painful as the research progressed. This vignette introduces the related and often-felt emotion held by researchers – that of feeling 'blocked', which could again be interpreted as another type of defence mechanism to avoid further pain; however, it also illustrates the importance of the capacity to 'stay with' emotion in the research process, with the prospect that deeper insights into self as researcher, and into the phenomena being researched, might emerge:

> *After three years' work, I experienced a 'block' and ceased most levels of work on the research for some months, apart from some reading. During this three to four month 'block' there were times when I lost confidence and assumed that I might not be able to return to the research in the same way again, but I had a more persistent intuition that this enforced respite had some purpose and that I would 'return' to my research. This experience stimulated my interest in the power of Keat's concept of 'negative capability' to inform a fuller understanding of qualitative research. This type of 'block' is not an uncommon experience for research students – but I had some insights about the emotional nature of this 'block' when it was over and I found that I took up my research project with increased drive and, importantly, openness to a more enhanced critical approach. It appeared to me that this 'block' had been an emotional respite – a form of effective emotional dissociation. It had not simply been a 'resting period' but it led to greater comfort with a more critical approach to issues surrounding construction of the self. This relatively fallow period appeared to increase my critical capacity by providing space to enable some form of unconscious 'shift' to take place.*

In this vignette we see the fine line between creative pleasure and pain. Writer's block can make one feel powerless to do anything, as frustration mounts and words refuse to come. The harder one tries (and I speak from experience here), the worse it can be as anxieties and insecurities come to the fore; the art of writing is necessarily both creative and unpredictable so it disregards the need to conform to any 'plan' or schedule which has been drawn up. We can view such tension in terms of the artificial rational–emotional dichotomy, as the experience appears to confound the seemingly logical expectations of the writer. This frustration and anxiety relating to 'writer's block' is palpable in the following extract from one PhD student:

> *The only noise is the tap tap tap of the pen on the desk. This is the sole activity in the room. I stare blankly, paralysed with fear, the words do not come, stubbornly refusing to appear on my screen, unable to leave my head, continuing to go round and round like a washing machine. I want to scream, there is nobody to ask, nobody except me is doing this PhD; yes they ask me (bewildered) 'how is that PhD going?' But nobody understands, not even me. I am alone, alone with (out) my thoughts. As the hours tick by I become increasingly desperate, and feel worthless. What have I achieved today? I have got nothing to show for myself.*

Here we see how the author is attempting to impose a rational and linear frame-work on the activity of writing. Increasingly desperate, isolated and anxious in her writing (or lack of it), she attempts to reconstruct this as a logical activity which must result in regular, productive and visible output in order to be 'worthwhile'. This desire for achievement and maximising one's own potential is tied intimately to ideals of self-discipline, which as Foucault (1982; 1984) argues may be one of the most onerous modes of self-regulation. The illusion of following the so-called success ethic can trap us into relentless strivings for unrealizable achievements and constant feelings of dissatisfaction. In addition, the student in the vignette con-structs herself as being deviant from an idealised norm ('on track'), yet as Heller's quote indicates, writing is like that for very few people – indeed this is arguably an *idealized* view of writing, or even a *fantasy* of how we would like the process of writing to be. Since the majority of people who write do not appear to be 'on track', perhaps we need to revise our own expectations of the art of writing, seeing it instead as an extremely frustrating, anxiety provoking, complex but potentially joyful process, rather than a simple unidirectional linear and rational task. Such dominant views of rationality as efficient and effective routes to the achievement of output are deeply rooted in Western ideals which rest on the notion that emotion *interferes* with these laudable aims: whether consciously or unconsciously, most peo-ple believe that emotions are messy, unproductive and interfere with clear thought (Plas and Hoover-Dempsey, 1988).

Fineman (2000) argues that emotion is ubiquitously positioned as *interfering* with rationality, or alternatively *serving* rationality (allowing us to make intuitive decisions where there is too much information). He suggests instead that they are actually *interpenetrated* since pure cognitions or pure emotions do not exist, so thinking is never feeling-free, and feeling is never thinking-free. Surfacing and reframing this artificial dichotomy of rationality and emotionality is an important part of understanding the tensions which their separation provokes, and allows us to provide an alternative notion whereby they are enmeshed seamlessly (Domagal-ski, 1999). This also means that neither term assumes greater importance over its opposite other, for dualistic oppositions are often regarded as hierarchical in their interpretation (Derrida, 1978).

In the following excerpt, Marilyn Strathern illustrates how the recognition of one's emotion can help:

> *I write all the time, but what marks off new tasks from old (or going over old ground) is finding myself plunged into something close to despair. I lose confidence, my self-esteem plummets, it is clear that everyone has already said things better, and it had been quite absurd to take on a task that now seems insuperable. . . . An air of unreality hangs over my beginning efforts, though if I am lucky that can temporarily clear by my hanging the argument on someone's else words (you know how real other people's words appear, solid and sensible things as they are!), just as I began this piece. It depends how much time I have as to what kind of panic may also accompany this lack of nerve. . . .*

[I] have begun to understand what falling down this gap does. It is a moment of dissolution, when past certainties melt away, and everything one thought was at one's fingertips (materials, notes, analyses) slips out of grasp. For myself, at least, it is climbing out of the crevasse, emotionally speaking, that is the writing. . . . The process of writing is dealing with the crisis.

(excerpt taken from www.dur.ac.uk/ writingacrossboundaries/writingonwriting/)

Here, Strathern describes how her depression actually facilitates her creativity and ability to progress. In common with many other tasks, once we have endured or overcome the challenges of writing, it can ultimately bring joy, exhilaration and an incredible sense of accomplishment. Writing is not only a function but also an aesthetically creative process which moves beyond ideas of pure cognition because 'some emotional reactions, such as the joy of being deeply "into" a task . . . the pleasure/pain principles that can attend aesthetic creation or art appreciation, defy a simple cognitive-appraisal analysis' (Fineman, 2000: 12). This is similar in many ways to Csikszentmihalyi's idea of flow (1990) whereby (artistic or creative) experiences are accompanied by such intense feelings of concentration and absorption that any concerns over issues of materiality such as food and drink are disregarded. Of course, where a 'block' continues, the opposite may occur, since eating and drinking offer a (temporary) escape from confronting the difficulty, or simply provide a displacement activity.

Writing is sometimes a tedious and painstakingly slow process which perhaps researchers may not appreciate or find hard to accept. Here a researcher talks about the diligence, dedication and patience involved in his writing and how he allows himself permission to take time over his craft:

I can easily spend a morning writing a paragraph. This may seem over the top to some people but I keep going until it feels right. What that means is that it looks and sounds as beautiful as it can be. That is a good morning's work, in my opinion.

It is a commonly held view that nobody is a good writer, only a good re-writer or editor, and therefore to finesse and craft text elegantly an iterative process is necessary. Writers may not anticipate having to practice and hone their craft in the same way that, say, concert musicians or artists need to repeatedly refine their craft.

Do it everyday; don't worry about whether it's the posh kind or for fun; try different ways of doing it; think of it as a skill, like wall-papering or baking or plumbing but requiring less dexterity.

(Stanley, www.dur.ac.uk/writingacrossboundaries/writingonwriting/)

In practice, the continuity of process and repetition bears little resemblance to the prescriptive step 1, step 2 and step 3 approach commonly advocated in *'how to'* textbooks, which only appear to reinforce unrealistic and idealized expectations, privileging rational processes which eschew and 'write out' setbacks, blind alleys, despair, confusion and frustration – precisely the emotions we are seeking to demystify here. The endless frustration of refining something which never appears to be actually 'finished' can also be exhausting, as well as bewildering, as this researcher describes:

> In the book 'the elves and the shoemakers' the tailor goes to bed one night and gets up in the morning to see that some beautiful shoes have been crafted by the elves. With my writing, it's like the antithesis of this. I go to bed with what I think is an elegantly written page of text, and somehow in the night it changes into a stilted piece of clunky prose so that when I turn my computer on in the morning I think 'who on earth wrote that?'. When I look at the page, it's almost as though I cannot believe I had previously thought this was good.

Apart from *how* to write, there is also a concern with *what* to write, particularly when making decisions about large amounts of qualitative data. How can we say it all? In the introduction to *One Way Street,* Susan Sontag says of Benjamin's writing, 'Each sentence is written as if it were the first, or the last . . . it was as if each sentence had to say everything' (Walter 1979: 24). However, Fletcher (2001) reminds us that even the most comprehensive of studies can only hope 'to tell one part of the story among many others that could be told' (p.8), and it is most important to understand that it is you the researcher who possesses both the power and the responsibility in deciding what to privilege and what to silence. The emotions of the researcher inform the type of accounts that will be constructed and should in no way be expected to be detached, separated out or excluded from the writing-up process because they shape, as well as reflect, what is said by the participants. There is no 'invisible hand' at work in crafting the research; there is only your own:

> The researcher composes the story; it does not simply unfold before the eyes of an objective viewer. The story reflects the viewer as well as the viewed.
>
> *(Charmaz, 2002: 515)*

In summary, writing is both a task and a creative process that cannot necessarily be planned in advance through a series of sequential steps. Although structure may help (or constrain) the writing, the emotional experience and feel of 'getting it right' is almost ineffable, especially when it is experienced as *flow* (Csikszentmihalyi, 1990). Writing is rarely an orderly progression, and constant re-reading and editing should be seen as the 'norm' rather than an exception.

We now turn to a section on defending our work, an experience which often comes after writing has been completed.

That's me in the spotlight

Once we have finished putting pen to paper, so to speak, and made some claims, or introduced some new ideas (our *contribution* to a field), we must submit our work and be prepared to defend it. This defence may take place in a number of forms, such as a *viva voce*, a conference paper, or a submission to a peer-reviewed journal. Whatever route is chosen, considerable trepidation often accompanies this experience. It is perhaps interesting then to reflect on the masculine connotations of the word *defend* – indicating combat, attack, war, defeat and doing battle. Of course there is also the implication here that, in defending our work, this may involve attacking the work of another, an individualised rather than collective approach within the scholarly community which also implies winners and losers. When we consider this language, it is not surprising that we may feel vulnerable or under siege in submitting our work for critique. Conversely, however, there will also be feelings of excitement that our research efforts are finally going to be shared with others. Ambivalence is a common experience as there can surely be few educational situations which provoke such anxiety as the *viva voce*. The potential for anguish over this is deep and multi-faceted, and imposter fears (I'm not good enough to gain a PhD) are common at this stage. These feelings can be reinforced by the fear or experience of rejection (by supervisors, or by internal or external examiners) or by the prospect of criticism and humiliation, stemming from anxiety over whether a 'proper' thesis or article has been produced. Students may also be concerned as to whether they have done justice to the voices of those who participated in the study, missed out key bits of literature, or even have not fully understood a great deal of what they have written. Such anxieties are bound up with notions of successful identities, of portraying a competent self, as well as the fear of being found lacking in one or many respects.

What appears to be ubiquitous (but by no means universal) is the intensity of feeling that surrounds the 'end' of the PhD or any research process. This is understandable since so much time and emotion has been invested over a long period of time, which means that stakes are high as failure is potentially devastating, both emotionally and professionally.

> *The funny thing was that once the machine started whirring to print out the God knows how many pages of the final version of my PhD, I felt a moment of sheer elation such that I momentarily squealed out loud and did a little dance around the room. This was quickly followed (literally about 30 seconds later) by terror – what if this final version had typos? What if by accident a few pages had been deleted. What if the formatting on the contents page had gone askew again. I wanted to look at it, to check, to drink from 'the poisoned well' but I also felt that I never wanted to see it again. I quickly drove to the University and handed it over in a cardboard box. I was racked with guilt – I felt like I had given a baby over for adoption. When I thought about the thesis on the way home I realised of course that it was all rubbish. It was all so obvious; how could I think it was good enough? I*

would be found out for sure, in the viva. The date loomed like an execution, I think I even wore black. I'd heard stories of course about people being locked into combat for seven or eight hours at a time. I walked in the room and they were both there, they smiled and looked encouraging but I braced myself and visibly stiffened as I prepared for the attack. I didn't get my PhD on the day but I got it 6 weeks later after a little more work, but the viva was nowhere near the sort of experience that I worried it would be. Horror stories abound, and in a state of vulnerability these naturally played on my mind.

This vignette illustrates how this PhD student fantasizes about her viva, concentrating on the negative aspects of what could go wrong so that it becomes not only probable but possible. In contrast the following viva experience tells a different story. It is also full of emotion, but this time they are in a less predictable form:

I entered the examiners' room for my viva, clutching my PhD thesis. I was actually more excited than nervous, psyched up for the event. I'd lived with the beast for around four years, and knew every word. But here was my chance to really engage with the only people in the world who had read it cover to cover, with whom I could explain and defend my ideas.

The two professors shook my hand, offered me a glass a water, and – congratulated me; I'd got my doctorate. I was baffled. Where were the testing questions? The debate? The arguments? I felt really cheated! Yes, they did then ask me some questions, and made a lot of the odd typos, but I felt a real sense of anti-climax. I wanted to fight my corner, but now what was the point? It was like knowing 'who did it' before reading a 'who done it'. Of course I was pleased to call myself 'Dr', but I really did want to play out the final act in the traditional way.

In this vignette we see the 'other side' of pre-viva emotions: the anticipation of the challenge and the excitement which replaces trepidation. The student is relishing an opportunity for intellectual sparring to discuss his ideas with those who are 'expert' in his field, but the whole experience falls short of the kind of ritual he was expecting, resulting in disappointment. While this account is necessarily partial, so we cannot appreciate the experience of the examiners, it does illustrate the wide range of possible and potential emotions on offer in this initiation ritual or *rites de passage*. Passing through this routine and transitional state does to some extent offer the student a confirmation of competence, although like all attempts to secure an identity the relief may be temporary before the next challenge is presented. Many students fix on the award of their Masters or PhD as the end of a process, which it is in one sense. Yet, it is also very often the start of another process such as building a career in academe, taking a post-doc research post or even getting a 'real' job.

In the penultimate section we will look at the process of presenting our work to others through talk, rather than text.

The show must go on

The live presentation of academic work almost always requires a performance which requires a particular show suitable for a particular audience (Goffman, 1959). The author (and academic) David Lodge writes in detail about the academic conference circuit in his book *Small World* (1984) in a way which portrays it as more of a circus than a show where the individual characters are often variously involved in scenes of politicking, drunkenness and romance. Lodge positions the conference as a form of academic 'jolly':

> It's June, and the conference season. . . . The whole academic world seems to be on the move. . . . For that's the attraction of the conference circuit: it's a way of converting work into play, combining professionalism with tourism, and all at someone else's expense.
>
> *(1984: 231)*

According to Lodge, the reality of going to a conference is less about the academic content and far more about 'networking' or schmoozing opportunities to liaise with colleagues and raise one's academic profile:

> it's this kind of informal contact of course that's the real *raison d'être* of a conference, not the programme of papers and lectures which has ostensibly brought the participants together, but which most of them find intolerably tedious.
>
> *(Lodge, 1984: 233–234)*

In practice most conference attendees congregate with the people they know, so only at the margins is networking going on – except for those who deliberately set out to do it. Since 1984, when Lodge wrote this book, the internet has facilitated perhaps more frequent virtual relationships and collaborative research with colleagues outside our own institutions. While conferences do still offer the opportunity for physical meetings, groupings can also consist of 'self-defining exclusive entities' (Lodge, 1984: 233) because of their masculine and 'gladiatorial' nature (Knights, 2006). So, while the conference experience can be an invigorating and inspiring event, it can also be a potentially marginalizing event for newcomers who are not yet well connected (Bell & King, 2010) and who can offer very little in terms of opportunities for advancement to others. The academic conference can also be an arena for point scoring, which can be made very public, as small agendas are played out, as this vignette from an established lecturer illustrates:

> *It had been a great conference – a small, really friendly and supportive arena where the 'great and the good' had offered only positive comments on how to improve the research presented. We filed in for the last session and like a grey cloud forming the atmosphere*

began to change. A senior academic was giving his paper. I'd been in a session with him the previous day where he had picked on a PhD student simply because he didn't like the kind of research he was doing and didn't like the university he was at.

He announced that he had changed the paper he was going to give. This is unusual. Often people might change their title or deviate a little from the submitted paper but this was altogether a different paper we'd not seen or read. It turned out to be a critique of a 2006 paper about identity which employed a methodology he didn't like. Gradually he read from a prepared script, dissecting the paper bit by bit. A deliberate disembowelment; a lion picking over the bones. We all listened in stunned silence.

When he finished nobody spoke. Finally my friend raised her hand, 'I feel like I've been hijacked' she said, 'you have presented a paper which feels like it is a personal attack on two people who aren't here to defend themselves with a critique which we haven't been able to read. I don't like the feel of that'. He stared at her, inscrutable, unreadable, and simply replied, 'I don't think that comment is even worthy of a reply'.

On one level this incident seems to connect well with Chapter 7 of this book as both politically and emotionally charged, and as a way of managing meaning to both 'create legitimacy' for oneself and at the same time 'de-legitimise' others (Hardy, 1994: 85). Although such extreme events are rare, it is these kinds of incidents at conferences which can fill inexperienced (and experienced) presenters with dread. After all, when presenting work at a conference, the presenter makes a claim towards some kind of familiarity with a body of knowledge, if not a degree of expertise in the subject. Since knowledge is infinite and we cannot know everything about anything, it is quite likely that many people in the room will know more than you do on the topic of your choice. This, as well as a possible fear of presenting in public, is one of the primary concerns that presenters have at conferences, for as Butler suggests we have 'a vulnerability to a sudden address from elsewhere that we cannot pre-empt' (2004: 29).

What is interesting is that few people will admit to fragility in public, the fear of 'out of control exposure' (Levinas, 1978). Why not? It would perhaps appear *unprofessional* and unpersuasive to stand up and apologise for our own inadequacies prior to presenting our work. Instead, presenters work hard to exercise iron control and assume the mask of competence (Goffman, 1959) in order to put on a good show without disruption (an example of both identity work and emotion work). No matter how terrified the performer is, the mask of competence must not slip to ensure 'success', because success means that the audience is left with an impression of the actor which the actor intended (Goffman, 1959). The masculine cultural norms of academia (Knights, 2006; Bell & King, 2010) appear to reinforce and uphold the idea that presenters must not reveal any emotion or feeling of inadequacy.

Consider this honest and humbling excerpt from the auto-ethnographic work of Michael Humphreys, an academic (now a professor) reflecting on the experience of presenting at his first conference:

This is really scary! What am I doing here? Why did I agree to present this paper? I am not an academic, I'm a teacher! Look at all those people in the audience . . . there's Andrew sitting next to Mary Jo . . . why did THEY have to come? I'm going to let them down, they're going to be really embarrassed at being associated with me as co-authors. The other two presenters look really confident, as have all the people I've seen do presentations in the last few days. I really shouldn't be here, I'm out of place, I'm not in their league. My God, some of the academics I've seen presenting papers are actually in the audience! Oh no, there are some of my new Nottingham colleagues coming in at the back of the room, what will they think when I freeze up and can't speak? I should have stayed in the U.K. and carried on working at Bolton, at least I was well respected there, small fish but in a very small pond; I feel like a minnow in a lake here, and there are some predatory-looking big fish around! OK, stay calm, I'm on my feet now, my dry mouth is subsiding, the script seems to be working, they are responding to me and laughing at my little jokes. This is going better than I could have expected, it's just like teaching a group of postgraduates, it actually feels alright, I am starting to get the famil-iar feeling of weightlessness and oneness with the group. People seem to be interested in what I am saying. They even want to hear more, everyone seems to want copies of the paper, they're thrusting business cards into my hand and asking questions that are giving me ideas for further work. This is a real buzz.

(Humphreys, 2005: 846)

What Humphreys writes here, I would suggest, is an account of what most people feel before going out 'on stage' to perform. It is an experience which the majority of people feel, but few can or will share it as openly or eloquently as Humphreys in his very 'human' account of conference presentation. Again there are feelings of being an imposter – *'I really shouldn't be here, I'm out of place, I'm not in their league'* – and a fear of not acquitting one's self satisfactorily – the 'what ifs' that may arise if the performance is not up to scratch. All these anxieties result from an idealized expectation of what constitutes a perfect performance, but what is also fascinating is that these experiences are not just restricted to 'newbies' or first timers as this similar story from a senior academic illustrates:

> *Well the time has come. Paul and I are presenting in the first session after lunch. Look-ing again at the programme I have reminded myself that we're presenting after Penny and Richard's paper. At least I now know that Richard isn't at the conference. That would make me even more nervous than I'm currently feeling because he's a big name in the field – I cited him in my thesis and previous papers and, although I've never met him, I am in awe of what he has done (a colleague tells me that actually Richard is also a really nervous presenter but I can't seem to take this in). I'm also aware of the other 'names' in the audience some of whom I'm seeing for the first time at this conference because this is my first time here.*

Paul is going to kick off our paper and although we'd decided who was going to speak to which slide, I wish we'd had a chance to go through the slides together. At least I'm talking about the bits I feel most confident about. The paper is based on data from my thesis and I know that well, so it should be ok. I also know that, in the past, people have complimented me on my presentation style, even when I know that I'm not confident in what I'm saying. I stumble at the start. From the first question after the presentation, I realise that I didn't mention that I had interviewed the participants! That was on my 'notes page' aide memoire but I'd forgotten to say it. Another question is challenging our perspective on the key theoretical concept. He seems to know more about the origins of the concept than I have researched and I don't think I answer his question particularly well. Anyway, it's over now. Paul is making some notes as the last speakers in this session are talking. I'm not sure that I would be able to do that as I can't recall the specific points that were made in the questions because I am still more focussed on how well, if at all, I answered them.

Interestingly, this relatively senior academic is intimidated by 'big names', revealing feelings of inferiority and constructing an idealized view of Richard, even though an attempt at dispelling this myth is made by a colleague. The presenter also knows that on some level she comes across well while presenting, but such cognitive or rational reassurances fail to eliminate her anxieties as she undertakes significant identity work. Towards the end of the vignette she admits to being preoccupied with her own identity as a competent presenter, to the extent that the feedback and learning points from the presentation itself become lost: 'I am still more focused on how well, if at all, I answered [the questions]'. Such feelings of insecurity about performance are by no means confined to academics but pop up in all spheres of life, both inside and outside of work. It has been suggested (e.g. Swenson, 2011) that up to 75 per cent of the population suffer from *glossophobia,* a fear of public speaking which is the most common phobia in the general population and is based on anxieties around the possibility that the speaker will be embarrassed or humiliated. Many people experience a fear of being exposed which cannot be alleviated despite excessive 'diligence and hard work' (Clance & Imes, 1978: 244), and a sense of relief can be gained from realising that we are by no means alone with these fears and insecurities. Ironically, while working hard on our emotions, suppressing what we do not want others to see, and expressing that which perhaps we do not feel (Hochschild, 1983; Fineman, 1993; 2000), we fuel the illusion of competence by intimidating others through our own successful identity work.

Of course the upside of performance is that when it 'works', it can be extremely exhilarating and gratifying as Humphreys detailed with reference to people laughing at his jokes during the conference presentation, and in his reflections of having 'a familiar feeling of weightlessness and oneness with the group', which is often similar to a good teaching experience. Speaking in front of individuals who are connected and visibly appreciative of what you are saying is extremely rewarding, and such intense and enjoyable experiences can evoke feelings of harmony whereby a kind of 'freedom from the ego comes from [an] immersion in the present flow of events' (Reedy & Learmonth, 2011: 122).

If we are able to understand that feelings of worry and anxiety are common and natural, and if they are not too overwhelming in terms of crippling our performance, we can also see how they may be part of the necessary emotions which fuel the creative process and keep us from complacency. For as the singer Willard White has argued, the base of insecurity is uncertainty, which stimulates the creative process and prevents us being blasé in our performance (*In Tune*, UK Radio 3, 23.4.12) so that even the most seasoned and experienced performers will disclose feelings of nervousness and apprehension. In the next (and last) section of this chapter we turn our attention to the tricky but often necessary process of getting our work published.

Publish and perish?

The final section in this chapter looks at the process of publishing our work. After writing our research, defending or presenting it, the next stage often involves a process of dissemination through a journal or book. Increasingly, being a serious researcher appears to equate with publishing successfully in highly rated journals consistently, and yet these same journals reject on average 95 per cent of the submissions made to them (Gabriel, 2010: 763). Submitting to a peer-review journal means that the work will be sent out to two or three reviewers who write in the field and who will read the work and provide a recommendation to the journal editor which falls largely into four outcomes: the first outcome is that the journal accepts the work immediately for publication (this is nirvana – and a rare outcome); the second outcome is that the author is asked to undertake some minor revisions to the manuscript prior to publication; third, the author is asked to undertake some major revisions to the paper before it returns to the reviewers again for another review; and the final possible outcome is that the paper is rejected by the journal. In some circumstances the editor can reject the paper without sending it out to review if it is felt that it is underdeveloped. The review process is undertaken anonymously by reviewers, which arguably allows reviewers to sometimes be harsh and brutal in their reviews, and this process can be 'enough to discourage and depress most sensitive people' (Gabriel, 2010: 763). Consider this anonymous reviewer's comment which (at best) could be interpreted as a little personal, and at worst an aggressive attack:

> *the paper talks about the authors' own experience of culture at conferences and publishing but perhaps the reference to Bell & King suggests they should get out more and stop going to CMS conferences.*
>
> *(Anonymous Reviewer)*

Our identities as researchers are fragile because they can at any moment be socially denied or disconfirmed (Watts, 1977), and so we often seek to secure our selves through aspirations and hopes of success, or through apprehensions of failure. In this sense, a concern with insecurity can be seen as one of the main drivers of our preoccupation with own identity (Knights & Willmott, 1999; Collinson, 2003), and this fuels our desires to do well. A rejection of our potential publication can be difficult to manage, for as Gabriel reminds us this is a very sensitive part of academic work:

> Few things are dearer to scholars than the paper, their 'baby' on which they have toiled for months or years. Few things are more important for their self-esteem or identity as researchers. And few things hurt as much or engender such deep anxieties as negative criticisms of their work.
>
> *(Gabriel, 2010: 764–765)*

The following vignette nicely illustrates the emotion which may accompany a rejection of one's work:

> *I read the review in disbelief. I was very angry at first, and upset, and could not believe it had been rejected. This rejection, although dressed up in fine and supportive language was a body blow. What it said to me is 'this is no good'. What that meant to me was 'you are no good'. What that led to was 'you probably won't be any good in the future'. I felt strongly that these reviewers were trying to blight my career; that they were responsible for my failure; that they were not pleasant people and lacked judgment. After a while (a few weeks) I calmed down and realised that many of their points were valid. I put that paper in a plastic wallet though, on the bottom shelf. I have never been able to face resuscitating it.*

In this vignette we see that the researcher has interpreted a rejection of the paper as a rejection of the self. Knights and Clarke's (2014) study endorses these ideas, as they found that publishing evoked intense emotions and passion for academics at all levels which may be almost inevitable where our research reflects our self-construction, and is likely to be more problematic when we have undertaken research to address deeply rooted issues within our personal histories. Thus a degree of 'resilience' is required in order to survive, especially, but not confined to, those starting out, as Knights and Clarke (2014) show:

> The fear of failure can be difficult and especially, I think, when you're newer and you don't know what you're going into and you've not had as much experience, your confidence can become very fragile.
>
> *(Professor)*

> It's quite daunting because whatever level you're at, the fear of rejection … it's an emotionally difficult thing to do and it requires a great amount of resolve.
>
> *(Professor)*

We catch a glimpse here of some of the prevailing feeling rules in academia (Harris, 2002). In order to 'survive' it is advised that researchers must limit (at least externally) their sensitivity to any rejection of their work – which is constructed simply as 'the way things are done'. Advice implies that emotions should be controlled and regulated through stoic resilience. This attempt to separate out emotions from thought is partly due to the mind/body dualism (Descartes), and although this dualism has not gone unchallenged it still remains extremely dominant in Western society. However, such 'feeling rules' can be rejected, resisted and reshaped as well as embraced and reproduced by individuals, although transgressions can often attract penalties which act as a deterrent.

By way of contrast, although it may appear devastating and invokes a number of defence mechanisms, a thorough review of our work by others can often help us to strengthen and clarify our research in terms of the contribution we make and the presentation of our texts. A different focus may lead to a more persuasive argument and a more convincing piece of research, so it is important to appreciate that defensiveness about feedback from others can be a form of denial, which can inhibit growth and development. Often feedback can seem inappropriate or harsh and can render the author powerless or helpless, and of course the review process itself is open to many criticisms (see for example Gabriel, 2010). Despite this, the 'pain' of publishing often brings pleasure, and the ultimate acceptance of our work in a book or journal is a reason for celebration, for as researchers we should rejoice that our findings will be read by others, who will hopefully use it to inform their own work. The following vignette gives us some hope that this is something worth striving for:

> When I saw the e-mail in my inbox I could see that the title read 'manuscript decision'. I started to shake and could not for a few seconds bring myself to open it. Of course curiosity got the better of me very quickly and I clicked on the envelope. A huge number of words appeared in front of me and I searched frantically for the all important message. Somewhere in the middle of this I found the sentence 'pleased to recommend acceptance of your paper' and I shouted 'yes!!!' at the top of my voice. I was on holiday at the time, and in the bedroom with my children trying to get a signal from an intermittent mobile connection. I nearly wept with joy at this news – my first publication. All those hours spent on it, and all those iterations and unreasonable requests from the reviewers. It felt like a validation of my work, no, of me as a researcher and as a scholar. At the same time I reflected that I should not need this sort of external legitimation to say my work is 'good'.

The final sentence of this vignette is rather telling as the researcher implies that confirmation of her researcher identity can only be secured (albeit on a briefly temporal basis) through external approbation. Perhaps this is so because 'if we have enough evidence of material achievement we won't be haunted by feelings of inadequacy' (Sennett, 1998: 119) and we can use visible accumulations both as a recourse to self-doubt and as a way of validating ourselves to others. Arguably, writing for its own sake and through channels other than highly rated journals can provide meaning and joy in itself (Reedy & Learmonth, 2011), rather than adopting the vain hope that publications, just as a means to an end, can secure our identities (and career and happiness) in some way (Knights and Clarke, 2014).

Concluding comments

In this chapter we have looked at what happens after field work is complete. Although we have referred to this as the 'aftermath', it is of course part of the research process itself, for as Broussine and Grisoni deliberate in Chapter 4, is there a point where research actually ends? The recurring theme in this chapter is that all aspects of research are unpredictable, messy and potentially filled with feelings of despair, embarrassment and frustration through to joy and exhilaration. This experience of doing research can only ever resemble a pale version of clinical, chronological and rational accounts of 'how to' research, and in particular the neatly ordered post-rational narratives of 'how I did' my study. Much is missing from such accounts, and yet it seems that there is a lot to commend the inclusion of these experiences: shared connections, reassurance, confidence and above all the wisdom that when our research activities are vexatious, they are not 'off track' but rather what most people experience and what we should expect. Mind you, we still did not fully expect this ourselves in the process of assembling this book – for a full account of this 'off track' process, see our final chapter, Chapter 11.

Perhaps, then, instead of becoming frustrated and hoping that these emotions can be eradicated so that 'normal service [can] be resumed as soon as possible' (Fineman & Gabriel, 1996: 157), we would be better off understanding that such struggles *are* 'normal' service.

References

Becker, E. (1971). *The Birth and Death of Meaning*. New York: Free Press.

Bell, E., & King, D. (2010) The Elephant in the Room: Critical Management Studies Conferences as Sites of Body Pedagogic. *Management Learning*, 41(4) 429–442.

Brannan, M. J. (2011) Researching Emotions and the Emotions of Researching: The Strange Case of Alexithymia in Reflexive Research. *International Journal of Work Organisation and Emotion,* 4 (3/4) 322–339.

Burkitt, I. (1997) Social Relationships and Emotions. *Sociology*, 31(1) 37–55.

Butler, J. (2004) *Precarious Life: The Powers of Mourning and Violence*. London: Verso.

Charmaz, K. (2002) 'Grounded Theory: Objectivist and Constructivist Methods'. In N. Denzin & Y. Lincoln (Eds), *Handbook of Qualitative Research* (2nd edn), 509–535. Thousand Oaks, CA: Sage.

Clance, P. R. (1985) *The Impostor Phenomenon: Overcoming the Fear That Haunts Your Success*. Atlanta: Peachtree Publishers.

Clance, P. R., & Imes, S. A. (1978). The Imposter Phenomenon in High Achieving Women: Dynamics and Therapeutic Interventions. *Psychotherapy: Theory, Research and Practice*, 15, 241–247.

Clarke, C., & Fineman, S. (2009) 'What We Had to Do Was Brutal: An Exploration of the Emotionologies Surrounding Downsizing', *EGOS* conference, July, Barcelona.

Collinson, D. L. (2003). Identities and Insecurities: Selves at Work. *Organization*, 10, 527–547.

Collis, J., & Hussey, R. (2003) *Business Research: A Practical Guide for Undergraduate and Postgraduate Students, Second Edition*. Basingstoke: Palgrave Macmillan.

Csikszentmihalyi, M. (1990) *Flow: The Psychology of Optimal Experience*. New York: Harper and Row.

Dawson, J. (2012) 'Getting Started'. In P. Daoust (Ed), *Write*. London: Guardian Books.

Derrida, J. (1978) *Writing and Difference*, trans. Alan Bass. Chicago: University of Chicago Press.

Domagalski, T. (1999) Emotion in Main Organizations: Main Currents. *Human Relations*, 52(6) 833–852.

Ekman, P. (1992) 'An Argument for Basic Emotions'. *Cognition and Emotion*, 6(3/4) 169–200.

Fineman, S. (1993) *Emotion in Organizations*. London: Sage.

Fineman, S. (2000) *Emotion in Organizations* (2nd edn). London: Sage.

Fineman, S., & Gabriel, Y. (1996) *Experiencing Organisations*. London: Sage.

Fletcher, J. K. (2001) *Disappearing Acts: Gender, Power, and Relational Practice at Work*. Cambridge, MA: MIT Press.

Foucault, M. (1982) 'The Subject and Power'. In H. L. Dreyfus & P. Rabinow (Eds), *Michel Foucault: Beyond Structuralism and Hermeneutics*, 208–226. Brighton: Harvester Press.

Foucault, M. (1984) 'What Is Enlightenment?' In P. Rabinow (Ed.), *The Foucault Reader*, 32–50. Harmondsworth: Penguin.

Freud, S. (1914) On Narcissism: An Introduction. *Standard Edition*, 14, 73–102.

Gabriel, Y. (2010) Organization Studies: A Space for Ideas, Identities and Agonies. *Organization Studies*, 31(6) 757–775.

Goffman, E. (1959) *The Presentation of Self in Everyday Life*. Harmondsworth: Penguin.

Hardy, C. (1994) 'Power and Politics in Organizations'. In *Managing Strategic Action – Mobilizing Change Concepts, and Cases*. London: Sage.

Harris, L. C. (2002) The Emotional Labour of Barristers: An Exploration of Emotional Labour by Status Professionals. *Journal of Management Studies*, 39(4) 553–584.

Hochschild, A. R. (1983) *The Managed Heart: Commercialization of Human Feeling*. London: University of California Press.

Humphreys, M. (2005) Getting Personal: Reflexivity and Autoethnographic Vignettes. *Qualitative Inquiry*, 11, 840–860.

Kenny, K. (2008) Aesthetics and Emotion in Organisational Ethnography. *International Journal of Work Organisation and Emotion* 2(4) 374–388.

Knights, D. (2006) Authority at Work: Reflections and Recollections. *Organization Studies*, 27(5) 699–720.

Knights, D., & Clarke, C. (2014) It's a Bittersweet Symphony, This Life: Fragile Academic Selves and Insecure Identities at Work. *Organization Studies*, 35(3) 335–357.

Knights, D., & Willmott, H. (1989) Power and Subjectivity at Work: From Degradation to Subjugation in Social Relations. *Sociology*, 23(4) 535–558.

Knights, D., & Willmott, H. (1999) *Management Lives, Power and Identity in Work Organizations*. London: Sage.

Levinas, E. (1978) *Existence and Existents*. Dordrecht: Kluwer.

Lodge, D. (1984) *Small World: An Academic Romance*. Harmondsworth: Penguin.

Plas, J., & Hoover-Demsey, K. V. (1988) *Working Up a Storm: Anger, Anxiety, Joy, & Tears on the Job*. New York: Ivy Books.

Rafaeli, A., & Sutton, R. I. (1987) Expression of Emotion as Part of the Work Role. *Academy of Management Review*, 12(1) 23–37.

Reedy, P., & Learmonth, M. (2011) Death and Organization: Heidegger's Thought on Death and Life in Organizations. *Organization Studies*, 32, 117–131.

Richardson, L. (1998) 'Writing – a Method of Inquiry'. In N. Denzin & Y. Lincoln (Eds), *Collecting and Interpreting Qualitative Materials*. London: Sage.

Sartre, J-P. (1943) *Being and Nothingness*. London: Routledge.

Schwartz, H. S. (1987) Anti-social Actions of Committed Organizational Participants: An Existential Psychoanalytic Perspective. *Organization Studies*, 8(4) 327–340.

Sennett, R. (1998) *The Corrosion of Character*. New York: W.W. Norton.

September, A. N., McCarrey, M., Baranowsky, A., Parent, C., & Schindler, D. (2001) The Relation between Well-being, Impostor Feelings, and Gender Role Orientation among University Students. *The Journal of Social Psychology*, 14, 218–232.

Swenson, A. (2011) You Make My Heart Beat Faster: A Quantitative Study of the Relationship between Instructor Immediacy, Classroom Community, and Public Speaking Anxiety. *UW-L Journal of Undergraduate Research XIV,* 1–12.

Waldron, V. R. (2000) Relational Experiences and Emotion at Work in Fineman, S (ed) *Emotion in Organizations* (2nd edn), London: Sage.

Walter, B. (1979) *One Way Street*. (Intro. by Susan Sontag. Transl. Edmund Jephcott and Kingsley Shorter.) Noldon: NLB.

Watts, A. (1977) *Psychotherapy East and West*. Harmondsworth: Penguin.

Ybema, S., Keenoy, T., Oswick, C., Beverungen, A., Ellis, N., & Sabelis, I. (2009) Articulating Identities. *Human Relations*, 62, 299–332.

10

RESEARCHING WITH FEELING

The case for an affective paradigm in social and organisational research

Chris James and Megan Crawford

Introduction

Researching feelings in various organisational contexts and for different purposes has been a fascination for both of us for a number of years, so we felt the best way to introduce this chapter would be for us to explain why that is the case and to set out why we have chosen to write this chapter. We do however come to this chapter via different pathways, so we thought it best for one of us to explain what has brought us to this point, why researching with feelings is so captivating and what has led to the writing of this chapter. So, what follows is Chris's story as an introduction.

I'm often intrigued by why I find doing research so very interesting. Finding things out has always been a fascination of mine ever since I was a child. My Uncle Ron and Aunty Phyllis spotted it when I was about nine. They gave me a chemistry set one Christmas – excellent – followed by a microscope the next – even better! That interest in finding things out has stayed with me all my life.

Perhaps unsurprisingly, I followed a science route at school and university. My first degree was in physiology, which is essentially finding out how 'bodies' (human and otherwise) function. I think I wanted to find out how the 'machine' I inhabited all day and every day worked. My PhD was also in physiology, this time trying to find out how the brain works. I researched how the brain processes visual information – totally fascinating. Following several years working in that field, I changed track and became a school teacher. Even as a science teacher, class experiments and the students' science projects were always really interesting, to me at least.

In parallel with that 'scientist script' has been a lifelong concern with feelings. I've always felt that I was a very 'affective person' – feelings seem to be 'big' in my life. I was always referred to as a very sensitive boy in our family circles. I found myself moved by events, often more so than my fellows, and impelled to do things often by forces which I could not fully rationalise or explain.

Those two dimensions – research and an interest in feelings – came together in the mid-1990s – and my fascination with researching feelings began. A colleague put me onto it, suggesting I read Obholzer and Roberts' excellent edited text 'The Unconscious at Work' (1994). It's a remarkable book. The first few chapters explain the essentials of system psychodynamics, which are then followed by some enthralling chapters which explore various illustrative cases from a systems psychodynamics perspective. All the component concepts of system psychodynamics seemed to make sense for me. For the first time, I found a set of ideas that enabled me to make sense of 'what might be going on here' – individually, interpersonally, in groups, in organisations – and even more widely. The ideas in systems psychodynamic theory provided me with a way of making sense of the experience of feelings. Importantly, the ideas gave me a way of understanding the social world how and explaining why we do what we do.

That idea of sense making – interpretation – is crucial in researching with feelings. How to make sense of the world from an affective standpoint is the central concern of this chapter. We are seeking to make the case that what is needed is an affective paradigm – a group of underlying and central principles and convictions (Guba and Lincoln, 1994) – that enables robust sense making to take place.

In writing the chapter, we are very conscious of the extensive work undertaken by other academic colleagues and that we are seeking to build on their work. In the last fifteen years or so, the rich and valuable insights in their published works have drawn attention to the ever-present interplay between feelings, experience and practice – in a range of settings. Published accounts of research have also shown that the process of attempting to understand feelings is complex and challenging. Our intention in this chapter is to analyse and reflect upon some of those complexities and challenges and to make the case for an affective paradigm in social and organisational research. Our idea for an affective paradigm was initiated in part by the work of Barsade, Brief and Spataro (2003), who argue for an affective paradigm in organisational studies generally.

We start the chapter with a short section that summarises the case we are making – our general thesis – then the chapter is organised into sections that address the issues set out above. In the first substantive section, we discuss the nature of feelings with a view to revealing the difficulties associated with researching them. In the subsequent section, we consider the nature of, and similarities and differences between, the three different forms of affect – feelings, emotions and moods. The third main section is where we begin to build the case for an affective paradigm. We distinguish between three kinds of mental processes that occur in individuals as they relate to others and events in the social world – affection, cognition and volition. In the fourth section, we clarify the nature of an affective paradigm and argue for, and illustrate the nature of, interpretation within an affective paradigm. In the final section, we explore the usefulness of the affective paradigm and raise some issues for further consideration.

So, by way of a conclusion to this introduction, we need to draw attention to a very significant issue for us, which is of course at the heart of this book and adds to the fascination of the research we do in this field. Here we are, researching feelings, and yet at the same time, the research process itself is imbued with feelings. Our research into feelings is in itself an affective practice that can be understood through the lens of affect. Research into feelings, like any other action, has an affective rationale, and the research process can be interpreted as such. That's an important idea for all researchers but especially so for those who research with feelings. A reflexive stance when researching allows deep insights to emerge for the researcher's own understanding and for the phenomenon being researched.

The case for an affective paradigm in social and organisational research: our central thesis

In essence, our argument is a simple one. Feelings and moods are essentially internal states. Describing those states is extremely difficult for a variety of reasons. Emotions are feelings and moods that are shown to others – crying, smiling and shouting, for example – but even they can be difficult to describe and explain. Very importantly, people show feelings in a whole variety of actions, not just those we would describe as emotions. All actions, including showing feelings as emotions, are the outcome of a complex interplay between the key three mental processes: affection (the experience of feelings), cognition (thinking and knowing) and volition, which is the term used to describe processes that tend towards activity or change and that underlie purposive action. Our first vignette illustrates some of the complexity around feelings, emotions, cognition and actions.

> *I've got some great colleagues. I had a quick word with one of them after a meeting the other day. He'd taken a particularly contrary view on a departmental teaching matter – nit-picking and being negative, not like him at all, very unusual.*
>
> *'You took an "unusual line" in there on that new initiative', I tentatively suggested.*
>
> *'Did I?' he replied, 'I have to say I thought the changes being suggested were plain daft, just bonkers'. He did have a bit of a point I have to say, but the meeting had agreed some sensible changes in the end.*
>
> *I looked at him, uncertain what to make of his frame of mind. 'Everything alright?' I asked.*
>
> *'Yes, I'm fine', he replied in a somewhat resigned manner (round here, we refer to being 'Fine' as Functionally Incapable of Normal Expression).*
>
> *I left it at that and wandered off back to my office.*

Half an hour later there was a knock at the door and in he walked.

'Hi, thought I should tell you that I heard I'd had an article rejected first thing this morning, got the email just before the meeting, it's that article I've been telling you about, that piece I was really pleased with'.

'Oh, hard luck', I replied, trying to be understanding and knowing just how he was feeling.

'Luck!' he retorted. 'Useless referees more like!'

'Didn't they do a good job?' I enquired rather cautiously .

'Huh, that's just the point. They were spot on. I hadn't realised where the weakness was. I thought it was one of the best I'd done'.

'Well', I said, 'you know 'the rules'. When that kind of thing happens, you're allowed 24 hours of wild fury – best not directed at your colleagues – and then knuckle down and re-work it using the referees' comments'.

'Yeh, yeh, I know', he said indicating that he did know and that he knew his behaviour in the meeting wasn't the proper thing to do either. 'Meanwhile, if you hear a big crash coming from my office, it'll be me throwing my laptop out of the window in frustration', he added.

'Hah!' I replied, knowing that his jokey tone showed he was getting over it a little. 'Just keep going, that's all you can do'.

'I guess so. Thanks'.

We will be using this vignette during the chapter to illustrate the complex nature of affective experience.

In this chapter, we argue that because feelings cannot be known as objects, they can only be known through the interpretation of actions they initiate, which can be known as objects. Acceptance of this argument requires a shift away from feelings as objects to feelings as rationales for and explanations of practice. This shift elevates the importance of interpretation from an affective standpoint, which is, we argue, the central feature of the affective paradigm. Feelings can only be understood and explained through an interpretation of social and organisational practices, and in turn, they can only be fully understood by understanding the affective experience that initiated them.

In developing the arguments in this chapter, we acknowledge that we are building on the work of a number of significant contributors to the field – for example, Hochschild (1983) and Fineman (1993; 2003), who have studied the affects of organising from a range of perspectives. They in turn have founded their contributions on the work of other renowned theoreticians such as Spinoza, Darwin, James and Harre, who themselves have built upon the long-standing interest of numerous eminent philosophers. Our reflections on our own previous work have also been important. Through this chapter, we are seeking to take that work on further.

The nature of affects

Affects are the particular mental states we experience, and usually three categories are differentiated: feelings, emotions and moods (Forgas, 2000). Distinguishing between the three states – especially between feelings and emotions – can be particularly problematic, as we discuss below. In the literature, writers generally agree that feelings and moods can be segregated on the basis that feelings are temporary and intense, whereas moods are persistent and low in intensity. Feelings also usually have an identifiable rationale and definable content, which is typically not the case with moods.

The literature on the categories of feelings is extensive, and, although there is some disagreement amongst theorists on which experiences are discrete states, five feature consistently: happiness, sadness, anger, disgust and fear (Niedenthal, Krauth-Gruber and Ric, 2006). Here, we are concerned with these social feelings rather than sensations that are apprehended specifically through the senses, such as temperature and taste, although of course social feelings can be elicited via these sensations. Neither feelings nor moods are necessarily made apparent to others (Fineman, 2003).

In the wider literature, the term 'emotion' is used interchangeably with feelings/moods. A number of writers, such as Fineman (1999), take the view that feelings are what we experience, whilst emotions are feelings that are shown. Emotions are thus *'personal displays of feelings'* (Fineman, 1999: 292 [our emphasis]). This distinction is helpful analytically, and we use it in this chapter. So, particular facial expressions and other demonstrations of feelings, such as crying or laughing, are depictions of internal affective states and are considered to be emotions. This distinction between feelings and emotions – on the basis that a feeling is what is experienced, whilst an emotion is a feeling that is shown – raises two interesting issues.

The first issue is the role of volition, which are processes that underpin purposive action, in the display of feelings as emotions. There are circumstances when the display of feelings may be controlled by force of will, though of course this control is not always possible in every case. Strong feelings can swamp and overcome the power of the will to prevent their display. Nonetheless, there is the potential for feelings to be hidden by force of will and not displayed as emotions. The display of feelings is a form of willed behaviour, though of course this display may not be possible in every circumstance. Such display of feelings can be considered to be a purposeful act. This potential for willed control over the display of feelings has important implications for researching feelings as we discuss below.

The second matter of interest is that feelings, even extreme feelings, can be made apparent as personal displays in an enormous variety of ways as actions of a range of kinds, some of which would not be considered to be emotions.

The problematics of researching affects

In this section, we consider the problematics of researching feelings. We begin with a consideration of ontological issues because they are fundamental to any research endeavour, and then go on to consider epistemological and methodological matters. We also consider the determinist-voluntarist dimension of human nature in relation to the experience of feelings.

Ontological considerations

We contend that feelings do not exist as objects in the world external to the individual. They are subjective phenomena, a notion which may be difficult to acknowledge because feelings may be socially embedded as familiar, intrinsic and expected aspects of interactions with others. Even so, feelings are substantively different from other objects, such as an individual's work colleagues, an office or a project planning document, which may or may not exist in the individual's external world.

The subjective experience of the external world may instigate feelings within an individual. It influences the individual's actions, as we have discussed above, which may then be experienced directly by the individual concerned and others as 'objects' in the outside world. Such actions may call up feelings within all those who experience them.

Individuals may not be consciously aware that they are displaying their feelings and that those unconsciously displayed feelings may be experienced by others consciously and unconsciously. Other people may become aware of an individual's or group's feelings consciously through the processes of projection and transference (Likierman, 2001). During projection, individuals and groups 'locate' feelings in others, rather than retaining them. The feelings become associated with the other, and as a result the individual or the group starts acting on that basis. Projected feelings may be experienced by the other consciously or unconsciously in a process known as transference. Those others experiencing the transference may then start acting on the basis of the projected feelings they have 'taken in', a process which is known as counter-transference (Likierman, 2001). A consequence of all these processes is the difficulty, or even the impossibility, of people, as individuals or in groups, distinguishing between the feelings that are generated solely within them and the feelings that have been projected by others and been taken in or introjected.

Epistemological questions

Epistemological questions relate to how one might begin to understand and communicate knowledge about the world. Knowing and measuring affective experience is problematic for a number of reasons. In this section, we use fictional quotations to illustrate the points we are trying to make. They all relate to reactions to the experience of having a journal article rejected that we discussed in the first vignette earlier, but of course other examples about other organisational matters, settings and experiences could be used.

1. Feelings may vary temporally. For example, affective experience may be transient (*'I felt really angry when I read the referees' comments, but I eventually calmed down'*), or persistent (*'I feel in a bad mood this morning, though I can't seem to understand why. I've not felt right since I had that article rejected but that was ages ago'*), to the extent that it becomes a permanent feature of an individual's internal world (*'I just always feel as though the whole world is trying to judge me'*). Over time, an affective response to an event may change (*'I felt so disappointed when I read the referees' comments. I'm over it now of course and actually it was quite helpful in the end'*). The affective experience may be delayed (*'The referees' comments didn't really affect me at the time, it wasn't until later that I started to feel really upset'*).

2. Affective responses vary. Individuals' experience of feelings and what is shown as emotions or actions may vary with apparently similar events eliciting different responses in different individuals. Some slightly negative referees' comments might elicit a very strong affective response in some academics but only a slight response in others. This difference in affective response can be interpreted in a range of ways. For example, feelings of self-doubt or insecurity may exacerbate some people's feelings when they receive negative feedback. Negative feedback could threaten some people's sense of themselves – their identity – which can cause considerable anxiety. Some people may experience feelings more strongly than others. This affective experience may be seen disproportionate to the apparent reason for them. The experience of feelings and their expression may not be closely or even directly linked. The feelings a person shows about an incident and that person's emotions or other actions may be different from what one might expect. As we discuss below, the relationship between feelings and emotions/actions is not a deterministic one.

Feelings can often be complex and contradictory. Individuals may experience a range of different feelings simultaneously in response to an event or incident of some kind. It is also quite possible – perhaps even usual – to have strong opposing feelings about objects and events. To have 'mixed feelings' (ambivalence) about an event is a familiar experience, as our second vignette shows, and these mixed and contradictory feelings can be difficult to describe accurately.

> *I feel myself very fortunate to work with some excellent colleagues. We have a very good team working in my field, they score ten out of ten on the bright (clever or at least willing to work hard at being clever) and nice (good to work with) categories.*

> *'When one of them told me he was leaving I was really very sad and, yes, upset but I was also very pleased for him. He was moving on to other things that would be of considerable benefit to him and his family. In truth, it was 'right' for him to move and I knew he eventually would. He'd leave a big hole as it were but I also felt it'd give us an opportunity to re-shape things a little, which I was pleased about.'*

> *'I was very sorry to see him go. We had an excellent 'good-bye do' for him. Interestingly, I felt strangely energised by the opportunity his departure gave us. I managed to keep that hidden during my farewell speech though!'*

If feelings are difficult to know and to measure, then communicating knowledge about feelings and emotions will also be difficult. This difficulty is exacerbated for a variety of other personal, interpersonal and cultural reasons. Some people's feelings may be so unacceptable to them, perhaps because they are associated with other feelings such as embarrassment or guilt, that revealing them to others may be difficult, even impossible. Feelings may be socially unacceptable in nature or degree, so much so that an individual may be unwilling to disclose them. People may have feelings but lack the vocabulary and the means of expression to describe them (Sturdy, 2003). Feelings may be so well repressed that there is no conscious experience of them to describe to others. The feelings being experienced may be unusual in that they may not have been experienced before and may therefore be difficult to communicate correctly. The act of articulating feelings may alleviate the experience of them, perhaps in a therapeutic or cathartic sense. So, describing them to another may dissipate the affective experience.

Individuals may split their difficult feelings from the more acceptable ones and project them elsewhere as a form of social defence (Likierman, 2001), as we have discussed above. In this way the unacceptable feelings are no longer experienced. This splitting and projection is a familiar practice in many organisations (Halton, 1994), including educational organisations (Dunning, James and Jones, 2005; Crawford, 2007; 2008).

People in work organisations may seek to remove any affective content from their work, although as we discuss above such extreme affective control by force of will can be very difficult. So, for example, the colleague in the first vignette may well say, *'That message from the journal editor was just another email; I just took it in my stride, no problem'*. This de-emotionalisation as Fineman (1993) calls it may have a number of purposes – for example, to keep life simple, to distance those concerned from the boring and repetitive nature of their work, to look strong and powerful or as a form of social defence that protects them from potentially painful feelings. Under these circumstances, ascertaining and communicating such individuals' affective experience may be difficult.

Sometimes feelings are expressed through metaphors (*'When I read the referee's comments, I just felt as though I'd been knocked over by a bus'*), which then have to be interpreted appropriately. Broussine and Vince (1995) found that metaphors at different levels of an organisation provided insights into the emotions present in relation to large-scale organisational change, and their study showed how metaphor can act as a container for emotional and unconscious forces at work.

For researchers of others' feelings, there is the additional difficulty which results from the creation of an emotional zone in the data-gathering process, such as interviews or group discussions. Such zones have particular display rules (Ashforth and Humphrey, 1993), which guide individuals on the feelings that may be publicly expressed, and feeling rules (Hochschild, 1979), which are the socially shared guidelines that govern how individuals want to try to feel in particular settings. These emotional zones can distort the reporting of affective experience.

Given that it is difficult in practice for a researcher to capture the knowledge of the feelings of another and to communicate that knowledge in an authentic way, feelings may be best known and understood through the actions including emotions they initiate and carry through. Understanding feelings in this way requires an interpretation of actions from an affective standpoint which we discuss below.

Human nature questions

People's feelings about the external world and their subjective experience of those feelings in their internal worlds both contribute to their total environment. However, a key issue here is that the objects in the external world, such as journal article review, do not determine the subjective experience of feelings even though they may well explain the evoking of feelings. Similarly, feelings subjectively experienced do not necessarily determine actions, but they may be the reasons for actions and can provide explanations for them. Broadly, the same arguments may be made about unconscious affective influences. They may not determine actions, but they may provide reasons and explanations for them. So, whilst there is no deterministic relationship between feelings and actions, we argue that feelings are central in the motivation and rationale for actions and that actions can be understood by exploring those motivations and rationales – both conscious and unconscious – for them. Moreover, feelings can be better understood by exploring what people do as a consequence of them.

In summary, feelings cannot be ascertained and communicated about easily for ontological, epistemological and methodological reasons and yet are an implicit part of practice. Even though there is no deterministic relationship between feelings and actions, we argue that the affective experience – the feelings – inherent in human activity, relationships and social processes can provide the rationales for and explanations of practices. Eliciting these rationales requires interpretation from an affective standpoint which is a central part of an affective paradigm for social research and practice. At the heart of interpretation is an acceptance of the interplay between the three basic mental processes: affection, cognition and volition, to which we turn our attention next.

Affection, cognition and volition

The development of the concepts

There is a widespread and longstanding acceptance that mental processes are of three basic kinds: affection, cognition and volition (Hilgard, 1980). Affection refers to the experience of feelings, and cognition relates to thinking and knowing, the processes of knowledge acquisition. Volition is the term given to the mental processes, which are sometimes referred to as willing or conation, that tend towards activity or change. Volition and conative processes underpin purposive action and are manifest in individuals as, for example, desire, determination, striving and trying. Hilgard (1980) refers to this tripartite categorisation as the 'trilogy of the mind', and Tallon (1997) uses the term 'triune' similarly.

The nature of and relationship between different forms of mental process has been a long-standing fascination of Western philosophers from as far back as Aristotle. Despite this history, during the last century, affect and volition were neglected, and two major theoretical standpoints – behaviourism and cognitivism – dominated the study of mental processes (Forgas, 2000). Behaviourism failed to take sufficient account of individuals' capability for purposive mindful behaviour, and volition was thus neglected. Cognitivists sought to separate thought from affect and to deal 'predominantly with the study of cold, affectless ideation' with the 'historical neglect of affective phenomena' (Forgas, 2000: 4, 5). This neglect has been reflected in the study of feelings in organisations. One explanation of this dominance of behaviourism and cognitivism was the prevalence of modernist thinking during the last century and the resulting emphasis on the measurement of psychological phenomena. Feelings are difficult to measure (as we have discussed above), as is volition, hence the desirability of attending to actions and performance, which are easily measured. Only towards the turn of the twentieth century did the importance of affect and volition begun to return to the fore.

Affection and cognition

Affection and cognition – the mental processes of feeling and thinking, respectively – may be distinguished analytically as different kinds of phenomena. There is evidence from experimental psychology – for example, Elliott and Dolan (1998) – which shows that feeling and thinking are separate processes. Recent physiological evidence also appears to confirm the existence of the two neural pathways; see, for example, LeDoux (1986).

Whilst there may be two separate affection and cognition systems, in social settings in everyday life there is clearly an interaction between the two, although the interaction varies in extent. Feelings may serve, support and enhance cognition (Fineman, 1999), or they may interfere with cognitive processes and be disruptive influences (Argyris, 1990). Many contemporary writers such as Harre (1986) and Forgas (2000) consider that thinking and feeling are parts of a single, integrated cognitive symbolic representational system, echoing the view of Bain (1868) over a century ago. The representational role of thinking and feeling for the purpose of bringing about knowledge and apprehension distinguishes them from volition, which is essentially concerned with action and activity.

Volition

Hershberger (1988) and others argue for the foundational significance of volition in understanding human mental processes and behaviour. One problem with understanding volition is ascertaining precisely the part it plays in bringing about intentional actions. Wittgenstein (1953) argues that willing, as he calls it, is an action of a particular kind. It is about trying, attempting and making an effort. In relation to speaking, for example, he distinguishes the action of speaking from the action of trying to speak. Zhu (2004) takes a similar line, arguing that volition initiates actions. But Zhu then extends the scope of volition to define it 'as a mediating executive process that bridges the gaps between deliberation, decision and voluntary bodily movements' (p.248). This conceptualisation of volition sees it as harmonising and overseeing essentially conscious cognitive processes that lead to actions. However, volition surely has a more substantial role than that of 'bridging the gap between thought and action' as Zhu asserts (p.249).

The interplay between affection, cognition and volition

There is, of course, an interplay between feeling/thinking as representational systems of knowing/apprehending and willing as an initiator and sustainer of purposeful activity. First, to think one has the capacity do something interacts with the will to do it (Bandura, 1997). Similarly, thinking that doing something can bring about a desired state, or thinking that an action is worth taking, will influence the will to do it. Second, there is an interaction between what is felt and volition. Our everyday experience indicates that feeling that a course of action is right (or indeed is wrong) significantly influences the will to do it. Similarly, feeling that one's identity is under threat can significantly influence the will to act to protect it, typically strengthening it. Many would argue – for example, Frank (1993) – that feelings are typically at least as significant as rationales for actions as are cognitions, if not more so. Thus motivation theorists from as far back as Murray (1938) have sought to substantiate the role of feelings in motivation because of the positive effect resulting from willed, voluntary behaviour. Conversely, the interruption of motivated activity is associated with negative affect (Srull and Wyer, 1985). Other writers more recently – for example, Gabriel (1999) – have argued for a central role of affect in motivation. We support this standpoint. An affective paradigm for social and organisational research accepts as axiomatic that affective rationales for willed voluntary actions are at least as significant as cognitive ones, and are almost certainly more significant.

There is thus a significant interplay between affection and cognition in a representational system. There is also significant interplay between this representational system and volition – which initiates and carries through purposeful actions that are intended to bring about a desired state. Achieving a desired state represents a rationale for the purposeful action. Understanding affective rationales for actions is therefore important and is in itself a rationale for an affective paradigm for social and organisation research and practice.

An affective paradigm for social and organisational research – the importance of interpretation from an affective standpoint

An affective paradigm

A paradigm may be regarded as 'a set of basic beliefs that deals with ultimates or first principles' (Guba and Lincoln, 1994: 108). It denotes a particular world view. A paradigm defines the nature of the world, the place of individuals within the world and the range of potential relationships to the world. The ultimate truth-fulness of the beliefs that underpin a paradigm may not be knowable for certain and may have to be accepted on faith. By implication, research paradigms define researchers' central concerns and characterise and delimit the scope of their research. Practice paradigms – for example, those of leaders and managers – perform a similar function for practitioners.

At the heart of the affective paradigm is the notion that feelings cannot be ascertained and communicated about easily for ontological, epistemological and methodological reasons, as we discussed above. They nonetheless influence actions, though not in a deterministic way, which we have established in the previous section. To understand actions fully, they have to be interpreted and made sense of on the basis of the affect and on the assumption that actions have affective rationales.

Interpretation from an affective standpoint

In social research texts, interpretation is seen as having a relatively minor place in comparison with the coverage given to other aspects of the research process – for example, data collection methods. We would therefore argue that, generally in social research, interpretation is underplayed. In this context, interpretation provides reasons, rationales and explanations for individual and group behaviours. So, an organisational event or process of some kind can be described using very robust data collection methods, but it cannot be explained until it is interpreted. The interpretive process requires a framework of linked concepts that enables empirical data to be considered and explained. In a metaphorical sense, it provides a lens through which data can be examined. The interpretive lens enables sense to be made of 'what is going on' in the event or the process. In published research into the affective aspects of organising, four interpretive frameworks can be readily identified: system psychodynamics, social constructionist, Marxist and feminist.

The system psychodynamics framework uses analytical psychological concepts and systems theory in its widest sense to interpret individual and group behaviours in social settings. In system psychodynamics, a number of concepts are central. The first is the notion of social defences where individuals and groups adopt behaviours to protect themselves against unacceptable feelings that threaten their deep but nonetheless vulnerable senses of identity, legitimacy and value. Anxiety is typically considered to be the most significant unacceptable feeling. The second central concept is the idea that the unconscious mental activity can be important in explaining individual and group behaviours. The third is the notion of boundaries and the affective influence upon them. Boundaries in this context are places of discontinuity in an individual's external social world, within an individual's inner psychic structure, and between an individual's internal and external worlds. Other significant concepts include basic assumption tendencies in group behaviour, the primary task of work groups and affective containment by individuals and in organisations. Examples of those working with this perspective, generally, are Obholzer and Roberts (1994), Hirschhorn (1988) and James *et al.* (2006).

A social constructionist perspective on the affective aspects of organising and human experience is grounded in the notion that our affective world is collectively formed through a prolonged experience of socialisation which begins in the earliest stages of life and is ongoing. From a social constructionist perspective, the continual socialising influence is mediated by others' explanations of the communal world with the consequence that a shared set of understandings, rationales and axioms is established in relation to feelings, emotions and moods. This social construction includes cognitive elements such as beliefs, judgements, cultural norms and language. The interpretation of organising practices in human systems from a social constructionist standpoint makes sense of them through the social and cultural influences upon individuals and groups and the established social norms. This perspective became established through the work of Berger and Luckman (1966) and has of course been taken forward substantially by others, and in relation to the social construction of feelings it was developed in particular by Harre (1986). In the context of organisational studies, generally Fineman's work is grounded in this perspective – see, for example, Fineman (2003) – as is the work of Crawford (2007; 2008).

Interpretation of workplace practices in the affective paradigm from a Marxist perspective is concerned with the way that feelings are used in the service of capitalism and corporate financial profit. Work from this perspective, especially work in service occupations, is considered to be emotional work or emotional labour. Emotional work is undertaken whenever employees need to control their feelings in undertaking their functions and responsibilities. When employees engage in emotional labour, they are required to undertake emotional work as a specific job requirement, and their remuneration depends on it. Employees are expected to display feelings as emotions authentically in a way appropriate to the work setting as a condition of their employment. This emotional labour is undertaken at considerable personal cost. Arguably, most if not all work occupations require some measure of affective control, and thus emotional work is a characteristic of almost all occupations. If, as we have argued above, feelings are implicit in all actions including

those at work, then arguably almost all work is emotional labour because the correct feelings have to be shown in appropriate work practices. This perspective was
established by the seminal work of Arlie Hochschild (1983).

The feminist interpretive perspective considers feelings and their expression
as emotions (or non-expression) and as a means of defining and distinguishing
between men and women. Male 'rationality', where cognition holds sway over
affect, is considered to take precedence over female 'irrationality', where feelings
are considered to dominate cognitive processes, and a male hegemony is established.
Inter alia, the perspective argues for more affective authenticity in the work place,
the legitimisation of a wider and fuller expression of feelings as emotions in the
work place, and the affective interaction between home life and work life. Martin,
Knopoff and Beckman's (2000) work is an example of writing from this perspective
in the organisational studies field.

In summary, there is a range of conceptual frameworks for interpreting individual and organisational practices from an affective standpoint. We consider that
there is value in maintaining their distinctiveness in the way that Martin, Knopoff
and Beckman (2000) seek to distinguish feminist and Marxist perspectives on the
role of feelings in work organisations. At the same time, we also accept that there is
common ground between them – for example, between social constructionist and
systems psychodynamics perspectives (Fineman, 2000). Furthermore, our purpose
here is not to evaluate the various interpretive perspectives. What we are seeking
to do is to argue the case for interpretation from an affective standpoint within an
affective paradigm. Interpretation from any of these perspectives gives an opportunity to understand social processes and practices and their affective rationales.

The usefulness of an affective paradigm for social research and practice

In this chapter, we have argued the case for an affective paradigm for social research
and practice. The value of an affective paradigm is that it gives enhanced insights
into practice and human experience. It provides a basis from which practices and
experience can be better understood, explained and interpreted. Such a paradigm
therefore has widespread utility.

From a research perspective, the usefulness of an affective paradigm lies in the
way it brings observation and interpretation closer and could thereby enhance
theorisation. In this paradigm, it is assumed that there is an affective explanation for
practices and it is that affective explanation and its link with practice and human
experience that needs to be explored. Thus researching in the affective paradigm
enables the explanation of individual and social actions and processes (why people
do what they do) and takes further the simple description of practice (what people
do) and their affective experience (what they feel while they do them). Importantly,
it opens up legitimate ways of 'researching with feeling'.

From a practice perspective, an affective paradigm is useful because it brings
practice and rationale closer. It is assumed that there is an affective reason for practices and it is these affective rationales that can be explored. This standpoint gives

people a potentially richer understanding of their experience and practice and the link between the two. It opens up the possibility of gaining an enhanced understanding of the rationales for practices and the potential for learning and practice improvement.

From a research perspective, understanding the affective experience of 'being a researcher' brings a number of benefits. For all researchers – not just those undertaking organisational/social research – making sense of the affective experience of researching enables an understanding of how feelings influence their research practice. Using an affective paradigm to reflect on research actions (Schon, 1983) enables research practice to be improved and also enables a deeper personal understanding. It allows researchers to learn about themselves potentially in some depth as well as simply to learn how to improve practice in a technical/rational way.

For researchers who focus on affective aspects of organisational and social practice and experience – as do many of our fellow contributors to this text – interpreting the feelings experienced as they research brings particular benefits. Such researchers – and we include ourselves – can gain additional insights into the phenomenon they are researching by reflecting on and seeking to explain their own research practice within an affective paradigm.

By reflecting on the research process, researchers can come to understand how their own affective state influences their research practice – we certainly find that to be the case. Those insights enable improved research practice. The experience of all aspects of the research process, which are often imbued with intense feelings, are amenable to interpretation from an affective standpoint: creative thinking, gathering resources to undertake the research, conceptual analysis, research design, data collection, presentation, analysis and interpretation, and communicating research to others – colleagues in one's own institution, at conferences and through written accounts. Our own experience is that reflecting on and making sense of the research process from the perspective of an affective paradigm presents an opportunity to practice the interpretation process, thereby gaining fresh insights and exploring the paradigm's limitations.

Very importantly, viewing and reflecting on the research process through the lens of an affective paradigm can also enhance the authority and legitimacy of the research – and the researcher. It enables the research process to be explored, understood and become securely grounded. Such reflection can facilitate a move to self-authorisation and autonomy (Keegan, 1982) and an inter-independent position (McCauley et al., 2006), which allow theory, principles and practice to be linked productively, complex systemic interactions to be fully understood, and the transformation of the individual and others (Rooke and Torbert, 2005).

References

Argyris, C. (1990) *Overcoming Organizational Defences: Facilitating Organisational Learning*. London: Allyn and Bacon.

Ashforth, B.E., and Humphrey, R.H. (1993) Emotional Labour in Service Roles, *Academy of Management Review* 18: 88–115.

Bain, A. (1868) *The Senses and the Intellect*. New York: D. Appleton.

Bandura, A. (1997) *Self-efficacy: The Exercise of Control*. New York: W.H. Freeman.

Barsade, S.G., Brief, A.P., and Spataro, S.E. (2003) The Affective Revolution in Organisational Behaviour: The Emergence of a Paradigm, in J. Greenberg (ed.) *Organizational Behavior: The State of the Science*. Hillsdale, NJ: Erlbaum.

Berger, T., and Luckman, T. (1966) *The Social Construction of Reality*. New York: Doubleday.

Broussine, M., and Vince, R. (1995) Working with Metaphor towards Organisational Change, in C. Oswick and D. Grant (eds.) *Organisation Development: Metaphorical Explorations*. London: Pitman: 57–72.

Crawford, M. (2007) Rationality and Emotion in Primary School Leadership: An Exploration of Key Themes, *Educational Review* 59(1): 287–298.

Crawford, M. (2008) *Getting to the Heart of Educational Leadership*. London: Sage.

Dunning, G., James, C., and Jones, N. (2005) Splitting and Projection at Work in Schools, *Journal of Educational Administration* 43(3): 244–259.

Elliott, R., and Dolan, R.J. (1998) Neural Response during Preference and Memory Judgments for Subliminally Presented Stimuli: A Functional Neuroimaging Study, *Journal of Neuroscience* 18(12): 4697–4704.

Fineman, S. (1993) The Emotional Organization: Organizations as Emotional Arenas, in S. Fineman (ed.) *Emotions in Organisations* (First edition). London: Sage.

Fineman, S. (1999) Emotion and Organizing, in S. R. Clegg and C. Hardy (eds.) *Studying Organisation: Theory and Method*. London: Sage: 289–310.

Fineman, S. (ed.) (2000) *Emotion in Organizations*. London: Sage.

Fineman, S. (2003) *Understanding Emotion at Work*. London: Sage.

Forgas, J.P. (2000) Introduction: The Role of Affect in Social Cognition, in J.P. Forgas (ed.) *Thinking and Feeling: The Role of Affect in Social Cognition*. Cambridge: Cambridge University Press.

Frank, R.H. (1993) The Strategic Role of the Emotions, *Rationality and Society* 5(3): 160–194.

Gabriel, Y. (1999) *Organizations in Depth*. London: Sage.

Guba, E.G., and Lincoln, Y.S. (1994) Competing Paradigms in Qualitative research, in N.K. Denzin and Y.S. Lincoln (eds.) *Handbook of Qualitative Research*. London: Sage: 105–117.

Halton, W. (1994) Some Unconscious Aspects of Organisational Life: Contributions from Psychoanalysis, in A. Obholzer and V.Z. Roberts (eds.) *The Unconscious at Work*. London: Routledge: 206–210.

Harre, R. (1986) The Social Construction of Emotions, in R. Harre and R. Finlay-Jones (eds.) *The Social Construction of Emotions*. Oxford: Blackwell.

Hershberger, W. (1988) Psychology as a Conative Science, *American Psychologist* 43(10): 823–824.

Hilgard, E.R. (1980) The Trilogy of the Mind: Cognition, Affection and Connation, *Journal of the History of the Behavioural Sciences* 16: 107–117.

Hirschhorn, L. (1988) *The Workplace Within: Psychodynamics or Organisational Life*. Cambridge, MA: MIT Press.

Hochschild, A.R. (1979) Emotion Work, Feeling Rules and Social Structure, *American Journal of Sociology* 85: 551–575.

Hochschild, A.R. (1983) *The Managed Heart: Commercialisation of Human Feeling*. Berkeley: University of California Press.

James, C.R., Connolly, M., Dunning, G., and Elliott, T. (2006) *How Very Effective Primary Schools Work*. London: Sage.

Keegan, R. (1982) *The Evolving Self: Problems and Process in Human Development*. Cambridge, MA: Harvard University Press.

LeDoux, J.E. (1986) Sensory Systems and Emotions, *Integrative Psychiatry* 4: 209–235.

Likierman, M. (2001) *Melanie Klein: Her Work in Context*. London: Continuum.

Martin, J., Knopoff, K., and Beckman, C. (2000) Bounded Emotionality in the Body Shop, in S. Fineman (ed.) *Emotions in Organisations* (Second edition). London: Sage.

McCauley, C.D., Drath, W.H., Palus, C.J., O'Connor, P.M.G., and Baker, B.A. (2006) The Use of Constructive-Developmental Theory to Advance the Understanding of Leadership, *The Leadership Quarterly* 17: 634–653.

Murray, H.A. (1938) *Explorations in Personality*. New York: Oxford University Press.

Niedenthal, P.M., Krauth-Gruber, S., and Ric, F. (2006) *Psychology of Emotion: Interpersonal, Experiential and Cognitive Approaches*. London: Psychology Press.

Obholzer, A., and Roberts, V.Z. (eds.) (1994) *The Unconscious at Work*. London: Routledge.

Rooke, D., and Torbert, W. R. (2005) Seven Transformations of Leadership, *Harvard Business Review* 83(4): 66–76.

Schon, D.A. (1983) *The Reflective Practitioner: How Professionals Think in Action*. New York: Basic Books.

Srull, T.K., and Wyer, R.S. (1985) The Role of Chronic and Temporary Goals in Social Information Processing, in R.M. Sorrentino and E.T. Higgins (eds.) *Handbook of Motivation and Cognition*. New York: Guildford Press: 503–549.

Sturdy, A. (2003) Knowing the Unknowable? A Discussion of Methodological and Theoretical Issues in Emotion Research and Organizational Studies, *Organization* 10(1): 81–105.

Tallon, A. (1997) *Head and Heart: Affection, Cognition, and Volition as a Triune of Consciousness*. New York: Fordham University.

Wittgenstein, L. (1953) *Philosophical Investigations*. New York: Macmillan.

Zhu, J. (2004) Understanding Volition, *Philosophic Psychology* 17(2): 247–273.

11

AUTHORIAL CONFESSIONS

Revealing our hands

Caroline Clarke, Mike Broussine and Linda Watts

In this book we have repeatedly and explicitly reminded the reader that no research process entirely goes to plan, remains within the control of the researcher or is experienced as a unidirectional rational-linear or cognitive enterprise. It would therefore be disingenuous of us as authors to pretend that this neatly bound book now in your hands is any exception to this; indeed at times it seemed that the process between the initial idea and what has now become the finished product could have faltered at any point.

On your marks . . .

The original idea for the book, which has had a long gestation period, actually started just after Linda finished her PhD when a few friends planted a seed:

> *I finished my thesis in summer 2005. A while after the award ceremony that autumn, I had supper with some friends, two of whom had published books in the past that focussed on their research topics. One of them asked if I was going to do the same. I instantly said 'no' as I had no desire to produce such a book – I had envisaged that I ought to try to have a few journal articles published focussing on my research findings. One of them pressed me and put a scenario to me – if I did work on a book, what would it be about? I replied without conscious thought and said that I'd like to produce the book that was 'missing' when I did my research. This reply was intriguing – not least to myself! What was 'the missing book' that I subconsciously wanted to appear? When the conversation moved on to other topics I had some space to reflect and had a clear realisation that I was talking about a book about the deeply challenging and exciting research process that I had experienced, rather than a book about my research findings. I had doubts about my capacity to author such a book as I had no experience of that form of writing and publishing. I also understood on one level that my subconscious*

had generated an idealised metaphor. In the event the collective experience of co-editing generated editorial capacity, and brought together experience that was 'more than the sum of its parts'. The 'missing book' metaphor was powerful and has been a 'lodestone' for me during the editorial journey.

This initial spark resulted in a deep dialogue between Linda and Mike (Linda's PhD supervisor) where they sketched out and debated a model attempting to capture what exactly they were both curious about. The discussion evolved into an idea for a relatively low-key collaborative inquiry group set up and participated in by Linda and Mike at the University of the West of England back in 2006–7. Their original message to colleagues was as follows:

[We] are starting a small research project on the lines of emotions in doing research. This project is in its infancy. As well as our own experiences as researchers, we have a substantial amount of anecdotal stories from people we have worked with that research makes potentially significant emotional demands of us. Some talk about the emotional "roller-coaster" of undertaking research, for example. Our thinking so far is that research can involve a range of emotions, conscious and unconscious processes, which may be accessed through reflections our own experiences and the stories we have to tell. These experiences might include the feelings associated with coming up against the politics of doing research, anxiety, contending with potentially painful truths, the "impostor syndrome" (e.g. can I do this? Is it legitimate/acceptable/valid?), the long-lasting and deep effects on us, our values commitments and attachments when doing research, and considerable learning about self in the process. . . . We are at the early stages of doing this, but [we] decided that a fruitful way forward might be to see whether we could establish an inquiry group (6–8 people currently engaged in doing research) that might be committed to working with us on this. The modus operandi of the group would be subject to discussion with anyone willing to participate, but we envisage it will provide a space in which researchers can together reflect critically on their emotional journeys in the process of doing research. . . . As well as being the convenors of such a group, we would also participate in the process. We do not intend that this work would be a substantial burden to already busy and committed researchers, but that we might go lightly together through a modest and finite programme of inquiry group meetings. The potential benefits to participants are that they would have access to a forum in which they can process their experiences. If you think there is any mileage in this (and comments would be welcome), would you be willing to circulate this invitation around your PhD students who would be welcome to contact us . . . about this project? Please let us know.

(email to colleagues, 18 September 2006)

In many senses, looking back on this episode, in that email we set out the *raison d'être* of this book, and we can trace the enthusiasm that we have held for this project ever since to the reactions of the group of six participants at the first meeting of the inquiry group in January 2007. It is this enthusiasm – and, in a very real way, a commitment to honour those colleagues and research students who set us off on this path – that has sustained our determination to widen and deepen an interest in academia into *Researching with Feeling,* through the publication of this book and (hopefully) its wider dissemination. The very first collaborative inquiry group session indicated that there was a fundamental need for researchers to be able to participate in a forum where they could work with their sometimes very strong emotions as these emerged during their research:

> *A participant remarked that the inquiry group felt like "play time" – "at last some free time", because otherwise what do we do with all our emotions – the projections, transferences, etc.? How do we deal with this particularly in the absence of supervision opportunities? Other colleagues mentioned that just recalling particular events, telling our stories, "makes me emotional in the recollection" – "these things never get discussed – we need someone else to work such feelings through".*
> (Emotions in Research Inquiry Group – Notes from session on 30 January 2007)

In the same session, participants offered several stories about the pressures to 'wear masks', to be defended, 'to keep the real me out of it' and to dehumanise oneself in the complex relationship between the researcher and the research. Someone in the group thought it was relevant to Arlie Hochschild's (1983) work on 'deep acting' and emotional labour of the researcher:

> *So we talked about what happens when the "data" becomes upsetting; situations in which interviewees could disclose much of themselves (leading possibly to embarrassment on the part of the researcher); or to a sense of narcissism ("God, I'm such a good interviewer!"); and that there can be (invariably are) unequal relations. One colleague recollected interviewing a man for whom she felt particular compassion and how his psychological injury may have reminded her of her own injury.*
> (Emotions in Research Inquiry Group – Notes from session on 30 January 2007)

We also noted the relief expressed by participants at being able to talk and find their voice through this inquiry. It felt then, and still does, that it is crucial that researchers have the opportunity to be able to reflect critically on their feelings in conducting research in a non-judgemental and safe setting. Unfortunately, as participants reported, the supervision provided by academic institutions did not always allow for this (a topic which evolved into Chapter 7 of this book). The ability to share stories of anxiety within the group was inspiring and so were reports relating to the delights of carrying out social research, an aspect which created a rich picture as to why we get committed to our research:

> *We reminded ourselves also about the potential joy of research, the "buzz" that we can get out of the process. One colleague mentioned that in her experience it was more an*

"awakening" rather than a buzz – "I can see things differently, join the dots up, and I can't go back to my previous ways of thinking". She also suggested that research is values-driven because we observed how shoddily people can be treated in organizations. There was a passage of discussion where we shared how working with emotions with research participants could be "incredibly inspiring and motivating", feeling that we can be "sucking so much out of the research, and getting so much out of it".

(Emotions in Research Inquiry Group – Notes from session on 30 January 2007)

In a subsequent session, four participants wanted to further explore and reflect on why they did research at all:

My PhD was my kind of end-of-career statement. In particular it was about my being able to find my own space.

We have deep attachments to our research – there are instrumental reasons for doing research, but also it's very wrapped up in our identity, politics, commitments – so there's always something autobiographical in all research.

Research is something consuming, a passion.

Research exposes the joy and the poignancy of stories – it can be a reparative process as well as a political one.

And so it was that we had embarked on our journey to know more about *Researching with Feeling.* As we take a reflexive turn in writing this conclusion we realise just how moved, inspired and motivated by our participants we became to take the work further, beyond the life of the collaborative inquiry group. The experience indicated clearly that there was an unfulfilled need in the social and organizational research worlds to discuss explicitly what if feels like to 'do research', and we hoped that – by publishing our theories, thoughts and experiences, and importantly those of a wide group of researchers – we might be able to contribute to a legitimisation of discussion of emotion in research. As part of this process, we presented some preliminary findings about research supervision at an academic conference in 2009 (Broussine and Watts, 2009), and the feedback we received at this conference encouraged us to try to disseminate our work further. That is when our struggle to publish started.

In the following vignette, Linda recollects how her relationship with Mike in this period shifted from that of a PhD student and supervisor to one that was characterised by a more equitable and colleague-like relationship. She suggests that this story may act as a counterpoint to some of the rather more pessimistic findings about the research supervision experience as outlined in Chapter 7. The experience described in the vignette conveys the importance placed on the quality of the relationship between co-editors or co-authors – in terms of the need for mutual support and encouragement, or dealing with the feelings associated with set-backs – when embarking on the struggle to publish:

> *Mike was my PhD supervisor – one of three on a supervisory team – for four years. Relatively soon after the thesis submission and viva examination we were working jointly on a series of workshops at UWE initiated by Mike, inviting others within the university to join us to discuss their emotional experience of their research journey. I thought that the workshops were amazing – contributions were fast flowing, revelatory, frank, trusting and moving. Given that Mike had been my supervisor for several years, I could have assumed that our relationship in further joint working would be that of a leader and follower or a teacher and learner – a relationship that was 'patterned' by the previous supervisory relationship. This was not the case. Mike's knowledge of the academic institution and extensive contacts gained by being an academic over an extended period of time led him to convene the workshops and draw on his contacts but apart from that, our working relationship was very equitable and supportive with a high degree of mutual checking or consultation.*
>
> *My reflection is that the foundation of that relationship was built during supervision. I felt that the last year or two of my PhD supervision sessions were as much about my supervisors' learning and development as they were about my own learning and development. My three supervisors were from different faculties at my request and the sessions were generally full of quick fire ideas and insights, energised, sparky and vivid. My place in that scheme of things felt as if it was to bring the draft thesis chapters and questions that fuelled the spontaneity – supervision covered the ground that it was meant to cover in academic terms but it was also a rich experience that made me feel included as a member of an active group that looked forward to being together.*
>
> *That supervisory experience primed me for the research workshops that followed. The basic values of mutual regard, empathy and openness to others' experience were demonstrated in practice over some years in supervision and Mike and I took forward those values as an assumption that underpinned our joint working in this book.*

. . . Get set . . .

We submitted a book proposal to a publisher (not the one who has actually published this book) and corresponded with that publisher over many months. We refer you to Chapter 9 in which we point to the 'challenging series of experiences' in getting published. We do not want to go into the ins and outs of these experiences (they are somewhat painful and would betray confidences), but suffice it to say that Linda and Mike felt that by the end they had been 'ground down'. This is part of the feedback they received from that publisher's editor:

> *My first response is that this is a brilliant idea for a book. It would not be a big seller, but it would be an important, path-breaking and fascinating contribution to the Research Methods canon. That said, I'm not sure that this is really the type of book that [we] would want on emotions in research. It is I think too narrowly conceived and*

it is also too reliant on unspecified student and researcher case studies. So I would only want to proceed with a book on this subject if it were more ambitious, less case-driven and not contributed to by students.

Much of the content right now is focused on the emotional experience of the researcher. This is all necessary, but I think the book would also benefit from more discussion of the emotional experiences of those being researched, so that we can treat emotions in research in the round. . . . Also, I think one would want, ideally, to have a chapter or two on how we study emotions? What methods can we use? What are the different approaches that can be adopted when emotions are the object of research (or at least part of it)? This would be a discussion of the methodology of capturing emotions.

(email, December 2008)

Our response to the above message indicated that we wanted to throw in the towel:

We are persuaded that a book that tackled all aspects of emotions in research would be a great addition to the research methodology literature as it would cover a range of aspects about emotions in the process of researching, and in the process of being researched. However, we feel that we are not the ones to lead such a project. As you know [we have] experience of publishing an edited book . . . and we therefore have a realistic view of the effort and time that needs to be put into such a venture if it is to produce a good product. . . . Your message has prompted us to look within ourselves – our energy and time – and we feel that a book of the kind you are suggesting will be beyond our capacities.

(email, January 2009)

. . . Get set (again) . . .

After a few months of abeyance, Caroline and another colleague then offered to join in the process of assembling a book proposal and were made very welcome by Mike and Linda who generously offered access to their 'baby'. Many meals and afternoon teas were consumed during this time as ideas were swapped, elaborated and often rejected.

A particularly significant feature of our editorial discussions has been eating together – most often at restaurants. Our food ranged from cake to steak and chips and almost invariably, pudding. I am talking about food with quality ingredients, savoury, comforting and possibly a bit more indulgent than our everyday diet. We worked at restaurant tables in Bath and Bristol for hours. One time in the restaurant we had so many ideas for potential chapters that we wrote them excitedly on post it notes, which we stuck all around the table. The waiter brought over main courses, desserts and then tea and coffee while we moved all the post-it notes around time and time again placing them in a different order. At the end of the meal we paid the bill and left with some of the sticky yellow notes still strewn across the table. A backward glance showed the waiter clearing away those 'chapters' that didn't make the cut. In Mike's notebook though, our evening's work had culminated in 15 luminous notes stuck on a piece of paper in a very particular order. For the moment at least, they had been picked to form part of a 'book' – which was at best a conceptual idea, and at worst, a fantasy.

After this 'successful' meeting it soon became clear to us that one of our 'new' colleagues, although enthusiastic and creative in meetings, was not delivering along the way. Task after task, which we assigned ourselves, never brought anything from this person. This was an upsetting state of affairs and provided us with a quandary we neither invited nor expected. On the one hand, the colleague was also a friend, highly intelligent, whose creative and academic input we really valued and appreciated. On the other hand, if the friend could not even supply a simple document, how much of a problem would this become when we began to write and edit the book? In the end we agreed to email this colleague and co-editor, who said she was glad we had surfaced the problem and that she did not feel she could commit to the project, but had found it difficult to tell us. This was a major setback for us all on a number of levels. First, it was upsetting that our colleague and friend had placed us in a position where we had to confront her. Second, in attempting to create a book about the emotions of doing research, we had clearly been unsuccessful in providing a climate for us all comfortably to discuss this issue along the way. Third, we missed the company and creativity of this colleague in our subsequent meetings, and even in writing this now we are sad that she was lost along the way. Collaborations, then, are fraught with potential problems, especially where colleagues persistently do not deliver. On the other hand, as we comment later on, collaborations can also be a source of joy.

Shortly after the 'disappearance' of this colleague, another colleague expressed an interest in coming on board as part of the editorial team. Very soon, though, this person admitted that a heavy workload meant that this was not going to be possible. We were left licking our wounds yet again and feeling somewhat rejected and dejected. Paranoid thoughts and doubts began to creep in – did our would-be co-editors know something we didn't? Was there something wrong with our proposal? Or, worse still, was there something wrong with us?

Eventually after submitting three or four different proposals to our publisher, each one being changed to accommodate their requirements, our proposal for this book was turned down:

Finally being rejected by this publisher evoked feelings of sadness and anger in us. We felt we had been given the run around for 18 months, developing the proposal for a larger book, then for a smaller book, then for I can't remember what. What a waste of time! I think the meeting (dining experience) where we discussed this definitely involved chips! This was a turning point though, as the publisher who has finally published this book had always been waiting in the wings, saying they would publish it if the other publisher (we were already engaged with) didn't want it. True to her word, the representative for Routledge immediately sent out our proposal to reviewers, and then after positive reviews wrote to tell us she was accepting it and preparing a contract for us. Since then our dealings with our publisher have been pain free, supportive and intelligently kind. Just what we needed.

Go!

Most experiences we would argue are characterised by emotional ambivalence, and the acceptance of our book was no exception. Doubts about our own competence in writing and managing/editing the book began to pop up. We talked about these, albeit in a jokey fashion at one of our afternoon feasts, as Caroline recalls:

> *I think the three of us were both scared and elated when our proposal was accepted. We were elated because it was the end of a long process courting publishers and clarifying our own ideas, and also because somehow the acceptance of the proposal legitimised our identities as potential book writers and editors. We were also scared because this meant we finally had to write it, to get on with it, instead of talking about it, like a political party who never quite expects to get into power. This meant a potential for failure. I myself was also scared because writing a book as a full time academic is now considered 'career suicide', as in the current academic climate books 'don't count' – they are not part of the Research Excellence Framework by which academics are judged. Writing an academic book then is considered more as something you do in your 'spare time', although my institution was very supportive of this project. I was worried that the time I spent on the book was time I would not spend publishing journal articles, although my belief that this was a really worthwhile project meant that I intended to pursue it in any case. The support of my co-editors has been invaluable as I have never felt exposed or aggrieved that anybody was doing less or more than anyone else. This has been a particularly fine example of collaboration with only positive emotion.*

This vignette highlights how different forms of research are in themselves politically constructed – i.e. some activities are more 'OK', or legitimate, than others. Currently, writing journal articles appears to be what defines and provides and exchanges currency for many academics (Knights and Clarke, 2014).

Ironically, after our contract from the publishers, the meetings and 'eatings' that had characterised our activity up to that point suddenly stopped, for we had writing to do, which is mostly an individual activity best done alone. We were also responsible for buddying other authors to ensure that drafts were submitted on time and that redrafts incorporated some of our suggestions. Some authors were more 'on track' than others, and we had to be flexible about this, as for some authors writing had a lower priority than the 'day job', and others found the process and 'getting started' a little harder than others. Above all we had to manage ourselves, perhaps the hardest task of all, as we reviewed each other's chapters and suggested changes, which were sometimes substantial. In order to make this process more palatable we once again resorted to the consumption of food:

> *I realised early on that I would find it hard to face the intensity of the editorial group process including as it did constructive criticism of our own writing, without the balancing pleasure of eating – perhaps in the sense of self – nurturing or taking care of one's self. There is a familiar metaphor about the collective sharing of food symbolising*

mutual connection and regard among a social group such as a kinship group or ethnic group. But I felt that our editorial eating occasions were something different from that and I had an insight when I came across a short piece on the web about a therapeutic group eating together as a means of building a sense of belonging or inclusivity. So sharing the meal table while working together promoted cohesion amongst us as editors while enabling us to feel that we were taking care of our own needs. In that sense the editorial session could more easily function as a 'container' for spirited discussion, reaching mutual agreements while we 'held our own'.

Sometimes criticism was taken defensively, but never personally. We agreed that the feedback made our writing better and that multiple and different views of our writing helped us to reflect on the differences between our intended narratives and the ways in which the reader sometimes interpreted them. Although criticism was undoubtedly a threat to our identities as writers, I think most of the authors in this book, including ourselves, have been able to acknowledge that constructive feedback (although potentially threatening) has also been a valuable part of the process of being a writer, as discussed in the previous chapter. It was also incredibly helpful when another co-editor suggested, 'You can stop now it's finished', because our own writing never feels finished to us; it is always left wanting, or is imperfect.

Literature reflecting life – a concluding provocation

It seems then that the experience of assembling this book has almost entirely mirrored the themes set out in many of our chapters. This is simultaneously reassuring and anxiety provoking; for, on the one hand, publishing a book on a topic such as this while experiencing the process as antithetical to what we have portrayed would be perturbing and provoke us into questioning whether we were simply creating a fictional 'reality'. On the other hand, although our experiences reminded us all that forays into the academic unknown are both exciting and potentially disturbing for our own identities (we are simultaneously threatened by the idea of failure as well as seduced by the thought of success), the setbacks and blind alleys were not always pleasant, and they required a real resolve to continue. Perhaps this resolve would not have been met if any of us had been doing this project alone, but of course we are unable to say if this is the case.

To recap, Chapters 4 and 7 remind us about the political aspect of all relationships, and the diverse agendas that we each have, and the different values we place on these activities. For the two colleagues who at different times joined and left our venture, the book was less of a priority for them than other events in their lives. For the remaining editors though, this was partially seen as a rejection both of us and of our project, and this cast doubt on whether or not it was meaningful and worthwhile, and also made us wonder whether we would ever secure a contract. Chapter 9 reminds us that writing and dissemination is potentially fraught with problems, many of which we have experienced (can we write a chapter? Can we edit a book?) and many of which we are yet to experience (will the publishers approve of the finished 'product'? Will anyone buy it? Will anyone read it? Will anyone like it?).

In this final part of the book, we want to leave the reader with a challenge – a provocation if you like – which, we believe, will enable the reader to draw some personal threads together as we finish our exploration. We have recognised the value of such challenges ourselves as we have contributed and edited this volume. However, the posing of awkward questions for us, and offering them to our reader, enables us together to maintain a kind of critical self-awareness concerning what it is to *research with feeling* that has been discussed and advocated in the preceding chapters.

Our provocation concerns the potential problem that by concentrating reflexively on our emotions as researchers we could be seen, and see ourselves, as *self-indulgent, narcissistic* or *self-fascinated*. This accusation is far from novel; others have been similarly accused of navel gazing and producing writing which is egotistic 'gross self-indulgence'(Coffey, 1999: 132), or demonstrating narcissism (Delamont, 2009). Matthew Brannan, in Chapter 2, pointed to this danger in the event that we understood emotions simply as 'attributive to individuals or their actions', and he advocated a more fruitful view of emotion, as being the property of social relationships. We put forward a similar argument in Chapter 1, suggesting that we needed to be aware of the trap of seeing researchers' emotions in acontextual and apolitical ways, separated from the social and institutional realities in which, and about which, we may be inquiring.

Of course we are also aware that any 'reflexive project of the self' (Giddens, 1991: 52) is closely bound up with ideas about our own identities (Chapters 3 and 5) and identity work (Chapter 9) in attempting to author constructions and re-constructions. Stella Maile began Chapter 8 with a vivid posing of questions about her engagement with this project, suggesting that the possible accusation of being self-indulgent can be a major inhibitor to writing about one's engagement in research. She suggested also that she was not alone in holding this feeling, and that some of her colleagues had mentioned to her their reluctance to pursue any inquiries that involved personal writing because, although important on one level, it feels 'wince-making'. This made the three of us as editors wonder whether we really mind some 'wince-making' – if we reflect on this challenge though, we could regard this as a possible defence against self-exposure. On the other hand, we, and all the contributors to the book, have 'exposed' ourselves to help readers associate with their experiences, but this could be a high-risk strategy. What if we are alone with our neuroticism?

Similarly, Louise Grisoni and Mike Broussine in Chapter 4 uncovered their feelings for us in relation to their experiences of conducting 'insider research' – and also that writing in the first person can indeed feel exposing and 'at times self-indulgent'. Of course authorial confessions can be a convenient device for creating a (self-)indulgent space to revisit the past with perhaps the unconscious intention of 'airbrushing' out any unwanted flaws or blemishes. However, we are as confident as we can be that we have included, illuminated and even magnified some of our blemishes in order that readers can connect with their own perceived 'imperfections'.

Bearing in mind the critiques of, and warnings about, a focus on researchers' feelings in the foregoing chapters, it will be clear to the reader that discussions about reflexivity and the 'reflexive turn' permeate this book, though not in an uncritical fashion. While acknowledging the problematic aspects of researcher emotion and reflexivity, contributors' accounts of their experiences – and the feelings these provoked – reveal researchers' emotional and reflexive selves. These accounts will hopefully encourage the reader to develop her or his critical self-awareness by recognising that previous career, life and research experiences, ethical stances, political beliefs, and attachments to the proposed topic or site of inquiry are supremely relevant in social and organizational research. The researcher's personal history may contain experiences that she or he brings consciously or unconsciously to the study.

As Etherington (2004: 25) put it:

> By allowing ourselves to be known and seen by others, we open up the possibility of learning more about our topic and ourselves, and in greater depth. This then becomes a personal journey.

Finally, if there is one reassurance that we want to leave the reader with, it is this: that undertaking research to which you are committed will of necessity entail undergoing an emotional journey – a metaphor used regularly through this book. As Chris James and Megan Crawford emphasised in Chapter 10 we may be inquiring into and with research participants' feelings, but we cannot forget that undertaking the research process itself is imbued with feelings. This means that you will feel 'blocked' sometimes; you may very well feel anxious, angry, afraid or 'useless' from time to time; you may doubt that you are up to it; you may be warned by others that you need to get on with the 'proper' job of doing the research and that your emotions are not centrally relevant. But, you will also experience and feel the 'highs' – hopefully of completing your research; of enjoying the process and your interactions with your participants; that you are learning a lot about the subject of your study; growing in confidence and competence; and the exhilaration of your research coming to fruition by either being awarded a research qualification, being published, or disseminating in a way that is useful to those you are writing about. While we have all suffered the deep hurt when our articles or papers have been rejected or reviewed badly, there is nothing like the elation we feel when we get our work recognised. Ultimately, you will have learned much more about yourself and, at the same time, have contributed worthwhile new knowledge into the community. Good luck!

References

Broussine, M., and Watts, L. (2009) *Reflections on the Research Supervision Process*, presented to British Academy of Management Research Methodology Special Interest Group Fourth

Annual Workshop on *Teaching Research Methods to Business and Management Students*, University of Central Lancashire, 31st March.

Coffey, A. (1999) *The Ethnographic Self*, London: Sage.

Delamont, S. (2009) The Only Honest Thing: Autoethnography, Reflexivity and Small Crises in Fieldwork, *Ethnography and Education*, 4, 1, pp. 51–63.

Etherington, K. (2004) *Becoming a Reflexive Researcher*, London: Jessica Kingsley.

Giddens, A. (1991) *Modernity and Self-Identity: Modernity and Society in the Late Modern Age*, Cambridge: Polity Press.

Hochschild, A.R. (1983) *The Managed Heart – Commercialization of Human Feeling*, Berkeley: University of California Press.

Knights, D., and Clarke, C.A. (2014) It's a Bittersweet Symphony, This Life: Fragile Academic Selves and Insecure Identities at Work, *Organization Studies*, 35, 3, pp. 335–357.

INDEX